Guide to County Records and Genealogical Resources in Tennessee

Guide to
COUNTY RECORDS
and
GENEALOGICAL RESOURCES
in
TENNESSEE

Compiled by
RICHARD CARLTON FULCHER

Baltimore
GENEALOGICAL PUBLISHING CO., INC.
1987

INTRODUCTION

While researching family histories in Tennsssee I have often encountered difficulty in determining the precise dates of coverage of the records of the various counties within the state. This led me to compile this county-by-county catalogue of existing records, which, for the most part, are available at the Tennessee State Library and Archives in Nashville, Tennessee, or through your local Branch Genealogical Library of the Church of Jesus Christ of Latter-day Saints.

Several points should be made here concerning this Guide and the resources listed herein:

1. The dates listed for the microfilmed county records represent those records microfilmed, beginning in the 1960s for the collections of the Church of Jesus Christ of Latter-day Saints and the Tennessee State Library and Archives; therefore, records existing after the dates of microfilming are available in the county courthouse.

2. The inventory of the microfilmed county records available at the Tennessee State Library and Archives is expected to increase, as will the collection of secondary sources. A check from time to time of the library's card catalogue or new acquisitions lists should be made to acquaint yourself with the latest acquisitions.

3. General histories and family histories are not included in this Guide unless they contain substantial genealogical data on a large number of families.

4. It is possible that some resources were unknown to me, or that I had incomplete information about a published work at the time of this writing; therefore, I will endeavor to update this publication from time to time.

5. Many county and college libraries in Tennessee have excellent local history and genealogy collections, including vertical files or manuscript collections of unpublished data. Be sure to ask about this rich resource at your library.

I sincerely hope this Guide will serve you well in your research in Tennessee.

Richard Carlton Fulcher

ANDERSON COUNTY

CREATED: 1801 from Knox [1792 from Greene & Hawkins Cos.] and Grainger County [1796 from Hawkins & Knox Cos.].
COUNTY SEAT: Clinton, Tennessee 37716.

LIBRARIES:
  Andersonville Public Library, Andersonville, TN 37705
  Briceville Public Library, Briceville, TN 37710
  Clinton Public Library, Clinton, TN 37716
  Lake City Public Library, Lake City, TN 37769
  Norris Community Library, Norris, TN 37830
  Oak Ridge Public Library, Oak Ridge, TN 37830
  Forked Deer Regional Library Center, P. O. Box 158, Trimble, TN 38259

GENEALOGICAL SOCIETY: Pellissippi Genealogical Society, 108 Trevecca Lane, Oak Ridge, TN 37830. Publishes The Pellissippian (Quarterly).

PUBLISHED RECORDS:
  Petitions Of Anderson County, Tennessee. [Ft. Worth: American Reference Publications, 1969].
  "Early East Tennessee Taxpayers, I, Anderson County, 1802." Pollyanna Creekmore. East Tennessee Historical Society Publications, no. 23 (1951). 115-135.
  Historical Records Survey, Tennessee. Inventory of the county archives of Tennessee, no. 1, Anderson County. [Nashville: The Survey, 1941].
  History Of Tennessee...(East TN ed.) [Chicago & Nashville: Goodspeed Publishing Co., 1887] (Anderson Co., pp. 837-40; & 1104-1123)
  Gammell, Paula. Anderson County, Tennessee Marriages 1859-1882. [1984]. (Contains v.3 "Colored Marriages," & v.4 of Anderson Co., TN Marriage Records.)
  _____. Anderson County, Tennessee, 1850 United States Census. [1984].
  Hutton, Edith W. 1870 Census, Anderson County, Tennessee.
  Hutton, Edith W. & Imogene Thacker. Historic Leach Cemetery, Anderson County, Tennessee. [1983].
  Petracek, Ruth. Early Records Of Anderson County, Tennessee.
  _____. Marriages 1838-1858 Anderson County, Tenn.
  Sistler, Byron & Barbara. 1880 Census, Anderson County, TN [1978].
  Whitley, E. R. Marriages Of Anderson Co., TN 1838-1858. [Baltimore: Genealogical Publishing Co., 1983].

ANDERSON COUNTY
(continued)

W.P.A. TYPESCRIPT RECORDS (available at the Tennessee State
Library and Archives):
County Court Records, 1801-1809.
County Court Minutes, 1810-1814.
Minutes of first Pleas & Quarter Sessions, 1814-1819.
Wills and Settlements, 1830-42; 1842-47; 1847-53.
Marriage Book, I, 1838-58.
Transfers and Licenses, pt. 1, 1834-43; pt. 2, 1843-55.
Baker Cemetery Tombstone Records.

MICROFILMED RECORDS (available at the Tennessee State Library
and Archives):
1830-80; & 1900-10 Federal Census.
Clerk & Master Minutes, June 1836 - Jan. 1902.
Circuit Court Minutes, Mar. 1844 - Nov. 1902.
Marriages, Sept. 1838 - Dec. 1912; and "colored" Dec. 1866
- June 1879.
Marriage Bonds, Sept. 1890 - May 1916.
County Court Minutes, Apr. 1811 - Sept. 1900.
Inventories of Estates, May 1859 - Apr. 1947.
Deeds of Conveyance, Feb. 1856 - Jan. 1871.
Administrators' Bonds, May 1872 - Sept. 1886.
Executors' Bonds, Nov. 1872 - May 1887.
Administrators' & Guardians' Bonds, May 1887 - May 1902.
Guardian Bonds, Oct. 1894 - Apr. 1923.
Settlements, May 1859 - Mar. 1911.
Vital Statistics, Apr. 1881 - Dec. 1882; June 1891 - Dec.
1899; July 1909 - July 1912.
Deeds, May 1802 - Dec. 1900.
Trust Deeds, Mar. 1882 - May 1902.
Tax Books, 1838 - 1865.
Rail Road Tax Book, 1859-1862.
Road Book, Dec. 1881 - Apr. 1889.
Wills, Jan. 1830 - Jan. 1842; Apr. 1847 - Dec. 1912.

MANUSCRIPT MATERIAL (available at the Tennessee State Library
and Archives):
Cemetery Records for Valley View Methodist Church.
Cemeteries (1800-1974). #506. Records for approximately
160 church and family cemeteries in Anderson and surrounding counties; and records of Valley View Methodist Church,
1880-1930, in Clinton, TN, consisting of church history,
pastor register, infant baptisms, marriages, and members.

CHURCH RECORDS (may be purchased from the Historical Commission
of the Southern Baptist Convention, 127 Ninth Ave. N.,
Nashville, TN 37234):
Anderson County, Longfield Baptist Church (originally called
Clear Branch), 1831-1878 (microfilm reel #4916).

BEDFORD COUNTY

CREATED: 1807 from Rutherford County [1803 from Davidson
& Williamson Cos.].
COUNTY SEAT: Shelbyville, TN 37160.

LIBRARY: Argie Cooper Public Library, 100 S. Main St., Shelbyville, TN 37160.

HISTORICAL SOCIETY: Bedford County Historical Society, Shelbyville, TN 37160 (publishes quarterly; Vol. 1, Spring,
1975).

LAND OWNERSHIP MAPS (available from Library of Congress,
Washington, D.C.):
Bedford & Coffee Cos. (portion 1863), N. Michler, John
E. Weyss & C. S. Mergell, surveyors; scale 1:105,000,
#868.
Bedford (1878), D. G. Beers Co., surveyors; scale 1:50,688,
#869.

PUBLISHED SOURCES:
Bell, Family Records Of Bedford County, Tennessee.
Fulcher, Richard C. Family Notes From The Shelbyville
Times-Gazette Newspaper. [Brentwood: 1980].
Fulcher, Richard C. Clipped Obits From The Shelbyville
Times-Gazette Newspaper. [Brentwood, 1980].
History Of Tennessee...historical & biographical sketch
of Maury, Williamson, Rutherford, Wilson, Bedford, and
Marshall Counties. [Chicago & Nashville: Goodspeed
Publishing Co., 1887].
Helsey, Jodie. The Country Doctor 1910-1923. (Births,
deaths, and some marriages of Dr. Daniel Sneed's
patients).
Historical Records Survey. Tennessee. Inventory of the
county archives of Tennessee, Bedford County. [Nashville:
The Survey, 1941].
Jacobs. Duck River Valley In Tennessee And Its Pioneers.
[1964].
Marsh. Name Index To Goodspeed's History Of Tennessee.
Marsh. Cemetery Records Of Bedford County, Tennessee.
Sistler, Byron & Barbara. 1880 Census, Bedford County,
TN. [1978].

W.P.A. TYPESCRIPT RECORDS (available at the Tennessee State
Library and Archives):
General Index to Deeds, Vol. 1, 1808-1830.
Chancery Court Records, 1837-1845.
Chancery Court Minutes, 1846-1854.
County Court Minutes, 1848-52; 1852-55.
Court Minutes, 1849-1864.
Marriages, 1861-1864.

BEDFORD COUNTY
(continued)

W.P.A. TYPESCRIPT RECORDS (continued)
Will Book, 1847-1881.
Church Records: New Hope Lutheran Church, 1805-1836.
Bible, Family, and Tombstone Records, Miscellaneous.

MICROFILMED RECORDS (available at the Tennessee State Library
and Archives):
1820-80; & 1900-10 Federal Census.
Circuit Court Minutes, June 1840 Apr. 1965.
Clerk & Master Minutes, Aug. 1830 - May 1965.
Administrators' & Executors' Settlements, July 1865 - Apr.
1963.
Administrators' & Executors Settlements, July 1865 - Apr.
1963.
Marriage Records, Jan. 1861 - Jan. 1965.
Merchants' Bonds & Oaths, Oct. 1904 - Feb. 1929.
Minutes, Co. Highway Commission, July 1930 - Jan. 1934.
Nurses' Records, Sept. 1911 - Nov. 1950.
Optometry Register, Aug. 1909 - June 1939.
Personal Property Tax Lists, July 1840 - Nov. 1842.
Physicians' & Veternarians' Register, May 1907 - Sept.
1911.
Probate Court Minutes, Sept. 1870 - July 1902.
County Court Minutes, Oct. 1848 - Oct. 1963.
Quarterly Court Minutes, Jan. 1928 - Oct. 1959.
Road Minutes, Overseer's Book, Jan. 1873 - Apr. 1910.
Wills, 1861 - 1966.
Wills & Inventories, Sept. 1868 - May 1965.
Judgement Dockets, 1826 - 1834.
Charter Books, Mar. 1902 - May 1965.
Deeds, Mar. 1808 - May 1966.
Auto Registration Records, July 1910 - Nov. 1915.
Claims against Estates, Oct. 1921 - Dec. 1923.
Conservators' Bond Booik, June 1954 - May 1965.
Conservators' Settlements, Oct. 1956 - May 1965.
Guardian Bonds & Letters, Nov. 1869 - Sept. 1965.
Guardian Settlements, June 1860 - June 1959.
Land Grant Books, 1808 - 1809.
Land Book, Oct. 1824 - Feb. 1825 (compromise bock).
Military Discharges, Sept. 1919 - Dec. 1964.
Trust Deeds & Chattel Mortgages, Aug. 1868 - Dec. 1965.
School Board Minutes, July 1921 - Nov. 1952.
Tax Books, 1875 - 1965.

MANUSCRIPT MATERIALS (available at the Tennessee State Library
and Archives):
Scrapbooks - Bedford and Rutherford Counties, Tennessee;
1900-1968. 4 vols., 1 reel. #266. (includes newspaper
clippings on local people and obituaries)

BEDFORD COUNTY
(continued)

MANUSCRIPT MATERIALS (continued)
Church Records of First Presbyterian Church, Shelbyville, TN. 1827-1956. 13 vols. 2 reels. #478, (consists of congregational meeting minutes, new clippings of church happenings, members, marriages, etc.)
Church Records. Normandy Presbyterian Church; Normandy, TN, 1870-1956. 4 vols. 1 reel. #492, (includes register of elders, deacons, pastors, etc., and baptisms and deaths).

BENTON COUNTY

CREATED: 1835 from Humphreys County [1809 from Stewart Co.] and Henry County [1821 from Western District (Indian lands)].
COUNTY SEAT: Camden, TN 38320.

LIBRARY: Benton County Public Library, Camden, TN 38320.

PUBLISHED SOURCES:
History Of Tennessee. [Chicago & Nashville: Goodspeed Publishing Co., 1887]. (Benton Co., pp. 797-954.)
Benton Co., TN Marriages, 1832-1957. [Knoxville: Lydia Russell Bean Chapter Daughters of the American Revolution, 1962].
Douthat, James. Benton County, TN Marriages 1846-1850. [1980].
"Benton County, Tennessee Marriages, 1837-1846," Ansearchin' News, v.17 (1970), no. 3, pp. 132-36.
"1850 Mortality Schedule of Benton County, Tennessee," Ansearchin' News, v.17 (1970), no. 3, p. 140.
Smith. Benton Co., Tenn. Heritage Notes. [Memphis: R. H. Harris, printer, 1975].
Smith. Family Bible Records Of Benton County, Tennessee. [1976].
Smith. Genealogical Gleaning In Benton Co., Tenn. [Memphis: R. H. Harris, printer, 1974].

W.P.A. TYPESCRIPT RECORDS (available at the Tennessee State Library and Archives):
Minutes of the County Court, Book 2, 1824-1854, pts. I,II.
Index to Marriages Records, A, 1846-1851.

BENTON COUNTY
(continued)

MICROFILMED RECORDS (available at the Tennessee State Library
    and Archives):
1840-80; & 1900-10 Federal Census.
Circuit Court Minute Books, Apr. 1836 - Jan. 1968.
Clerk & Master's Chambers Minutes, Dec. 1920 - July 1967.
Clerk & Master's Enrollment Books, Aug. 1854 - July 1903.
Clerk & Master's Minute Books, Aug. 1854 - Apr. 1968.
Administrators' & Executors' Bonds & Letters, Aug. 1874
    - Jan.1967.
Administrators' Settlement Books, Aug. 1860 - Mar. 1968.
Guardian Bonds and Letters, Aug. 1874 - Apr. 1968.
Guardian Settlements & Accounts, Aug. 1860 - May 1956.
Minutes of Insanity Records, Oct. 1919 - Mar. 1944.
Insolvent Estates, July 1852 - Dec. 1943.
Marriage Records, Dec. 1938 - Apr. 1968.
Miscellaneous Records, 1836 - 1855 (includes wills, settle-
    ments, scholasatic records, guardian settlements, etc.)
Optometry Register, Aug. 1889 - Mar. 1953.
Quarterly Court Minutes, July 1926 - Apr. 1968.
Road Records, 1889 - 1907.
Vital Statistics, Mar. 1881 - Jan. 1882; 1908 - 1912.
Wills, Sept. 1855 - Apr. 1968.
School Board Minutes, Sept. 1943 - June 1968
Trustees' Cash Journals, Sept. 1943 - June 1968.
Trustees' Tax Books, 1836-43; 1868-74; 1876-79; 1909-.
Deed Books, June 1836 - Apr. 1968.
Notebook relating to Deed Book, I, Deeds (1871).
Land Entries, Dec. 1820 - Jan. 1849.
Military Discharges, June 1919 - May 1968.
Oil & Gas Leases, Aug. 1918 - Nov. 1932.
Plat Books, Mar. 1942 - May 1968.
Survey Books, Jan. 1821 - Jan. 1848.
Trust Deeds, Nov. 1874 - June 1968.
Vital Statistics, Administrators' & Guardians' Index Book,
    1908 - 1912.

BLEDSOE COUNTY

CREATED: 1807 from Roane County [1801 from Knox Co.].
COUNTY SEAT: Pikeville, Tennessee 37367.

LIBRARY: Bledsoe County Public Library, Pikeville, TN 37367.

BLEDSOE COUNTY
(continued)

PUBLISHED SOURCES:
    Appell. A Census Of Wesley Chapel Cemetery, Pikeville, Tennessee, Bledsoe County. [1982].
    Douthat, James L. 1840 Sequatchie Valley Census. [1982].
    Hutcherson, Willis Reed. 1850 Bledsoe County, TN Census. [1863].
    History Of Tennessee...(East Tenn. ed.) [Chicago & Nashville: Goodspeed Publishing Co., 1887] (Bledsoe Co.)
    Kirkeminde, Patricia B. 1870 Bledsoe County, TN Census. [1980].
    Sistler, Byron & Barbara. 1880 Census, Bledsoe, County, TN. [1978].
    Robnett, E. P. "A History of Bledsoe County." Dissertation, Peabody College, Nashville, TN, 1957.
    Robnett, E. P. A Short History Of Bledsoe County. [Pikeville: Bledsoe Co. High School, 1977].

W.P.A. TYPESCRIPT RECORDS (available at the Tennessee State Library and Archives):
    Deed Books, A,B,C,D,G,H,I, & L, 1807-26; & 1829-54.
    Circuit Court Execution Docket, 1810-1824.
    Minutes of Circuit Court, 1834-1841.
    County Court Minutes, I, 1841-1846.
    Baptist Church Minutes, 1882-1938.
    Chancery Court Minutes, 2, 1836-1847.
    Tombstone Inscriptions.

MICROFILMED RECORDS (available at the Tennessee State Library and Archives):
    Birth Records, 1908-1912.
    Death Records, 1908-1912.
    Circuit Court Minute Books, June 1845 - May 1969.
    General Sessions Minutes, Mar. 1943 - July 1969.
    Tax Sales Records, July 1915 - June 1917.
    Clerk & Masters' Minute Books, Dec. 1836 - Sept 1956; Sept 1872 - June 1969.
    Administrators' Bonds and Letters, May 1909 - June 1969.
    Executors' Bonds and Letters, Jan. 1909 - May 1969.
    Guardians' Bonds and Letters, May 1908 - May 1969.
    Marriage Records, Apr. 1908 - June 1969.
    County Court Minutes, Sept. 1841 - Mar. 1852; Apr. 1856 - Mar. 1860.
    Quarterly Court Minutes, Oct. 1962 - Oct. 1969.
    Wills and Inventories, Nov. 1884 - Jan. 1906; Apr. 1908 - July 1968.
    County Bond Book, Sept. 1942 - Sept. 1968.
    1830-80; & 1900-10 Federal Census.

BLEDSOE COUNTY
(continued)

MICROFILMED RECORDS (continued)
Deeds, Jn. 1808 - Aug. 1826; Sept. 1829 - 1969.
Land Entries, Dec. 1868 - Aug. 1900.
Land Survey, Apr. 1824 - Mar. 1878.
Military Discharges, June 1944 - May 1969.
Oil & Gas Leases, July 1928 - May 1969.
Trust Deeds, Dec. 1896 - Oct. 1968.
School Board Minutes, Apr. 1943 - May 1969.
Trustee's Tax Books, 1901 - 1968.

BLOUNT COUNTY

CREATED: 1795 from Knox County [1792 from Greene & Hawkins
Cos.].
COUNTY SEAT: Maryville, TN 37801.

LIBRARY: Harper Memorial Library, 300 E. Church St., Maryville, TN 37801.

PUBLISHED SOURCES:
History Of Tennessee...(East Tenn. ed.) [Chicago & Nashville:
Goodspeed Publishing Co., 1887]. (Blount Co.)
Historical Records Survey, Tennessee. Inventory of the
county archives of Tennessee, Blount County. [Nashville:
The Survey, 1941].
Brown, Kenneth A. 1870 Federal Census Of Blount County,
Tennessee.
Burns, E. I. From War Trail To Landing Strip 1795-1955,
History of Blount County, Tennessee. [Nashville: TN
Historical Committee, 1957]. (contains tax lists and
muster rolls)
Little, Edith B. Blount County, Tennessee Cemetery Records,
(including the Blount section of Loudon and Monroe Cos.).
[1981].
Little, Edith B. Blount County, Tennessee Marriages 1795-
1910. [1982].
Parham, Will E. Blount County, Tennessee Marriages, 1795-
1859. [1982].
Sistler, Byron & Barbara. 1880 Census, Blount County,
Tennessee. [1979].
Whitley, E. W. Marriages Of Blount County, Tennessee 1795-
1859. [Baltimore: Genealogical Publishing Co., Inc.
1982].

BLOUNT COUNTY
(continued)

W.P.A. TYPESCRIPT RECORDS (available at the Tennessee State
   Library and Archives):
Wills, Book 1, 1799-1858.
Marriage Record Index, Books O and 1, 1795-1870.
County Court Records, Books 1 and 2, 1795-1807.
County Court Records, 1808-1811.
County Court Minutes, Book 2, 1814-1817.
County Court Minutes, Book 3, 1818.
Entry Takers' Book, 1824-1826.
First Baptist Church Minutes, Maryville, 1886-1899.
Tombstone Records.

MICROFILMED RECORDS (available at the Tennessee State Library
   and Archives):
1830-80; & 1900-10 Federal Census.
Chancery Court Minutes, Nov. 1859 - Mar. 1958.
Delinquent Tax Dockets, Aug. 1953 - Mar. 1971.
Enrolling Dockets, Dec. 1871 - Mar. 1877.
Land Sale Records, 1908 - 1920.
Civil & Criminal Court Minutes, May 1852 - Sept. 1865;
   Sept. 1881 - Feb. 1924.
Civil Court Minutes, Feb. 1925 - June 1971.
Criminal Minutes, Apr. 1925 - May 1971.
Administrators' & Executors' Bonds and Letters, Aug. 1889
   - June 1971.
Guardians' Bonds and Letters, Nov. 1925 - June 1971.
Insanity Records, Dec. 1918 - June 1971.
Insolvent Estates Accounts and Minutes, 1879-1944.
Administrators' Estate and Settlement Inventories, July
   1857 - June 1971.
Marriages, 1795-1854; July 1854 - July 1971.
Board of Alderman Minutes; Corporation of Maryville, May
   1850 - July 1868.
County Court Minutes, Sept. 1795 - Aug. 1971.
Miscellaneous Court Records, 1796 - Mar. 1834.
Guardians' & Conservators' Settlements, July 1857 - Sept.
   1878.
Vital Statistics: Births & Deaths, Apr. 1881 - Aug. 1912.
Wills Index, 1857 - 1971, A-Z.
Wills, 1795-1869; Jan. 1896 - Aug. 1971.
Wills, 1857-1971. (See rolls 73-79; also Wills & Inven-
   tories, 1795-1818; & roll 101, County Court Minutes.)
Board of Education Minutes, Feb. 1947 - Aug. 1971.
Affidavit Releases, Jan. 1932 - Sept. 1971.
Record of Charters, June 1891 - Sept. 1971.
Deeds, June 1796 - Aug. 1971.
Federal Tax Liens, Feb. 1933 - Sept. 1971.

BLOUNT COUNTY
(continued)

MICROFILMED RECORDS (continued)
  Military Discharges, Aug. 1919 - Sept. 1971.
  Miscellaneous Records, May 1900 - Oct. 1971.
  Plats, July 1906 - October 1971.
  Record of Releases, Jan. 1932 - Oct. 1971.
  Trust Deeds, Dec. 1884 - Oct. 1971.
  Trustees' Cash Journal, July 1929 - August 1940.
  Trustees' Tax Books, 1845-1856; 1865-1970.

MANUSCRIPT MATERIAL (available at the Tennessee State Library
    and Archives):
  Associations, Institutions, etc. Confederate Veterans
    Association of Upper East Tennessee, 1861 - ca. 1895,
    1 volume, 1 reel, #167. (A roster containing name,
    county, state, date of enlistment, company and regiment,
    rank, wounds received, date and cause of discharge,
    etc., about members of the association.)
  Cemeteries. South Carolina and Tennessee, ca. 1850 - ca.
    1956. Approximately 125 items. 1 reel, #307.
    (Alphabetical listing, by county, of tombstone
    inscriptions from 25 South Carolina and 48 Tennessee
    cemeteries; including some in Blount County.)

CHURCH RECORDS: (can be purchased from the Historical Commis-
    sion of the Southern Baptist Convention, 127 Ninth Ave.
    N., Nashville, TN 37234):
  Townsend. Bethel Baptist Church, 1840-1924, Aug. 24, 1947
    - Nov. 1963. (Microfilm reel #2051).
  Walland. Chilhowee Association. Miller's Cove Baptist
    Church, 1813-1962. (Microfilm reel #2053).

BRADLEY COUNTY

CREATED: 1835 from Indian lands.
COUNTY SEAT: Cleveland, TN 37311.

LIBRARY: Cleveland Public Library, 833 Ocoee St., Cleveland,
    TN 37311.

HISTORICAL SOCIETY: Bradley County Historical Society, c/o
    Cleveland Public Library (see address above).

BRADLEY COUNTY
(continued)

PUBLISHED RECORDS:
  History Of Tennessee...(East Tenn. ed.) [Chicago & Nashville: Goodspeed Publishing Co., 1887]. (Bradley Co., pp. 798-804; 926-987.)
  Historical Records Survey. Tennessee. Inventoary of the county archives of Tennessee. No. 6, Bradley County. [Nashville: The Survey, 1941].
  Lillard, R. G. & W. R. Snell. History Of Bradley County. [East TN Historical Society; Bradley Co. Chapter, 1976].
  Corn, James F. Red Clay And Rattlesnake Springs. [1959]. (A history of Cherokee Indians of Bradley County.)
  McGee. Cherokee And Creek Indians Returns Of Property Left In Tennessee And Georgia 1838. [?1957].
  Manly, E. C. Marriage Book I 1864-1887. [1974].
  Manly, E. C. Chatata Valley Families And Their Neighbors. [1981].
  Randolph, Sheridan. 1840 Federal Census, Bradley County, Tennessee. [1974].
  Ross, E. L. Historical Cemetery Records Of Bradley County, Tennessee. 2 vols. [1973].
  Sistler, Byron & Barbara. 1880 Census, Bradley County, Tennessee. [1979].
  Snell, Wm. R. 1850 Federal Census, Bradley Co., TN. [1974].
  Snell, Wm. B. Name Index To The 1860 Federal Census Of Bradley County. [1983].
  Snell, Wm. B. Tax Lists Of Bradley County, 1837-1839. [1979].
  Snell, Wm. B. & Virginia F. Taylor. Death Notices In The Cleveland Banner, 1865-1883. [1981].
  Snell & Taylor. Marriage Records In The Cleveland Banner, 1865-1883. [1981].
  Wooten, J. M. A History Of Bradley County. [Cleveland, TN: American Legion & Tn Historical Commission, 1949].

W.P.A. TYPESCRIPT RECORDS (available at the Tennessee State Library and Archives):
  Circuit Court Minutes, 1837-1842, pts. I & II.
  Circuit Court Minutes, Book B, 1838-1841, pts. I & II.
  Chancery Court Book, 1840-1859, pts. I & II.
  Entry Takers' Book, 1840-1841.
  Canday's Creek Baptist Church Minutes, 1849-1892.
  White Plains Baptist Church Minutes, 1843-1844.
  Journal of Augustine P. Shannon, 1848-1850.
  Tombstone Inscriptions.
  Will Book, 1866? - 1884.

BRADLEY COUNTY
(continued)

MICROFILMED RECORDS (available at the Tennessee State Library
and Archives):
1840-80; & 1900-10 Federal Census.
Chancery Court Minutes, Mar. 1838 - Aug. 1900.
Enrollment Book, Mar. 1872 - Sept. 1875.
Naturalization Petitions, Apr. 1909 - May 1919 (unindexed).
Circuit Court Minutes, Aug. 1838 - Sept. 1899.
Administrators' Bonds & Letters, Jan. 1887 - Feb. 1908.
Guardian Bonds & Letters, Feb. 1887 - Nov. 1908.
Executors' Bonds & Letters, Feb. 1887 - Feb. 1931.
Guardians' Bonds, Dec. 1871 - Aug. 1886.
Insolvent Estates, Oct. 1889 - Oct. 1947; (see also, mf.
roll #15; Oct. 1891 - Sept. 1941.)
Settlements, Guardians & Administrators, Mar. 1865 - Aug.
1908.
Marriages, 1864 - Jan. 1914.
Vital Statistics; Births & Deaths, 1908 - 1912.
County Court Minutes, Nov. 1864 - Aug. 1900.
Wills, Feb. 1859 - Oct. 1905.
Deeds, June 1862 - Aug. 1903.
Trust Deeds, Dec. 1864 - Feb. 1902.
Claims against County, 1836 - 1848.
Tax Books, 1865 - 1898 (except 1881-84).
Circuit Court Minutes, 1837 - 1897 (except 1864-86).
Executors' Docket, 1845 - 1851.
Poor House Minutes, 1860 - 1884 (except 1877-79).
Chancery Rules & Orders, 1840 - 1859.
Inheritance Taxes, 1885 - 1906.
Physicians' Records, 1889 - 1906.
Claims under Act of Feb. 1868.
Road Dockets, 1871 - 1891.
Register's Office: 1841 Grant Nos. 2305-2918; & 3523-3990.

MANUSCRIPT MATERIAL (available at the Tennessee State Library
and Archives):
County Records, miscellaneous, ca. 1835-1960; #561. (Various
records including store account books, scrapbooks,
cemetery records, and assorted church records.)

CAMPBELL COUNTY

CREATED: 1806 from Anderson County [1801 from Knox & Grainger
Cos.] and Claiborne County [1801 from Hawkins & Grainger
Cos.].
COUNTY SEAT: Jacksboro, TN 37757.

LIBRARY: Jacksboro Public Library, Rt. 2, Jacksboro, TN
37757.

PUBLISHED SOURCES:
History Of Tennessee...(East Tenn. ed.) [Chicago & Nashville:
Goodspeed Publishing Co., 1887]. (Campbell Co., pp.
844-46; & 1125-35.)
"Early East Tennessee Taxpayers," (Campbell County Tax
Lists), XII, Pollyanna Creekmore, 1818; East Tennessee
Historical Society Publications, no. 36, [1964].
Hutton, Edith W. 1870 Campbell County, Tennessee Federal
Census Schedule.
Ridenour, G. L. The Land Of The Lake: A History of Campbell
County. [Lafollette: Lafollette Publishing Co., 1941].
Sistler, Byron & Barbara. Campbell County, Tennessee
Marriages, 1838-1881.
_____. 1880 Census, Campbell County, Tennessee. [1979].
Whitley, E. R. Marriages Of Claiborne County, Tennessee,
1838-1850 And Campbell County, Tennessee, 1838-1853.
[Baltimore: Genealogical Publishing Co., Inc., 1983].

W.P.A. TYPESCRIPT RECORDS (available at the Tennessee State
Library and Archives):
Tennessee Negro Cemetery Records (Campbell Co.)
Deeds, Grants, etc., 1806-1810.
Deed Book, D, Index, 1820-1826.
Wills, Bonds, Inventories, 1807-1841.
Cemetery, Bible, Family Records.
Court of Pleas & Quarter Sessions Minutes, 1813-1817.
Vol. 3, 1834-1839.
Vol. 4, 1839-1846.
Registers' Books, C & E, 1817-20; & 1825-31.
Surveyors' Record of Entries, 1825-1833.
Marriage Records, 1838-1860.
Estates, Wills, Inventories, Book C, 1860-1880.

MICROFILMED RECORDS (available at the Tennessee State Library
and Archives):
1830-80; 1900-10 Federal Census.
Chancery Minutes, Jun 1842 - May 1900.
Circuit Court Minutes, May 1849 - June 1903.
Enrolling Dockets, May 1860 - April 1869.

CAMPBELL COUNTY
(continued)

MICROFILMED SOURCES (continued)
  Marriages, 1838 - Jan. 1914.
  Probate of Deeds, 1833-47; 1882-1903.
  County Court Minutes, Apr. 1839 - Apr. 1901.
  Guardian Settlements, Oct. 1858 -Apr. 1909.
  Inventory of Estates, Apr. 1860 - May 1896.
  Will Book, Feb. 1877 - Nov. 1907.
  Estate Book, 1806 - 1841.
  Deed of Conveyance, July 1848 - July 1881.
  Deeds, Sept. 1820 - Feb. 1901.
  Entry Book, Dec. 1806 - Oct. 1868.
  Entry Takers, 1824 - 1902.
  Surveyors' Records of Entry, Sept. 1825 - July 1910.
  Trust Deeds, Nov. 1852 - Nov. 1902.
  Tax Duplicates, 1876 - 1900.
  Land Sold for Taxes, 1894 - 1900.

CANNON COUNTY

CREATED: 1836 from Warren [1807 from White], Coffee [1836
  from Bedford, Franklin, & Warren Cos.], Wilson [1799 from
  Sumner Co.], and Rutherford County [1803 from Davidson
  Co.].
COUNTY SEAT: Woodbury, Tennessee 37190.

LIBRARY: Adams Memorial Library, Woodbury, TN 37190.

PUBLISHED RECORDS:
  History Of Tennessee...with an historical & biographical
    sketch of White, Warren, Coffee, DeKalb, and Cannon
    counties. [Chicago & Nashville: Goodspeed Publishing
    Co., 1887] (Cannon Co., pp. 854-60; 987-92.)
  Brown, S. S. History Of Woodbury And Cannon County. [Man-
    chester: Doak Publishing Co., 1936].
  "Index to Cannon County, Tennessee Wills, 1836-1895," Mary
    Jewel Standefer; Ansearchin' News, v.16 (1969), no.
    2: 57-60, 66.
  Porch D. 1850 U.S. Census, Cannon County, TN.

W.P.A. TYPESCRIPT RECORDS (available at the Tennessee State
    Library and Archives):
  County Court Minutes, Book A, 1836-1841.
  Will Book, Vol. A, 1836-1895.
  General Index to Deeds, Vol. 1, Direct & Reverse, 1836-1897.

CANNON COUNTY
(continued)

W.P.A. TYPESCRIPT RECORDS (continued)
   Marriage Records, Vol. 6, 1850-1866.
   Bible, Family, and Tombstone Records.

MICROFILMED RECORDS (available at the Tennessee State Library
      and Archives):
   1840-80; & 1900-10 Federal Census.
   Enrollment Books, Sept. 1852 - Mar. 1857; Sept. 1865 -
      Feb. 1890.
   Chancery Court Minutes, Aug. 1840 - July 1902.
   Circuit Court Enrollment Books, June 1846 - Oct. 1847;
      Feb. 1858 - Mar. 1861; Oct. 1865 - June 1977.
   Circuit Court Minutes, Feb. 1862 - June 1906.
   Administrators', Executors', & Guardians' Settlements,
      May 1859 - Mar. 1868.
   Guardian Settlements, Feb. 1854 - Oct. 1908.
   County Court Enrollment Books, Mar. 1848 - June 1916.
   Inventory & Settlements of Estates, Mar. 1876 - JUne 1908
      (labeled Administrators' Bonds).
   Insolvent Estates, Feb. 1888 - Dec. 1926.
   Inventories of Estates, Apr. 1848 - Apr. 1859.
   Claims against Estates, Aug. 1871 - Sept. 1914.
   Administrators' & Executors' Settlements, Jan. 1868 - May
      1876.
   Administrators' and Executors' Bonds & Letters, March 1872
      - Dec. 1898.
   Guardians' Bonds, March 1872 - Oct. 1898.
   Marriages, Mar. 1838 - Dec. 1919.
   County Court Minutes, May 1836 - June 1902.
   Road Book, Feb. 1866 - Apr. 1885.
   Vital Statistics: Births, May 1881 - Feb. 1903; & June
      1908 - 1912.
   Wills, June 1836 - Aug. 1926.
   Deeds, Apr. 1836 - Nov. 1902.
   Oil Leases & Deeds, Apr. 1869 - Nov. 1881.
   Entry Takers' Book, May 1836 - Jan. 1897.
   Surveyors' Book, June 1836 - Nov. 1860.
   Trust Deeds, June 1868 - Nov. 1901.
   Tax Books, 1853-56; & 1875-1900.
   Woodbury Lodge #235, Jan. 1859 - Apr. 1873.

MANUSCRIPT MATERIAL (available at the Tennessee State Library
      and Archives):
   Church Records of First Baptist Church at Woodbury, 1844-1971;
   (contains minutes, letters, membership list [black & white],
   deacons, etc.) Available as item #514, Tennessee State
   Library and Archives; and available for purchase as microfilm
   reel #3484 from the Historical Commission of the Southern
   Baptist Convention, 127 Ninth Avenue, N., Nashville, TN
   37234.

CARROLL COUNTY

CREATED: 1821 from Western District (lands in Tennessee east of the Mississippi River ceded by Chickasaw Indians to the U. S. by treaty in 1818.)
COUNTY SEAT: Huntingdon, TN 38344.

LIBRARY: Carroll County Library, Court Square, Huntingdon, TN 38344.

PUBLISHED RECORDS:
History Of Tennessee...with an historical and biographical sketch of Carroll, Henry, and Benton Counties. [Chicago & Nashville: Goodspeed Publishing Co., 1887]. (Carroll Co., pp. 797-813; 847-88.
"Shiloh Cumberland Presbyterian Church Cemetery, McKenzie, Carroll County, Tennessee," Ansearchin' News, v.13 (1966), no. 1, pp. 11-22.
DeVault, M. A. Carroll County Sesquicentennial Booklet. [McKenzie: McKenzie Banner, 1922].
Nolan. Carroll County, Tennessee Records, some wills, marriages, church, cemetery, and misc. references. [1965].

W.P.A. TYPESCRIPT RECORDS (available at the Tennessee State Library and Archives):
Varied Records of Carroll Co. Minutes, Tax Reports, etc., 1821-1826.
County Court Minute Book, 1826-1833, pts. I & II.
County Court Minutes, Book 3, 1833-42, pts. I & II.
County Court Minutes, 1843-1850.
County Court Minutes, 1850-55; & 1855-59.
Will Book, A, ca. Sept. 1822 - 1864.
Marriage Records, 1838-1860.
Guardian Account Records, 1-3, 1842-1845.

MICROFILMED RECORDS (available at the Tennessee State Library and Archives):
1830-80; & 1900-10 Federal Census.
Delinquent Tax Dockets, 1920-1970.
Chancery Court Minutes, Oct. 1836 - Aug. 1972.
Chamber Minutes, July 1876 - Oct. 1932.
Circuit Court Civil Minutes, Feb. 1912 - Aug. 1972.
Circuit Court Criminal Minutes, June 1922 - Apr. 1972.
Circuit Court Minutes, General Sessions, Sept. 1960 - Aug. 1972.
Administrators' Bonds & Letters, Oct. 1936 - Oct. 1960.
Administrators' and Executors' Bonds & Letters, Sept. 1899 - July 1915; Oct. 1828 - Dec. 1942.
Executors' Bonds & Letters, Oct. 1937 - Nov. 1959.

CARROLL COUNTY
(continued)

MICROFILMED RECORDS (continued)
Guardians' Bonds & Letters, Jan. 1901 - Apr. 1958.
Insanity Records, Nov. 1926 - Jan. 1961.
Inventories of Estates, Feb. 1852 - Sept. 1939.
Marriages, Mar. 1838 - Sept. 1972.
County & Quarterly Court Minutes, Mar. 1822 - Dec. 1878.
Quarterly Court Minutes, Jan. 1881 - Oct. 1972.
Professional License Register, Dentists, July 1919 - July 1940.
Settlements, Administrators', Apr. 1847 - Oct. 1942.
Settlements, Guardians', Apr. 1887 - Feb. 1956.
Wills, Sept. 1822 - Sept. 1972.
Deeds, Apr. 1822 - Dec. 1972.
Land Entries, Dec. 1820 - Dec. 1838; Dec. 1842 - Nov. 1866.
Claims against Estates, Oct. 1868 - Aug. 1972.
Settlements, Administrators' & Executors', May 1893 - Mar. 1961.
Board of Education Minutes, Feb. 1923 - Sept. 1972.
Automobile Registrations, Feb. 1914 - June 1916.
Land Surveys, Nov. 1820 - June 1825; Feb. 1842 - Nov. 1857.
Military Discharges, June 1919 - Dec. 1972.
Oil & Gas Leases, Oct. 1919 - Dec. 1947.
Trust Deeds, Oct. 1904 - Feb. 1973.
Federal Trust Deeds, Jan. 1932 - June 1972.
Cash Journals, Jan. 1958 - Sept. 1972.
Tax Books, 1848-50; & 1928-71 (intermittantly). (Tax books prior to 1928 burned in Court house fire.)
Sheriff Trustee Account Books, 1821-1841.
Chancery Enrollments, Feb. 1860 - Aug. 1876.
Chancery Minute Book, Aug. 1842 - Mar. 1843.
Circuit Court Minute Book, Oct. 1921 - Oct. 1930.
Administrators' & Executors' Bonds, Jan. 1852 - Oct. 1882.
Administrators' & Executors' Bonds & Letters, Dec. 1882 - Aug. 1899.
Guardians' Bonds, Apr. 1852 - Nov. 1882.
Guardians' Bonds & Letters, Dec. 1882 - Jan. 1901.
Guardian Minute Books, May 1885 - Dec. 1885.
Insolvent Estates, Nov. 1854 - Apr. 1907.
Inventory of Estates, Jan. 1867 - Sept. 1891.
Quarterly Court Minutes, Jan. 1873 - Oct. 1880.
Administrators' Letters, Sept. 1870 - Mar. 1880.
Administrators' & Executors' Letters, Apr. 1852 - Mar. 1868.
Administrators' & Executors' Settlements, Aug. 1860 - Dec. 1869.
Guardians Settlements, Nov. 1842 - Mar. 1887.

CARROLL COUNTY
(continued)

MICROFILMED RECORDS (continued)
Road Book, July 1867 - Mar. 1891.
Judges' Minutes and Roll Docket, 1835-1858.
Vital Statistics, 1927-33; & 1931-38. Deaths, 1925-38.
Trust Deeds, Sept. 1873 - Jan. 1907.
Sheriff's & Trustee's Account Books, 1821-1841.
Tax Book, 1848-1850.
Tax Book, 1871 (15th Dist.).
Tax Sales, 1902.

MANUSCRIPT MATERIALS (available at the Tennessee State Library
    and Archives):
Scrapbooks, Mrs. Mollie Grizzard; fl. 1870-1920; Scrapbook,
    1869-1920, 1 vol. (consists of newspaper clippings of
    church activities such as weddings, deaths, and genealogi-
    cal data.)

CHURCH RECORDS (available at the Tennessee State Library
    and Archives):
Hopewell Presbytery of the Cumberland Presbyterian Church,
    1824-1892. 4 vols. 1 reel.
Hollow Rock Primitive Baptist Church, 1823-1885. 2 vols.
    1 reel.
First United Methodist Episcopal Church, McKenzie, TN,
    1867-1913; 1957-1970. 7 vols. 1 reel.
First Methodist Church, Huntingdon, TN, 1916-1972, 9 vols.
Mt. Nebo Baptist, Buena Vista, TN, 1898-1972. #407.
Mud Creek Primitive Baptist Church, 1825-1968. 2 vols.
    1 reel.
Enon Missionary Baptist Church, McKenzie, TN, 1909-1973.
    8 vols. 1 reel.
Concord Baptist, Christmasville, TN, 1858-1878. #408.
Macedonia Missionary Baptist, McKenzie, TN, #410.
Westport Missionary Baptist, 1896-1972. #411.
New Hope Presbyterian, Christmasville, TN, 1919-1971. #413.
McLemoresville Baptist Church, 1836 - Aug. 1954. Reel #528
    (may be purchased from the Historical Commission of
    the Southern Baptist Convention, 127 Ninth Ave. N.,
    Nashville, TN 38234).

CARTER COUNTY

CREATED: 1796 from Washington County.
COUNTY SEAT: Elizabethton, TN 37643.

LIBRARY: Elizabethton Public Library, Sycamore Road, Elizabethton, TN 37643.

PUBLISHED SOURCES:
History Of Tennessee...(East Tenn. ed.) [Chicago & Nashville:
Goodspeed Publishing Co., 1887] (Carter Co., pp. 906-12;
& 1289-1299)
Bishop, Brenda C. 1870 Census Carter County, Tennessee.
Creekmore & Nave. Carter County 1796-1850. [Knoxville:
Clinchdale Press, 1958].
"Early East Tennessee Taxpayers," IV, Carter County, 1796.
East TN Historical Society Publications, no. 30 (1958);
by Pollyanna Creekmore; pp. 104-11.
Fields, Cemeteries Of Carter County. [1976].
McIver, Mary. Abstracts Of The Deeds Of Carter County,
Tennessee, 1796-1825. [1985].
McIver, Mary. Abstracts Of Wills And Estates Records Of
Carter County, Tennessee. [1986].
Merritt, F. Early History Of Carter County. [Knoxville:
East TN Historical Society, 1950].
Sistler, Byron & Barbara. 1880 Census, Carter County,
Tennessee. [1978].

W.P.A. TYPESCRIPT RECORDS (available at the Tennessee State
Library and Archives):
Wills & Inventories, 1794-1847.
Court of Pleas & Quarter Sessions Minutes, 1804-1805.
Vol. 2, 1819-1820.
Vol. 3, 1821-1826.
County Court Minutes, 1826-29; & 1834-35.
Sketch of Sinking Creek Baptist Church.
Cemetery and Church Records.

MICROFILMED RECORDS (available at the Tennessee State Library
and Archives):
1820-80; & 1900-10 Federal Census.
Chancery Court Minutes, Nov. 1854 - Jan. 1970.
Circuit Court: Land Sale Records, Sept. 1897 - Mar. 1904;
June 1912 - june 1918; & 1920.
Circuit Court: Civil Minutes, Nov. 1881 - Jan. 1970.
Circuit Court: Criminal Minutes, Mar. 1848 - nov. 1853;
Mar. 1871 - Feb. 1970.
Administrators' Bonds & Letters, Dec. 1865 - Mar. 1970.
Executors' Bonds & Letters, July 1866 - Mar. 1970.

CARTER COUNTY
(continued)

MICROFILMED RECORDS (continued)
  Claims against estates, June 1929 - Mar. 1970.
  Insanity Records, May 1925 - Mar. 1961.
  Estates Inventories, Jan. 1839 - Feb. 1918.
  Marriages, 1790 - Mar. 1970.
  County Court Minutes, Feb. 1804 - Feb. 1806; Feb. 1819
    - Nov. 1820; Feb. 1826 - Feb. 1876.
  Quarterly Court Minutes, July 1856 - Jan. 1866; July 1889
    - Jan. 1970.
  Quorum Minutes, Mar. 1876 - Mar. 1970.
  Professional License Registers, 1889-1906; May 1907-Jan. 1962.
  Administrators' Settlements, Aug. 1886 - Mar. 1970.
  Executors' Settlements, July 1879 - Mar. 1970.
  Guardians' Settlements, Feb. 1887 - Mar. 1970.
  Vital Statistics of Births & Deaths, 1881-1912.
  Wills, June 1794 - Mar. 1970.
  Board of Education Minutes, Oct. 1937 - Mar. 1970.
  Deeds, July 1796 - July 1970.
  Land Entries, Apr. 1824 - Nov. 1887.
  Land Surveys, July 1824 - July 1923.
  Military Discharges, Dec. 1920 - July 1970.
  Miscellaneous Records, Nov. 1928 - Nov. 1970.
  Plats, Oct. 1925 - May 1956.
  Surveyors' Books, June 1825 - May 1901.
  Trust Deeds, Aug. 1874 - Nov. 1970.
  Trustee's Cash Journal, Nov. 1927 - Aug. 1934.
  Trustee's Road Book, Sept. 1905 - July 1917.
  Trustee's Tax Books, 1860-72; 1875-86; 1919-20; 1928; 1930;
    1938; & 1947-70.

MANUSCRIPT MATERIALS (available at the Tennessee State Library
    and Archives):
  Church Records.   Siam Valley Primitive Baptist Church,
    Carter County, Tennessee, 1891-1963. 6 vols. 1 reel,
    #166.   Records consisting of minutes of session, member-
    ship, baptismals, obituaries, & financial records for
    this church.
  Associations, Institutions, etc. Confederate Veterans Associ-
    ation of Upper East Tennessee, 1861 - ca. 1895. 1 vol.
    1 reel #167.   Roster containing name, county, state,
    date of enlistment, company and regiment, rank, wounds
    received, date and cause of discharge, and general remarks
    about members of association living in Carter County
    and several other counties.

CHURCH RECORDS (may be purchased from the Historical Commis-
    sion of the Southern Baptist Convention, 127 Ninth Ave.
    N., Nashville, TN 37234):
  First Baptist Church, 1842-1943, Elizabethton. Reel #1428.
  Sinking Creek Baptist Church Records, 1773-1893.   Johnson
  City. Reel #1918.

CHEATHAM COUNTY
(continued)

CREATED: 1856 from Davidson [1783 from Washington Co., NC], Robertson [1796 from Tennessee Co.], Dickson [1803 from Robertson & Montgomery Cos.], and Montgomery County [1796 from Tennessee Co.].
COUNTY SEAT: Ashland City, TN 37015.

LIBRARY: Cheatham County Public Library, Ashland City, TN 37015.

GENEALOGICAL SOCIETY: Cheatham Co. Genealogical Society, Ashland City, TN 37015.

PUBLISHED SOURCES:
  History Of Tennessee. [Chicago & Nashville: Goodspeed Publishing Co., 1887]. (Cheatham Co., pp. 947-974; 1358-1388.
  Historical Records Survey. Tennessee. No. 11, Cheatham Co. [Nashville: The Survey, 1941].
  Bishop. 1870 Cheatham County, Tennessee.
  Brinkley, Lois B. The Deserted Sycamore Village Of Cheatham County. (contains courthouse records, newpaper accounts and genealogy of many first families of Cheatham Co.)
  Sistler, Byron & Barbara. 1880 Census, Cheatham County, Tennessee. [1978].
                                    .

W.P.A. TYPESCRIPT RECORDS (available at the Tennessee State Library and Archives)
  County Court Minutes, Vol. A, 1856-60.
  Marriage Licenses, Vol. A, 1856-97; Vol. B, 1881-93.
  Wills and Inventories, Vol. A, 1856-71.
  Bible and Tombstone Records.

MICROFILMED RECORDS (available at the Tennessee State Library and Archives):
  1860-80; & 1900-10 Federal Census.
  Chancery Court Enrolling Dockets, Oct. 1871 - Sept. 1875.
  Chancery Court Minutes, Oct. 1857 - Sept. 1969.
  Circuit Court Minutes, Feb. 1877 - Aug. 1969.
  Administrators' Bonds, Aug. 1903 - Mar. 1965.
  Guardians' Bonds & Letters, June 1868 - July 1959.
  Claims against Estates, June 1920 - Sept. 1969.
  Commissioners' Book, Feb. 1856 - Nov. 1874.
  Insanity Records, Aug. 1923 - Mar. 1969.
  Insolvent Estates Accounts, Aug. 1859 - Aug. 1951.
  Administrators' Letters, June 1868 - Oct. 1906; Oct. 1938 - Feb. 1963.
  Marriages, May 1856 - Oct. 1969; with Black marriages, 1865-81, inserted in front.
  Military Discharges, World War I.

CHEATHAM COUNTY
(continued)

MICROFILMED RECORDS (continued)
County Court Minutes, May 1856 - Apr. 1969.
Quorum Minutes, June 1939 - July 1969.
Professional License Registers, July 1889 - Jan. 1947
Physicians' Registers, June 1914 - March 1925 (Optomotrist).
Ranger Book, 1857 - 1877.
Guardians' Settlements, Aug. 1856 - Sept. 1969.
Vital Statistics: Births & Deaths, 1881-82; 1908-12. Deaths:
    1925-41.
Wills, Inventories, & Settlements, July 1856 - Sept. 1969.
Board of Education Minutes, Dec. 1940 - Aug. 1969.
Deeds, July 1856 - Oct. 1969.
Deeds, Trust Deeds, & Chattel Records, Aug. 1921 - Jan.
    1960.
Land Entries, Sept. 1856 - Sept. 1915.
Military Discharges, Aug. 1919 - Sept. 1969.
Oil & Gas Leases, July 1919 - May 1965.
Plats (interfiled in the Deed Books).
Trust Deeds, Oct. 1875 - Sept. 1969.
Tax Books, 1856-61; 1865; 1868; 1872; 1875-79; 1883-84;
    1888-1968.

CHESTER COUNTY

CREATED: 1879 from Hardeman [1823 from Western District
    (Indian lands)], Henderson [1821 from Western District],
    McNairy [1823 from Hardin Co.], and Madison County [1821
    from Western District].
COUNTY SEAT: Henderson, TN 38340.

LIBRARY: Chester County Public Library, Henderson, TN 38340.

PUBLISHED SOURCES:
    History Of Tennessee. [Chicago & Nashville: Goodspeed
        Publishing Co., 1887]. (Chester Co., pp. 806-13; 862-69.)
    Reid, S. E. A Brief History Of Chester County. [Jackson:
        Mccowat-Mercer Press, 1967].
    Sistler, Byron & Barbara. Claiborne Co., TN Marriages
        1838-1868. [1985].
    Sistler, Byron & Barbara. Claiborne Co., TN Marriages
        1868-1891. [1985].

CHESTER COUNTY
(continued)

MICROFILMED RECORDS (available at the Tennessee State Library
and Archives):
1880; & 1900-10 Federal Census.
Clerk & Master Minutes, Sept. 1891 - Sept. 1902.
Circuit Court Minutes, July 1882 - Oct. 1903.
Criminal Case Minutes, Mar. 1895 - Mar. 1899.
Marriages, Apr. 1891 - Dec. 1916.
Wills, May 1891 - Sept. 1931.
Insolvent Estates, Apr. 1891 - Mar. 1935.
County Court Minutes, Apr. 1891 - Sept. 1902.
Deeds, Jan. 1891 - Dec. 1900.
Trust Deeds, June 1891 - Sept. 1900.
Tax Books, 1890 - 1900.

CLAIBORNE COUNTY

CREATED: 1801 from Hawkins [1786 from Sullivan Co.] and Grainger County [1796 from Hawkins and Knox Cos.].
COUNTY SEAT: Tazewell, TN 37879.

LIBRARY: Claiborne County Public Library, Tazewell, TN 37879.

PUBLISHED SOURCES:
History Of Tennessee. [Chicago & Nashville: Goodspeed
Publishing Co., 1887].
Bell. Abstract Of Pensions Of Revolutionary War, War Of
1812, And All Wars Prior To 1883 Of Claiborne County,
Tennessee. [1952].
Bell. Family Bible Records Of Claiborne County, Tennessee.
(includes 1850 U.S. Census of Claiborne Co.)
Bishop. 1870 Claiborne County, Tennessee Census.
Edwards, L. & J. E. Davis. Old Speedwell Families. [Easley,
SC: Southern Historical Press, 1980] reprinted 1983.
Hansard, Mary A. Old Time Tazewell. [1979].
Johnson, Paul. Cemeteries Of Claiborne County, Tennessee.
Sistler, Byron & Barbara. Claiborne County, TN Marriages,
1838-1868. [1983].
Sistler, Byron & Barbara. Claiborne County, TN Marriages,
1868-1891.
Whitley, E. R. Marriages Of Claiborne County, Tennessee,
1838-1850, and Campbell County, Tennessee, 1838-1853.
[Baltimore: Genealogical Publishing Co., Inc., 1983].

CLAIBORNE COUNTY
(continued)

W.P.A. TYPESCRIPT RECORDS (available at the Tennessee State
    Library and Archives):
General Index to Deeds, 1801-1865.
Court of Pleas and Quarter Sessions Minute Book Book, v.1,
    1801-1803; & v.2, 1803-06.
Minute Docket, Court of Pleas and Quarter Sessions, 1812-14;
    & County Court Minutes, 1815-17.
Minutes of Court of Pleas and Quarter Sessions, 1818-19;
    1819-21; & 1821-24.
Minute Docket Court of Pleas & Quarter Sessions, 1806-08.
Index to Quarterly Court Records, 1826-1829.
Will Book, A, 1837-1846.
Will Book, B, 1844-1850.
Marriage Records, No. 2, 1838-1850; & No. 3, 1850-1868.
Cemetery Records.
Deed Book, A, 1801-1808.

MICROFILMED RECORDS (available at the Tennessee State Library
    and Archives):
1820-80; & 1900-10 Federal Census.
Administrators' Bonds & Letters, Dec. 1878 - July 1921.
Inventory of Estates, Feb. 1848 - Mar. 1940 (also includes
    some early wills - 1848-1865).
Guardians' Bonds & Letters, Jan. 1879 - Mar. 1903.
Guardian Settlements, Jan. 1872 - July 1878.
Physicians' Records, July 1889 - June 1904.
Vital Statistics, 1902-1912.
Guardians', Administrators', and Executors' Settlements,
    Apr. 1878 - Feb. 1902.
Inventory and Settlements of Estates and Wills, May 1839
    - May 1892.
Marriages, June 1838 - Aug. 1899 (indexed 1838-1973).
Marriage Bonds, Nov. 1893 - Sept. 1918.
Minutes, Dec. 1801 - Oct. 1900.
Wills, May 1893 - Dec. 1932.
Deeds, 1801 - Feb. 1895.
Surveyors' Books, Apr. 1824 - 1836; Jan. 1838 - June 1861;
    Apr. 1899 - Dec. 1913.
Tax Books, 1850-73; 1881-82; 1899; & 1900.

MANUSCRIPT MATERIALS (available at the Tennessee State Library
    and Archives):
Associations, Institutions, etc. Confederate Veterans
    Association of Upper East Tennessee, 1861 - ca. 1895,
    #167. Roster containing name, county, state, date of
    enlistment, company and regiment, rank, wounds received,
    date and cause of discharge, and general remarks about
    members of association living in Claiborne Co., as well
    as other counties.

CLAIBORNE COUNTY
(continued)

MANUSCRIPT MATERIAL (continued)
  County Records. Claiborne County, Miscellaneous Records, 1846-1915, #540. Collection consists of indexed general merchandise books 1898-1915 of Newton Lafayette Holt; two letters, 1863, from Robert Earl; and a stage book, 1846-48, for route from London, KY to Russellville, TN.
  Church Records. Big Spring Primitive Baptist Church, Claiborne Co., 1795-1948, #557. Church records consisting of meeting minutes, 1800-1948; membership list for 1800; list of pastors; etc.

CLAY COUNTY

CREATED: 1870 from Jackson [1801 from Smith Co.] and Overton County [1806 from Jackson Co.].
COUNTY SEAT: Celina, TN 38551.

LIBRARY: Clay County Public Library, Celina, TN 38551.

W.P.A. TYPESCRIPT RECORDS (available at the Tennessee State Library and Archives):
  Marriage Records, Book A, 1871-1873.
  Bible and Tombstone Records.

MICROFILMED RECORDS (available at the Tennessee State Library and Archives):
  1820-80; & 1900-10 Federal Census.
  Clerk & Master Minutes, June 1871 - Mar. 1914.
  Enrolling Dockets, Apr. 1871 - Nov. 1907.
  Circuit Minutes, May 1871 - June 1898.
  Enrollments, Aug. 1871 - Feb. 1904.
  Marriages, Apr. 1871 - July 1917.
  Guardians' & Administrators' Bonds & Letters, Apr. 1871 - Sept. 1903.
  Administrators' Settlements, Apr. 1873 - Apr. 1909.
  Wills, Apr. 1871 - Jan. 1913.
  Insolvent Estates, 1871 - 1930.
  County Court Minutes, Mar. 1871 - July 1899.
  Vital Statistics, 1908-1912.
  Deeds, June 1871 - Sept. 1901.
  Trust Deeds, Jan. 1874 - Oct. 1904.
  Tax Duplicates, 1884-85; 1897-99.
  Guardian Settlements, Jan. 1875 - Oct. 1915.

CLAY COUNTY
(continued)

MANUSCRIPT MATERIAL (available at the Tennessee State Library
and Archives):
"Historical Sketches of Clay County," by W. C. Stone, Jr.,
Tennessee State Library and Archives, Nashville.
Unpublished, typescript, 1962.

COCKE COUNTY

CREATED: 1797 from Jefferson County [1792 from Greene & Hawkins
Cos.].
COUNTY SEAT: Newport, Tennessee 37821.

LIBRARY: Stokely Memorial Library, E. Broadway, Newport,
TN 37821.

PUBLISHED SOURCES:
"Cocke County Tax Lists, 1839," East Tennessee Historical
Society Publication No. 37.
O'Dell, R. W. The Misty Blue Hills: The Story of Cocke
County. [Newport, TN: the author, 1951]. (contains
information concerning deeds, tax, Indian names &
marriages, C.S.A. soldiers, U.S. soldiers in Civil War,
WW I, & WW II, militia commissions, and some family
sketches.)

W.P.A. TYPESCRIPT RECORDS (available at the Tennessee State
Library and Archives):
Minutes of Slate Creek Baptist Church, 1812-1876.
Minutes, Pleasant Grove Baptist Church, 1838-1860.
Minutes of East Tennessee Association of Baptists, 1841-1872.
Entry Book, E, 1856-1871; and Surveys, 1856-60.

MICROFILMED RECORDS (available at the Tennessee State Library
and Archives):
1830-80; & 1900-10 Federal Census.
Chancery Court Minutes, Feb. 1877 - Feb. 1900.
Circuit Court Minutes, Mar. 1877 - Nov. 1899.
Circuit Court Civil Minutes, Mar. 1883 - Nov. 1899.
Administrators' Settlements, Mar. 1877 - Feb. 1910.
Guardians' Settlements, Feb. 1877 - July 1901.
Guardians' Bonds, Feb. 1877 - July 1910.
Administrators' & Executors' Bonds, Feb. 1877 - Sept. 1901.

COCKE COUNTY
(continued)

MICROFILMED RECORDS (continued)
Insolvent Estates, Minutes of, Jan. 1879 - Feb. 1920.
Inventory of Estates, Jan. 1875 - Jan. 1922.
Marriages, Feb. 1877 - Dec. 1900.
Vital Statistics: Births & Deaths, Oct. 1908 - Feb. 1912.
Wills, Dec. 1876 - Dec. 1913.
County Court Minutes, Jan. 1877 - Apr. 1908.
Trust Deeds, Jan. 1877 - Mar. 1902.
Deeds, June 1865 - July 1902.
Surveyors' Book, Aug. 1856 - Apr. 1889.
Land Entries, Apr. 1874 - June 1898.
Tax Book, 1876 - 1900 (intermittantly).

MANUSCRIPT MATERIAL (available at the Tennessee State Library
    and Archives)
Associations, Institutions, etc. Confederate Veterans
    Association of Upper East Tennessee, 1861 - ca. 1895.
    #167. Roster containing name, county, state, date of
    enlistment, company and regiment, rank, wounds received,
    date and cause of discharge, and general remarks about
    members of the association living in Cocke County and
    other counties.
Church Records. Slate Creek Baptist Church, 1812-1876.
    #205. Church records consisting of minutes, membership
    lists, and formal organization of the church in 1818.

COFFEE COUNTY

CREATED: 1836 from Bedford [1807 from Rutherford Co.], Frank-
    lin [1807 from Warren & Bedford Cos.], and Warren County
    [1807 from White Co.].
COUNTY SEAT: Manchester, TN 37355.

LIBRARIES: Coffee County Lannon Memorial Library, 312 N.
    Collins St., Tullahoma, TN 37388.
    Branch Genealogical Library of the Church of Jesus Christ
    of Latter Day Saints, Old Shelbyville Hwy., Tullahoma,
    TN 37388.

HISTORICAL SOCIETY: Coffee County Historical Society, 304
    S. Erwin St., Manchester, TN 37355.

COFFEE COUNTY
(continued)

PUBLISHED SOURCES:
History Of Tennessee. [Chicago & Nashville: Goodspeed
Publishing Co., 1887] (Coffee Co.,pp. 827-45; 921-51.)
Bridgewater, B. A. 1860 Federal Census Of Coffee County,
Tennessee. [1980].
Ewell, L. History Of Coffee County. [Mancester, TN: Doak
Printing Co., 1936].
Helsey. The Country Doctor 1910-1923.
Jacobs, L. F. Duck River Valley In Tennessee & Its Pioneers.
[typescript; 1968].
Jernigan & Shepard. Tombstone Inscriptions Of Coffee County,
Tenn. [Manchester: typescript, 1971].
Martinez, Collier, & Shephard. Coffee County From Arrowheads
To Rockets. [Tullahoma: Coffee Co. Conservation Board,
1969].
Potter. Marriage Books A & C, 1853-1870, Coffee County.
[Tullahoma, 1973].
Ward, W. P. History Of Coffee County. [Spartanburg:
Reprint Co., (1930) 1978].

W.P.A. TYPESCRIPT RECORDS (available at the Tennessee State
Library and Archives):
Will Book, v.1, 1833-60.
County Court Minutes, v.1, 1836-41.
Marriage Records, v.1, Book A, 1853-62; Book 2, 1863-70;
& Book 3, 1870-86.
Bonds and Settlements, 1858-1868.
Bible, Family, & Tombstone Records.

MICROFILMED RECORDS (available at the Tennessee State Library
and Archives):
1840-80; & 1900-10 Federal Census.
Minute Book of Tullahoma, TN, 1852-1862.
Chancery Court Enrolled Cases, Sept. 1872 - Apr. 1918.
Chancery Court Minutes, Aug. 1874 - May 1969.
Chancery Court Chambers Minutes, June 1929 - May 1967.
Circuit Court Enrolling Book, Apr. 1869 - Mar. 1899.
Circuit Court Minutes, Jan. 1852 - June 1969.
Administrators', Executors', & Guardians' Bonds, Dec. 1910
- May 1969.
Conservators' Bonds & Letters, June 1960 - July 1968.
Inventories of Estates, Sept. 1870 - May 1869.
Insolvent Estates, Dec. 1865 - Mar. 1889.
Suggestions & Accounts of Insolvent Estates, Dec. 1865
- Mar. 1962.
Administrators' Letters, Apr. 1890 - May 1969.
Executors' Letters, May 1890 - May 1969.
Guardians' Letters, Mar. 1890 - May 1969.

COFFEE COUNTY
(continued)

MICROFILMED RECORDS (continued)
Marriages, Jan. 1853 - June 1969.
County Court Minutes, May 1836 - June 1969.
Quarterly Court Minutes, Jan. 1895 - June 1969.
Professional License Register, June 1920 - July 1960.
Overseers' Road Book, July 1883 - Jan. 1891.
Administrators' & Executors' Settlements, Jan. 1860 - Jan. 1969.
Guardians' Settlements, Mar. 1901 - June 1969.
Wills, May 1836 - May 1968.
Education Department Minutes, 1905 - 1968.
Deeds, May 1836 - May 1969.
Military Discharges, Aug. 1919 - Aug. 1969.
Plats, Index to, 1912 - 1969.
Roll Book, Confederate Soldiers, 1861.
Surveyors' Book, June 1836 - Oct. 1955.
Trust Deeds, July 1888 - July 1969.
Cash Journals, Jan. 1928 - June 1968.
Tax Books, 1836-39; 1856-67; 1870; 1875-1904; 1906-14; 1918; 1923; 1929; 1934; 1938; 1943; 1948; 1953; 1958-68.

MANUSCRIPT MATERIALS (available at the Tennessee State Library and Archives):
Church Records. Methodist Churches, Warren & Coffee Counties, 1898-1967. #375. Records consisting of church history, 1898-1910; and membership lists, pastors, marriages, baptisms of the Fountain Grove Methodist Episcopal Church of Coffee County, and some Warren County Churches.
Church Records. St. Barnabas' Episcopal Church, Tullahoma, TN, 1872-1972. #461. Records consisting of baptisms, communicants, confirmations, families, marriages, offerings, and rectors.
Church Records. Methodist Episcopal Churches, 1869-1974. #516. Records of Mudd Creek Methodist Episcopal Church, South, 1903-1971; Summitville Methodist Episcopal Church, South, 1911-1967; Methodist Laymen's Club, 1950-1971; First Methodist Church in Manchester, 1870-1944; and Fountain Grove Methodist Episcopal Church, South, 1907-1966. Included are registers of pastors, marriages, baptisms, some church members, and some minutes.
Church Records. Methodist Episcopal Churches, 1885-1931. #525. Records for Ashbury Methodist Episcopal Church, 1888-1916; Hillsboro Methodist Episcopal Church, 1887-1916; Hillsboro Methodist Episcopal Quarterly Conferences, 1898-1940; and Mt. Pleasant Methodist Episcopal Church, 1815-1916.

COFFEE COUNTY
(continued)

ADDITIONAL CHURCH RECORDS (may be purchased from the Historical
Commission of the Southern Baptist Convention, 127 Ninth
Ave. N., Nashville, TN 37234):
Beech Grove. Garrison Fork Baptist Church, 1809-1933.
(Microfilm reel #3250).
Tullahoma. Maxwell Baptist Church, 1830-1889 (incomplete).
(Microfilm reel #1221.)

CROCKETT COUNTY

CREATED: originally created 1845 by Legislative Act, but
ruled in 1846, not to be a constitutional county. Subsequent
act of 1870 created Crockett County from parts of Haywood,
Madison, Gibson and Dyer Counties [created from the Western
District (Indian lands) in the years 1823 except for Madison
which was created in 1821].
COUNTY SEAT: Alamo, TN 38801

LIBRARY: Crockett Memorial Library, Alamo, TN 38801.

PUBLISHED SOURCES:
Historical Records Survey. Tennessee. No. 17, Crockett
Co. Inventory of the archives of Tennessee. [Nashville,
The Survey, 1941].
History Of Tennessee. [Chicago & Nashville: Goodspeed
Publishing Co., 1887]. (Crockett Co., pp. 830-42; 947-71.)
Murray, Sara C. Y. Lebanon Methodist Church. [1965].

W.P.A. TYPESCRIPT RECORDS (available at the Tennessee State
Library and Archives):
Marriage Books, 1872-75; 1875-77; 1877-80; 1880-82.
Marriage Books, 1884-86; & 1886-88.

MICROFILMED RECORDS (available at the Tennessee State Library
and Archives):
1870-80; & 1900-10 Federal Census.
Circuit Court Minutes, Apr. 1872 - May 1903.
Chancery Court Minutes, May 1872 - Aug. 1908.
Enrolling Dockets, Dec. 1875 May 1878.
Marriage Records, July 1872 - Jan. 1916.
County Court Minutes, Dec. 1871 - July 1907.
Insolvent Estates, Jan. 1853 - Sept. 1951.
Administrators' Bonds, Apr. 1872 - Sept. 1927.
Executors' Bonds, Aug. 1878 - July 1924.

CROCKETT COUNTY
(continued)

MICROFILMED RECORDS (continued)
Administrators' Settlements, Jan. 1875 - June 1915.
School Accounts, Sept. 1888 - Sept. 1896.
Guardian Accounts, May 1872 - Jan. 1883; Apr. 1889 - May 1902.
Guardians' Bonds, Dec. 1882 - Dec. 1909.
Guardians' Settlements, Sept. 1882 - Feb. 1891.
Inventories, June 1872 - Feb. 1915.
Road Book, Apr. 1872 - Sept. 1878.
Deeds, Mar. 1872 - Feb. 1901.
Military Discharges, WW I, Oct. 1897 - July 1909.
Trust Deeds, Mar. 1872 - Dec. 1900.

MANUSCRIPT MATERIALS (available at the Tennessee State Library and Archives):
County Records. Miscellaneous Records, ca. 1800-1960. #567.
Assorted records concerning the history of Crockett County, including genealogical data for some early families; accounts & business papers; election commission minutes, 1871-75; and records for the Cox Chapel Church of Christ, ca. 1877-1907; and photographs.

CUMBERLAND COUNTY

CREATED: 1855 from White [1806 from Smith Co.], Van Buren Co. [1840 from White, Warren, & Bledsoe Cos.], Bledsoe [1807 from Roane Co.], Rhea [1807 from Roane Co.], Morgan [1817 from Roane Co.], and Putnam County [1842 from White, Overton, Jackson, Smith, & DeKalb Cos.].
COUNTY SEAT: Crossville, TN 38555.

LIBRARY: Art Circle Public Library, 306 E. First St., Crossville, TN 38555.

PUBLISHED SOURCES:
Bullard & Krechniak. Cumberland County's First Hundred Years. [Crossville, TN: Centennial Committee, 1956].
Castillo, Betty. Cumberland County Tennessee County Tennessee Cemetery Records. (all known cemeteries in Cumberland Co., and 27 cemeteries in surrounding counties).
Crossville Chronicle, July 12, 1956, Centennial Edition. [1956].
Kirkeminde, Patricia B. Crossville Newspapers, Vol. 1, 1878-1888; & Vol. 2, 1889-1895.

CUMBERLAND COUNTY
(continued)

PUBLISHED SOURCES: (continued)
Kirkeminde, P. B. 1860 Cumberland County, Tennessee Census.
Kirkeminde, P. B. 1870 Cumberland County, Tennessee Census.
Kiwanis Club. Short History Of Cumberland County, Tennessee.
[1952].
Ogle, G. A. & Co. Biographical Sketches Of The Cumberland
Region In Tennessee, Part II, Memoirs & biography.
[1898]. (contains 343 biographies of persons in the
Cumberland region.)
Roddy, Vernon. The Lost Town Of Bledsoesborough, Tennessee:
Its Beginning, Its End. [1984].
Stratton, Cora S. & Nettie M. Stratton. And This Is Grassy
Cove, [Crossville: Chronicle Publishing Co., 1938].

W.P.A. TYPESCRIPT RECORDS (available at the Tennessee State
Library and Archives):
Plat Book, A, 1856-97.
Entry Takers' Book No. 2, 1856-91; & Journal B, 1856-60.

MICROFILMED RECORDS (available at the Tennessee State Library
and Archives):
1860-80; & 1900-10 Federal Census.
Circuit Court Minute Books, Civil, June 1907 - Mar. 1969.
Criminal Court Minutes, June 1905 - Feb. 1969.
Clerk & Masters' Minutes, June 1897 - Nov. 1968.
Clerk Minutes, Chambers, Dec. 1943 - Apr. 1969.
Conservators' Bonds & Letters, Dec. 1957 - Apr. 1969.
Administrators' Bonds, Mar. 1905 - Apr. 1969.
Executors' Bonds & Letters, Apr. 1907 - Apr. 1969.
Guardians' Bonds & Letters, Mar. 1905 - Apr. 1969.
Cattle Marks & Brands, Apr. 1905 - Mar. 1955.
Insanity Proceedings, Sept. 1947 - Jan. 1969.
Administrators' Letters, Aug. 1905 - May 1967.
Marriage Records, Feb. 1905 - Apr. 1969.
Quarterly Court Minutes, Mar. 1905 - Jan. 1969.
Quorum Court Minutes, Dec. 1912 - Feb. 1969.
Physicians' Register, Sept. 1905 - June 1952.
Optometrists' Register, Jan. 1909 - July 1933.
Nurses' Register, Dec. 1938 - Dec. 1962.
Administrators' Settlement Books, July 1907 - Feb. 1969.
Guardians' Settlement Books, Nov. 1906 - Jan. 1969.
Will Book, Sept. 1904 - Feb. 1969.
Deed Books, Oct. 1854 - Mar. 1969.
Entry Takers' Book, Apr. 1856 - Apr. 1904.
Military Discharges, June 1920 - Apr. 1969.
Miscellaneous Records, June 1871 - May 1969 (includes Index
Books, Trust Deeds, Leases, Charters, etc.)

CUMBERLAND COUNTY
(continued)

MICROFILMED RECORDS (continued)
Oil & Gas Leases, Apr. 1939 - Jan. 1951.
Plat Books, Feb. 1939 - Dec. 1968.
Surveyors' Book, Mar. 1857 - Feb. 1896.
Board of Education Minutes, Jan. 1914 - June 1969.
Tax Books, 1904-05; 1907-14; 1917; 1923; 1928; 1933; 1943; 1948; 1953; 1958-68 (intermittantly).

MANUSCRIPT MATERIALS (available at the Tennessee State Library and Archives):
Cemeteries. South Carolina & Tennessee, ca. 1850 - 1956. #307. Alphabetical listing, by county, of tombstone inscriptions from 25 SC and 48 TN cemeteries including some in Cumberland Co.

CHURCH RECORDS (may be purchased from the Historical Commission of the Southern Baptist Convention, 127 Ninth Ave. N., Nashville, TN 37234.):
Cumberland County. Grassy Cove and Mt. Pleasant Baptist Church, 1833-1924. (Microfilm reel #1402.)

DAVIDSON COUNTY

CREATED: 1783 from Washington County, North Carolina.
COUNTY SEAT: Nashville, TN 37201.

LIBRARIES: Tennessee State Library and Archives, 403 7th Ave. N., Nashville, TN 37219.
Public Library of Metropolitan Nashville and Davidson Co., Nashviile Room of the Ben West Library, 222 8th Ave. N., Nashville, TN 37203.
Joint University Libraries, 419 21st Ave. S., Nashville, TN 37203.
Branch Genealogy Library of the Church of Jesus Christ of Latter Day Saints, 107 Twin Hills Dr., Madison, TN 37115.

HISTORICAL & GENEALOGICAL SOCIETIES:
Bellevue-Harpeth Historical Society, Bellevue, TN.
Brentwood Historical & Genealogical Society, P.O. Box 21, Brentwood, TN 37027.
Disciples of Christ Historical Society, 1101 19th Ave. S., Nashville, TN.
Middle Tennessee Society of Professional Genealogists, P.O. Box 21, Brentwood, TN 37027.
Tennessee Historical Society, War Memorial Bldg., Nashville, TN 37219.

DAVIDSON COUNTY
(continued)

PUBLISHED SOURCES:
Harpeth Gleanings, compiled by Bellevue Historical Society.
Clayton, W. W. History Of Davidson County, Tennessee.
   [Philadelphia: J. W. Lewis & Co., 1880].
"List of Taxable Property; and List of Slaves owned in
   Davidson County, Oct. 1, 1798," by Ruth Henley Duncan,
   Ansearchin' News, Vol. 8 (1961), No. 3, pp. 78-86.
Fulcher, Richard C. 1770-1790 Census Of The Cumberland
   Settlements. [Brentwood, TN, 1986]. With the loss
   of all early Tennessee Census Records, this as an extreme-
   ly important enumeration of the first settlers along
   the Cumberland River with cited references on each.)
Fulcher, Richard C. Tombstone Inscriptions Of Davidson
   County, Tennessee, 5 volumes. [Brentwood, TN, 1986]
   Revised edition. (The most complete collection available
   on the tombstone inscriptions from hundreds of private
   and church cemeteries in Davidson County, with plats
   of many of the cemeteries.)
Fulcher, Richard C. Concord Baptist Church Records. [1982].
Johnson, Lillian B. Historic Cane Ridge And Its Families.
   [1973].
Lucas, S. Emmett. Davidson County Marriage Record Book
   I, 1789-1837. [1979].
Polk's Nashville city directory, 1865-1926.
Nashville City & Business Directory, Vols. 1-5, [L. P.
   Williams & Co.].
Sistler, Byron & Barbara. Davidson Co., TN Marriages 1838-
   1863. [1985].
Waller, William, ed. Nashville In The 1890's. [1970].
Waller, William. Nashville 1900-1910, [1972].
Whitley, A. B. & E. R. Mill Creek Baptist Graveyard.
   [Nashville: 1929].
Whitley, E. R. Marriage Records Of Davidson County,
   Tennessee 1789-1847. [Baltimore: Genealogical Publishing
   Co., Inc., 1981].
"Revolutionary Soldiers of Davidson County, Tennessee,"
   by E. R. Whitley; William and Mary College Quarterly,
   Vol. 11, pp. 13-19.
Whitley, E. R. Davidson County Pioneers. [1965].
Williams, Charlotte A. Index To The Tennessee Gazette
   And The Tennessee Gazette And Mero-District Advertiser.
   [Nashville: 1979].
Index To Interments In Nashville City Cemetery, 1846-1962.
   [Nashville: Tennessee State Library and Archives].
   (no infant interments listed, and note that this is
   compilation of interments, not tombstone inscriptions.)

DAVIDSON COUNTY
(continued)

PUBLISHED SOURCES (continued)

The Montgomery County Genealogical Journal; Ann Evans Alley, publisher. Old Davidson County records, being with Vol. 9, no. 1.

W.P.A. TYPESCRIPT RECORDS (available at the Tennessee State Library and Archives):
County Court Minutes, Vol. A, 1783-1790, pts. I & II; Vol. B, 1791-1797, pts. I & II.
Register Book, A, 1784-1889, pts. I, II.
General Index to Deeds, 1784-1871.
Land Record, 1788-1793
Bill of Complaint, Hugh Gwinn vs. Williamson Rice, 1808-1813.
Re-Survey of Nashville, 1820, by Smith Criddle
Superior Court Minutes Of NC, including Mero District, 1788-1803, pts. I, II.
Superior Court Minutes of Mero District, 1803-1806, pts. I, II; and 1807-1809.
Marriage Record Book 1, Jan. 1, 1789 - Dec. 18, 1837. (DAR).
Marriages, v.2, 1838-1847; v. 3, 1848-49.
Wills & Inventories, v.1, 1784-1794.
    Vol. 2, 1794-1805, pts. I, II.
    Vol. 3, 1805-1811.
    Vols. 4-5-6, 1805-1816, pts. I,II.
    Vol. 8, 1821-1826, pts. I,II.
    Vol. 10, 1832-1836, pts. I,II.
MICROFILMED RECORDS (available at the Tennessee State Library and Archives):
1820-80; & 1900-10 Federal Census.
Deeds, 1794-1940.
Plat Books, 1860-1939.
Registers, 1784-1844; 1887-1890
Charter Register, 1877-1888.
Trust Deeds, 1856-1941.
Chattel Mortgages, 1887-1940.
Personal Conveyances, 1882-1939.
City Building & Loan, 1856-1861.
Nashville Building Association, 1854-1856.
Release Affidavits, 1938-1941.
Charters of Incorporation, 1926-1940.
Records of Charters, 1889-1935.
Military Records, 1919-1946.
Partial Payments, 1930-1936.
Wills, 1784-1941.
Marriage Records, 1789-1941.
Mero District Court of Equity, 1803-1809.
Mero District Daily Court Minutes, 1783-1823.

DAVIDSON COUNTY
(continued)

MICROFILMED RECORDS (continued)
County Court Minutes, 1783-1928 (1879 missing).
Circuit Court Minutes, 1803-1960 (1st through 4th).
Tax List, 1871-1948 (inside and outside Nashville).
Printed Index to Wills & Inventories, 1784-1794; 1794-1805.
Davidson County Tax Books (located in County Court Minute
    Book, B.) includes: 1841-46; 1846-50; Books D,E, & F.

MANUSCRIPT MATERIALS (available at the Tennessee State Library
    and Archives):
Morton B. Howell Collection. This a collection of letters
    and writings - primarily letters written by members
    of the Howelll family - and includes, among other things,
    writings of Baptist minister Robert Boyte Crawford Howell,
    a list of all the marriages performed by the minister,
    1827-1868; the pastor's book containing sketches of
    the churches in Richmond and Nashville with lists of
    members of both churches.
Federal Collection Records, 1863-1864, vol. 1. This volume
    contains official records of the Board of Claims, giving
    a partially alphabetized list of the claimants, the
    amount claimed, and the amount awarded for damage
    sustained during the occupation of Nashville and vicinity
    by the U.S. Army.
Church Records, First Presbyterian Church in Nashville,
    1823-1955. These records contain, among other things,
    a list of baptisms and communicants for the years
    1833-1853.
Parish Register, St. Ann's Episcopal Church, Nashville,
    Tennessee, 1858-1962. These include baptisms,
    confirmations, marriages, deaths, and a sketch of the
    church's history.
Sketches. "Biographical Glimpses of Early Nashville,"
    includes all the mayors of Nashville from 1806-1854,
    as well as a number of other early settlers. These
    sketches were written by William B. Nicholson.
Records of Nashville City Cemetery, 1843-1961. Three volumes
    contain deeds for the cemetery lots. The three other
    volumes contain the interments from 1846-1962.
Interment Records for National Cemetery, Madison.
Land Records. Real Estate Books, 1866-1870. (microfilmed,
    #144).
Associations, Institutions, etc. Cumberland Lodge No.
    8, Free and Accepted Masons, Nashville, 1812-1961,
    (microfilmed, #433). Minutes of lodge meetings; newsaper
    clippings of biographical-historical sketches and
    obituaries; lodge records, and special events.

DAVIDSON COUNTY
(continued)

MANUSCRIPT MATERIALS (continued)
Vital Statistics. Doris, Finley M. & Karsch Dorris & Co.,
Nashville, TN, 1902-1914, (microfilmed, #522). These
records for the Dorris family funeral home in Nashville
contain infomation on the name, age, race, sex, date
and place of birth, marital status, date and place of
burial, and funeral charges. Race and sex of deceased
not recorded until after January, 1908.
Church Records of Christ Episcopal Church in Nashville,
1829-1958, (microfilmed, #47). Contains records of
baptisms, births, deaths, and marriages.
Church Records of West End Methodist Church in Nashville,
1873-1959, (microfilmed, #65). Records consisting of
membership, baptismal, marriage, and death records;
Board of Stewarts' meeting minutes, and other related
church history.
Church Records of St. Ann's Episcopal Church in Nashville,
1858-1962, (microfilmed, #120). Baptisms, confirmations,
marriages births, and deaths; and a historical sketch
of the church from 1858-1904.
Church Records of Immanuel Baptist Church, Nashville,
1887-1952, (microfilmed, #196). These records consist
primarily of church business meetings, but does include
some membership lists and a few obituaries.
Church Records of Lockland Baptist Church, Nashville,
1903-1953, (microfilmed, #197). Baptisms, deaths,
marriages, and a membership list and membership
withdrawals, along with other church business records.
Church Records of First Presbyterian Church in Nashville,
1925-1966, (microfilmed, #265). Church records consisting
mainly of church minutes but does contain registers
of baptisms, marriages, and deaths for 1925-1961.
Church Records of The Church of the Advent, 1857-1959,
(microfilmed, #289). Baptisms, burials, communicants,
confirmations, marriages, offerings, etc.
Church Records, St. George's Episcopal Church in Nashville,
1949-1969, (microfilmed, #470). Contains some baptisms,
burials, confirmations, and marriages.
Church Records of Moore Memorial Presbyterian Church,
Nashville, 1873-1896, (microfilmed, #487). Contains
records of church organization, minutes, etc., along
with baptisms and deaths.
Church Records, First Baptist Church, Nashville, 1820-1863,
(microfilmed, #74). Records of church history,
pastorships, missionary work, Baptist State Convention,
& church during Civil War.

DAVIDSON COUNTY
(continued)

MANUSCRIPT MATERIALS (continued).
Church Records, Downtown Presbyterian Church, Nashville, 1954-1961. Records of minutes, list of members of steering committee, 1954; officers; organization; minutes of session; etc.
Church Records of Downtown Presbyterian Church, Nashville, 1961-1970, (microfilmed, #495).
Church Records of Woodmont Baptist Church, Nashville, 1941-1952, (microfilmed, #199). Records consisting mainly of business minutes with reports and records, and membership lists.
Church Records of Trinity Presbyterian Church, Nashville, 1942-1959, (microfilmed, #207 & #269). Contains material on the organization of the church; lists of baptisms, deacons, elders, members, and dismissals.
Church Records of First Presbyterian Church, Nashville, 1860-1869, (microfilmed, #256).
Church Records of McKendree Methodist Church, Nashville, 1900-1941, (microfilmed, #287). Records include church history; membership lists and baptismal records, etc.
County Records of Cumberland District, Davidson & Washington Counties, 1779-1806, (microfilmed #224). Records for Tennessee Courts of Pleas and Quarter Sessions recording court cases - land claims, tax assessments, wills probated, members of the county court, and commissioners appointed.

ADDITIONAL CHURCH RECORDS (may be purchased from the Historical Commission of the Southern Baptist Convention, 127 Ninth Ave., N., Nashville, TN 37234.)
Nashville Association, New Hope Baptist Church, Minutes, 1846-1883, (microfilm reel #402).
Nashville, Baptist Church of Nashville, (Old School Baptists), May 3, 1838; June 1939 - Feb. 22, 1878, (microfilm reel # 2272).
Nashville, Belmont Heights Baptist Church, 1909-1957, (microfilm reel #879).
Nashville, Central Baptist Church, Oct. 20, 1858 - May 1946, (microfilm reel #3835).
Nashville. Eastland Baptist Church, 1911-1961, (microfilm reel #1265).
Nashville, Edgefield Baptist Church, 1903-1969, (microfilm reel #4100).
Nashville, First Baptist Church, 1820-1966, (microfilm reel #294).

DAVIDSON COUNTY
(continued)

ADDITIONAL CHURCH RECORDS (continued)
Nashville, Glendale Baptist Church, 1950-1967, (microfilm reel #1595).
Nashville, Grace Baptist Church, Contents of 1913 cornerstone (microfilm reel #4715).
Nashville, Immanual Baptist Church, Vols. 1-8, 1887-1952, (microfilm reel #220).
Nashville, Lockeland Baptist Church, 1903-1973, (microfilm reel #238).
Nashville, Lockeland Baptist Church, Bulletins & Church History, 1940-1941, (microfilm reel #696).
Nashville, Woodmont Baptist Church, 1941-70; & 1971-77, (microfilm reel #252).

LAND OWNERSHIP MAPS (available from the Library of Congress, Washington, D. C.):
Davidson County (1871), W. F. Foster, surveyor; scale 1:37,000, #870.
Davidson County (1900?), W. B. Southgate, surveyor; scale 1:63,360, #871.

DECATUR COUNTY

CREATED: 1845 from Perry County [1821 from Hickman Co.].
COUNTY SEAT: Decaturville, TN 38329.

SPECIAL NOTE: Courthouse fire in July 1969 destroyed most records.

LIBRARY: Decatur County Library, Courthouse, Decaturville, TN 38329.

PUBLISHED SOURCES
History Of Tennessee. [Chicago & Nashville: Goodspeed Publishing Co., 1887]. (Decatur Co., pp. 814-19; 880-94.)
Younger, Lillye. History Of Decatur County. [Southhaven, MS: Carter Publishing Co., 1977].

W.P.A. TYPESCRIPT RECORDS (available at the Tennessee State Library and Archives):
Deed Book, 1, 1846-52; 1852-54.
Marriage Record Book, 1, 1869-74.
Marriage Record Book, 2, 1874-79.

DECATUR COUNTY
(continued)

W.P.A. TYPESCRIPT RECORDS (continued)
  Marriage Record Book, 3, 1879-81.
  Marriage License & Bond Book, 4, 1881-87.
  Marriage Record Book, 5, 1887-93.
  Marriage Record Book, 6, 1883-98.
  Survey Book #1, 1846-60.
  Record Book #3, 1854-57.

MICROFILMED RECORDS (available at the Tennessee State Library
    and Archives):
  1850-80; & 1900-10 Federal Census.
  Clerk & Master Minutes, June 1868 - Nov. 1891.
  Clerk & Master Enrollments, Dec. 1860 - Nov. 1876.
  Guardian Settlements, June 1869 - Sept. 1913.
  Administrators' and Executors' Settlements, Sept. 1869
    - Nov. 1905.
  Settlements, June 1887 - Jan. 1901.
  Administrators' Bonds, July 1869 - Oct. 1930
  Executors' Bonds, Dec. 1869 - Jan. 1975.
  Guardians' Bonds, July 1869 - Nov. 1921.
  Inventory of Estates, Sept. 1869 - Nov. 1905.
  Marriages, July 1869 - Apr. 1883.
  Marriages, May 1903 - Aug. 1912.
  Wills, July 1869 - Sept. 1927.
  Claims against estates, Aug. 1869 - Jan. 1921.
  Births, Apr. 1881 - May 1883.
  Administrative Settlements, Dec. 1871 - Feb. 1938.
  Minutes, July 1969 - Dec. 1905.
  Deeds, Ap. 1846 - Apr. 1902.
  Trust Deeds, Jan. 1869 - May 1900.
  Survey Books, Apr. 1891 - Mar. 1918.
  Tax Books, 1888-89; 1896-98.

CHURCH RECORDS (may be purchased from the Historical Commission
    of the Southern Baptist Convention, 127 Ninth Ave. N.,
    Nashville, TN 37234.)
  Decaturville. Decatur Co., New Hope Baptist Church, 1842
    - Mar. 1928, (microfilm reel #2113).
  Parsons, Decatur County. Bear Creek Baptist Church, 1842
    - Feb. 1929, (microfilm reel #2112).

DEKALB COUNTY

CREATED: 1837 from White [1806 from Smith Co.], Warren [1807 from White], Cannon [1836 from Warren, Coffee, Wilson, & Rutherford Cos.], Wilson [1799 from Sumner Co.], and Jackson County [1801 from Smith Co.].
COUNTY SEAT: Smithville, TN 37166.

LIBRARY: Justin Potter Public Library, Smithville, TN 37166.

PUBLISHED SOURCES:
  History Of Tennessee. [Chicago & Nashville: Goodspeed Publishing Co., 1887]. (DeKalb Co., pp. 845-53; 951-87.).
  Marler. The Name Index To History Of DeKalb County. [Nashville: 1971].
  Love, Jolee. Love's Valley. [Nashville: Ambrose Printing Co., 1954].
  Hale, W. T. History Of DeKalb County. [Nashville: Hunter, 1915].

W.P.A. TYPESCRIPT RECORDS (available at the Tennessee State Library and Archives):
County Court Minute Book, A, 1837-1849.
Will Book, A, 1838-1854.
Marriage Book, H, 1848-59.
Salem Baptist Church Minutes, 1809-1908.
Tombstone Inscriptions.

MICROFILMED RECORDS: (available at the Tennessee State Library and Archives):
1840-80; & 1900-10 Federal Census.
Circuit Court Clerk Minutes, Oct. 1860 - May 1866; July 1881 - July 1968.
Clerk and Masters' Minutes, July 1955 - Mar. 1969.
Clerk and Master Enrollments, Mar. 1845 - May 1936.
Guardian Bonds, Dec. 1952-June 1964.
Guardian Settlements, Feb. 1925 - Nov. 1966.
Minutes, Mar. 1844 - Mar. 1857; Apr. 1883 - Nov. 1968.
Administrators' Bonds, May 1860 - Jan. 1892; May 1902 - Apr. 1969.
Administrators' Inventories, May 1885 - Mar. 1969.
Administrators' Letters, Feb. 1888 - July 1914.
Administrators' Settlements, May 1846 - Oct. 1865; Oct. 1870 - Sept. 1873; Sept. 1886 - Apr. 1969.
Guardian Bonds, Jan. 1874 - Apr. 1969.
Guardian Settlements, Oct. 1871 - Mar. 1969.
Insolvent Estates Minutes, June 1856 - May 1879; Jan. 1899 - Nov. 1946.
Land Sales Records, Aug. 1878 - Feb. 1886; Mar. 1903 - Aug. 1921.

DEKALB COUNTY
(continued)

MICROFILMED RECORDS (continued)
Marriage Records, Aug. 1848 - Apr. 1968.
County Court Minutes, Apr. 1842 - Sept. 1849; Dec. 1856
  - June 1871; Apr. 1878 - Dec. 1887; Sept. 1890 - Feb.
  1968.
Optometry, Physicians' and Dentists' Registers, Feb. 1907
  - Apr. 1942; Aug. 1889 - Aug. 1946.
Quarterly Court Minutes, Oct. 1849 - Nov. 1856; July 1871
  - Mar. 1878; Jan. 1888 - Aug. 1890; Jan. 1915 - Apr.
  1969.
Road Commission Minutes, July 1919 - Jan. 1932.
Wills, Aug. 1838 - Jan. 1968.
Deeds, Mar. 1838 - Jan. 1968.
Entry Takers' Books, Mar. 1838 - Sept. 1849; July 1890
  - Aug. 1905.
Lease Records (Gas & Oil), Mar. 1896 - Aug. 1909.
Military Discharges, June 1919 - Apr. 1969.
Trust Deeds, Apr. 1869 - Apr. 1969.
Trust Deeds & Mortgages Index, 1940 - 1968.
Board of Education Minutes, Oct. 1915 - June 1921; Apr.
  1938 - May 1969.
Tax Books, 1857-70; 1889-99; 1901; 1905; 1919; 1924; 1928;
  1933; 1938; 1943; 1948; 1952-53; 1958-68.

DICKSON COUNTY

CREATED: 1803 from Montgomery [1796 from Tennessee Co.]
  and Robertson County [1796 from Tennessee Co.].
COUNTY SEAT: Charlotte, TN 37036.

LIBRARY: Dickson County Public Library, 305 Hunt St., Dickson,
  TN 37055.

HISTORICAL SOCIETY: Dickson County Historical Society, 113
  West Lake Circle, Dickson, TN 37055.

PUBLISHED SOURCES:
  History Of Tennessee. [Chicago & Nashville: Genealogical
    Publishing Co., 1887]. (Dickson Co., pp. 920-47; 1329-
    1357.)
  Corlew, R. E. History Of Dickson County. [Nashville:
    TN Historical Commission, 1956].
  Garrett, Jill K. & Iris H. McClain. Dickson County, Tennes-
    see Cemetery Records. [Columbia, TN: 1967].

DICKSON COUNTY
(continued)

PUBLISHED SOURCES (continued)
Garrett, Jill K. & Iris H. McClain. Dickson County, Tennes-
see Cemetery Records. [Columbia, TN: 1967].
Rowe, Imogene. Dickson County, Tennessee 1820 Federal
Census. [1974].

W.P.A. TYPESCRIPT RECORDS (available at the Tennessee State
Library and Archives):
County Court Minute Book, Vol. I, 1804-07.
County Court Minute Book, Vol. II, 1810-15.
Circuit Court Minute Book, 1839-1845.
Will Books A & B, 1804-65; 1865-08.
Marriage Records, 1838-48.
Marriage Records (Negro), 1865-1881.
Tennessee Negro Cemetery Records (Dickson Co.)

MICROFILMED RECORDS (available at the Tennessee State Library
and Archives):
1820-80; & 1900-10 Federal Census.
Circuit Court Minutes, Sept. 1810 - Sept. 1815; Apr. 1818
- July 1823; Mar. 1825 - Sept. 1827; Feb. 1839 - Oct.
1965.
Clerk & Masters' Minutes, Apr. 1836 - Dec. 1965.
Accounts of Insolvent Estates, May 1860 - Aug. 1896.
Administrators' Bonds & Letters, Sept. 1912 - May 1966.
Administrators' Settlements, Apr. 1823 - Feb. 1860; Nov.
1874 - Dec. 1966.
Conservators' Bonds & Letters, Dec. 1958 - Jan. 1967.
County Court Minutes, Mar. 1804 - Jan. 1807; Jan. 1812
- Jan. 1814; July 1816 - July 1828; July 1830 - Dec.
1852; Jan. 1853 - Apr. 1861 (mf. roll #2); & May 1861
- Sept. 1964.
Dentist Register, 1891 - 1945.
Guardians' Bonds & Letters, June 1900 - Nov. 1966.
Guardians' Settlements, Aug. 1842 - Aug. 1866; Nov. 1894
- Feb. 1967.
Marriage Records, Jan. 1817 - Oct. 1836; Mar. 1837 - Sept.
1966.
Index to Guardians' & Administrators' Settlements, 1898
- 1900.
Trustees' Office Enrollment Books, 1871 - 1877.
Docket Book of B. A. Collier, J. P.
Trust Deeds, July 1875 - July 1966.
Board of Education Minutes, July 1918 - Jan. 1967.
Tax Books, 1831 - 1836; 1847-71; 1873-78; 1880-1965.
Trustees' Books, Oct. 1868 - June 1875.

DICKSON CCUNTY
(continued)

MICROFILMED RECORDS (continued)
  Merchants' Bonds, Oaths, & Licenses, Dec. 1898 - Apr. 1916.
  Board of Equalization Minutes, 1900-34.
  Physicians' Record, 1855 - 1950.
  Probate of Deeds, Oct. 1894 - Sept. 1938.
  Quarterly Court Minutes, Jan. 1936 - Jan. 1965.
  Physcians', Nurses', and Veterinarians' Register, May 1907
    - Nov. 1915.
  Tax Sales, Sept. 1897 - June 1920.
  Birth & Death Records, 1908 - 1930.
  Wills, Dec. 1803 - Dec. 1966.
  Deeds, Mar. 1804 - May 1966.
  Military Discharges, Oct. 1920 - Jan. 1964.
  Oil & Gas Leases, July 1918 - June 1935; Apr. 1944 - May
    1966.
  Plat Book, Aug. 1899 - June 1966.
  Road Minutes, May 1889 - Mar. 1891.

MANUSCRIPT MATERIALS (available at the Tennessee State Library
    and Archives):
  Church Records. Turnbull Primitive Baptist Church, Dickson
    Co., 1806-1935. (4 vols., 1 reel #164). Consists of
    minutes of sessions; and membership lists which include
    the date of death of many members.
  Church Records, McAdoo Memorial Cumberland Presbyterian
    Church, 1890-1940. (1 vol., 1 reel #168). Consists
    of minutes of sessions; registers of elders, deacons,
    communicants, baptisms, marriages, and deaths; and finan-
    cial reports of the church, which is located near the
    town of Burns.

DYER COUNTY

CREATED: 1823 from Western District (Indian lands).
COUNTY SEAT: Dyersburg, TN 38024.

LIBRARIES:
  McIvers' Grant Public Library, Dyersburg, TN 38024.
  Forked Deer Regional Library Center, Trimble, TN 38259.

PUBLISHED SOURCES:
  History Of Tennessee. [Chicago & Nashville: Goodspeed
    Publishing Co., 1887]. (Dyer Co., pp. 842-52; 1024-73.)
  Alexander. Dyer County, The Garden Spot Of The World.
    [Dyersburg: Wallace Printing Co., 1974].
  Carpenter, V. K. Dyer County, Tennessee 1850 Federal Census.
    [1969].

DYER COUNTY
(continued)

PUBLISHED SOURCES (continued)
Glass, Mrs. Quintard. Cemetery Inscription Of Dyer Co.,
Tennessee. [Southern Historical Press, 1977].
Ridens, A. H. Dyer County and Newbern, Tennessee. [1979].

W.P.A. TYPESCRIPT RECORDS (available at the Tennessee State
Library and Archives):
County Court Minutes, 1852-56, pts. I, II.
Entry Book #1, 1820-55.
Deed Book, A, 1824-27.
Wills, Vol. A, 1853-93.
Marriage Records, 1860-80.
Sketch of Life and Imprisonment of Mary Neely.

MICROFILMED RECORDS (available at the Tennessee State Library
and Archives):
1830-80; & 1900-10 Federal Census.
Enrolling Dockets, Jan. 1853 - Oct. 1885.
Minutes, May 1854 - May 1969.
Civil & Criminal Minutes, June 1863 - Mar. 1969.
Circuit Court Criminal Minutes, Apr. 1915 - Apr. 1917.
Circuit Probate Minutes, Mar. 1922 - May 1945.
Administrators' Bonds, Nov. 1871 - July 1927.
Guardians' Bonds, Dec. 1870 - July 1969.
Administrators' Bonds & Letters, July 1927 - July 1969.
Executors' Bonds & Letters, Dec. 1883 - Jan. 1969.
Insanity Records, Oct. 1919 - July 1969.
Insolvent Estates, Feb. 1915 - Jan. 1969.
Estate Inventories, Mar. 1897 - Nov. 1962.
Administrators' Letters, Dec. 1871 - July 1927.
Executors' Letters, Jan. 1886 - Apr. 1948.
Executors', Administrators', and Guardians' Letters, Aug.
1865 - July 1969.
Marriages, April 1860 - Sept. 1969.
Marriages (Negro), Jan. 1881 - Sept. 1969.
County Court Minutes, Mar. 1848 - Apr. 1856; Feb. 1865
- July 1941.
Drainage District Minutes, Aug. 1913 - Apr. 1937; Jan.
1964 - Nov. 1968.
Probate Court Minutes, Apr. 1927 - Feb. 1969.
Quarterly Court Minutes, July 1941 - Sept. 1969.
Road Commission Minutes, Jan. 1937 - Aug. 1946.
Professional Licenses, Nov. 1901 - Aug. 1963.
Administrators' & Executors' Settlements, Jan. 1885 - Oct.
1968.
Guardians' Settlements, Oct. 1865 - Oct. 1968.
Births & Deaths, 1908 - 1912.

DYER COUNTY
(continued)

MICROFILMED RECORDS (continued)
Wills, Oct. 1853 - Feb. 1969.
Board of Education Minutes, July 1907 - June 1970.
Deeds, May 1824 - July 1969.
Land Surveys, Jan. 1827 - Jan. 1860.
Military Discharges, Dec. 1918 - June 1970.
Probate Minutes, May 1945 - Dec. 1959.
Oil & Gas Leases, May 1950 - Mar. 1969.
Oil & Gas Leases & Liens, July 1933 - May 1970.
Plats, Apr. 1928 - Nov. 1969.
Survey Entries, Dec. 1820 - May 1911.
Trust Deeds, Jan. 1912 - July 1969.
Cash Journals, 1922 - 1962.
Tax Books, 1862; 1873-84; 1885 - 1966 (intermittantly).

MANUSCRIPT MATERIALS (available at the Tennessee State Library
and Archives):

Church Records. Hopewell Presbytery of the Cumberland
Presbyterian Church, 1824-1892. (4 vols., 1 reel #176).
Records of Carroll, DYER, Gibson, Obion, and Weakley
counties in West Tennessee. There are four volumes,
some containing minutes, membership lists, lists of
ministers and elders, and a statistical report.

FAYETTE COUNTY

CREATED: 1824 from Hardeman [1823 from the Western District]
and Shelby County [1819 from Hardin Co.].
COUNTY SEAT: Somerville, TN 38068.

LIBRARY: Fayette County Public Library, Somerville, TN 38068.

PUBLISHED SOURCES:
History Of Tennessee. [Chicago & Nashville: Goodspeed
Publishing Co., 1887]. (Fayette Co., pp. 797-817; 840-887.)
"1840 Census, Fayette County, Tennessee," Ansearchin' News,
v.17 (1970), no. 3; 106-112.
Carpenter, V. K. Fayette County, Tennessee 1850 Federal
Census. [1969].
"1850 Mortality Schedule for Fayette County, Tennessee,"
Ansearchin' News, v.17 (1970), no. 3; 113-15.

FAYETTE COUNTY
(continued)

PUBLISHED SOURCES (continued)
"Fayette County, Tennessee Marriages, 1838-1841," Ansearch-in' News, v.17 (1970), no. 3; 117-24.

W.P.A. TYPESCRIPT RECORDS (available at the Tennessee State Library and Archives):
Court of Pleas & Quarter Sessions Minute Book A, 1824-29.
Marriage Record A, 1838-57.
Church Minutes of Immanual Episcopal Church, La Grange, Tenn. 1848-54.
History of St. Thomas Episcopal Church, Somerville, Tenn.

MICROFILMED RECORDS (available at the Tennessee State Library and Archives):
1830-80; & 1900-10 Federal Census.
Circuit Court Minutes, June 1829 - Sept. 1900.
Guardians' & Administrators' Settlements, Feb. 1868 - Feb. 1902.
Marriages, Feb. 1838 - July 1859.
Marriage Records, May 1859 - July 1875.
Marriage Bonds, Oct. 1866 - De. 1869.
County Court Minutes, Dec. 1824 - Apr. 1833; July 1833 - Jan. 1900.
Administrators' Letters, Nov. 1891 - Apr. 1965.
Guardians' Settlements, Aug. 1885 - May 1914.
Quarterly Minutes, Oct. 1877 - Jan. 1904.
Inventory, Jan. 1854 - Mar. 1856.
Settlements Book, May 1858 - Apr. 1860.
Wills, June 1836 - Nov. 1905.
Vital Statistics: Deaths with ages and places of birth, 1925-1927.
Entry Bock, June 1821 - Mar. 1881.
Deed Books, Apr. 1825 - Mar. 1900.
Masonic Lodge #75, Minutes, 1829-1910.
Willison Methodist Womans' Society.
Sesquicentennial Edition Fayette Falcon.
Account Book, 1878 - 1879.
150 Years in Fayette County, 1824-1974.

MANUSCRIPT MATERIALS (available at the Tennessee State Library and Archives):
Associations, Institutions, etc. Confederate Veterans Association of Upper East Tennessee, 1861 - ca. 1895. (1 vol. 1 reel #167). Roster containing name, county, state, date of enlistment, company and regiment, rank wounds received, date and cause of discharge, and general remarks about members of the association living in Fayette and other Tennessee Counties.

FAYETTE COUNTY
(continued)

MANUSCRIPT MATERIALS (continued)
County Records. Fayette County, TN. Miscellaneous Records, ca. 1807-1944. (40 items, 11 vols., 2 reels #569). Assorted records including those of Somerville Masonic Lodge; records of the Williston Methodist Church; photographs; historical sketch of the county; and various cemetery records.
Church Records. St. Thomas Episcopal Church at Somerville, 1872-1916 (1 vol.). Mt. Pleasant Cumberland Presbyterian Church at Macon, 1847-1935, (4 vols., 1 reel #225). Church minutes along with a list of baptisms, confirmations, communicants, memberships, marriages, births, deaths, burials, etc., at both churches.
Church Records. Moscow Methodist Church, 1890-1970, (1 vol., 1 reel #360). Register of baptisms; lists of pastors and members, etc.
Church Records. Mt. Pisgah Primitive Church, 1832-1901, (2 vols., 1 reel #361). Records consisting of membership lists, including some death dates; etc.

FENTRESS COUNTY

CREATED: 1823 from Morgan [1817 from Roane Co.] and Overton County [1806 from Jackson Co.]
COUNTY SEAT: Jamestown, TN 38556.

LIBRARY: Fentress County Public Library, Jamestown, TN 38556.

HISTORICAL SOCIETY: Fentress County Historical Society, Box 324, Jamestown, TN. 38556.

PUBLISHED SOURCES:
Carpenter, V. K. Fentress County, Tenn. 1850 Federal Census. [1970].
Hogue, A. R. History Of Fentress County. [Nashville: Williams Printing Co., 1916].

W.P.A. TYPESCRIPT RECORDS (available at the Tennessee State Library and Archives):
Entry Book, A, 1824-1836.
Deed Books, A & B, 1824-38.
Circuit Court Minute Book, 1, 1842-44.

FENTRESS COUNTY
(continued)

MICROFILMED RECORDS (available at the Tennessee State Library
and Archives):
1830-80; & 1900-10 Federal Census.
Enrolling Book, Aug. 1847 - Sept. 1912.
Clerk & Masters' Minutes, Sept. 1854 - Apr. 1904.
Marriages, Jan. 1905 - Aug. 1915.
Deeds, Nov. 1820 - Sept. 1901.
Trust Deeds, June 1889 - Nov. 1901.
Land Entries Books, Apr. 1824 - Nov. 1901.

MANUSCRIPT MATERIALS (available at the Tennessee State Library
and Archives):
Diaries, Memoirs, etc. Colditz, B. M., 1870-72; 1885-89,
(2 vols., 1 reel #68.)
Papers of Albert Ross Hogue, 1790-1960, ca. 50 items, (2
vols., 1 reel #140). Autobiography containing copies
of some early census records, land grants, lists of
county officials, lists of soldiers in various wars
from this county, and other items of genealogical and
historical interest.
Cemeteries. Anderson County, TN, 1800-1974, ca. 160 items,
(1 reel #506). These cemetery records for Anderson
County also include some cemetery records for Fentress
and other Tennessee counties.

FRANKLIN COUNTY

CREATED: 1807 from Warren [1807 from White] and Bedford
County [1807 from Rutherford Co.].
COUNTY SEAT: Winchester, TN 37398.

SPECIAL NOTE: Some of the county records were burned in
1863.

LIBRARY: Franklin County Library, Winchester, TN 37398.

HISTORICAL SOCIETY: Franklin County Historical Society,
105 S. Porter, Winchester, TN 37398.

PUBLISHED SOURCES:
Burks, Billie & Hall. Marriage Records Of Franklin County,
Tennessee, 1838-1875.
Carpenter, V. K. U.S. Census Office, 7th Census 1850.
[Huntsville: Century Enterprises, 1970].

PUBLISHED SOURCES (continued)
Cemetery Records Of Franklin County, Tennessee. Franklin
County Historical Society.
History Of Tennessee. [Chicago & Nashville: Gocdspeed
Publishing Co., 1887]. (Franklin Co., pp. 785-804;
820-846.)
Rhoton, T. F. "A Brief History Of Franklin County," Thesis,
University of TN, Knoxville. 1941.
Rogers, E. Focus On Franklin County. [Winchester: The
Author, 1966].
Sherrill, Charles A. Revolutionary War Pension Applications
From Franklin County, Tennessee. [1883].
Swenson, Helen. Franklin County Tennessee 1860 Census
And Marriages For Head Of Household. [St. Louis: Francis
Terry Ingmire, 1981].

W.P.A. TYPESCRIPT RECORDS (available at the Tennessee State
Library and Archives):
Record Book, A, 1808-18.
Will Books, 1 & 2, 1808-76.
County Court Minutes, v.2, 1832-37, pts. I, II.
Settlements Book, v.1, 1837-43, pts. I, II.
Marriages, 1838-75.

MICROFILMED RECORDS (available at the Tennessee State Library
and Archives):
1820-80; & 1900-10 Federal Census.
Circuit Court Minutes, Jan. 1832 - May 1968.
Clerk & Masters' Chamber Minutes, Sept. 1921 - Nov. 1943.
Clerk & Masters' Minutes, July 1834 - Aug. 1845; Feb. 1850
- June 1968.
Administrators' Bonds & Letters, Nov. 1898 - June 1968.
Administrators', Executors' & Guardians' Bonds, Aug. 1872
- Dec. 1898.
Administrators', Executors' & Guardians' Letters, Sept.
1882 - Sept. 1898.
Administrators', Executors' & Guardians' Settlements, May
1844 - Apr. 1848; Feb. 1851 - Mar. 1854; Sept. 1857
- Apr. 1869; May 1875 - Aug. 1882; Sept. 1959 - July
1968.
Conservators' Bonds & Letters, Dec. 1956 - July 1968.
Executors' Bonds & Letters, Mar. 1898 - June 1968.
Guardians Bonds & Letters, Dec. 1898 - July 1968.
Guardians' Settlements, Sept. 1882 - Oct. 1959.
Inventories of Estates, Nov. 1952 - June 1968.
Marriages, Jan. 1838 - July 1968.
Merchants' Licenses, June 1879 - July 1895.

FRANKLIN COUNTY
(continued)

MICROFILMED RECORDS (continued)
  World War I Discharges; indexed.
  County Court Minutes, May 1832 - Apr. 1845; Nov. 1849 -
    July 1968.
  Nurses' Register, Aug. 1925 - Oct. 1952.
  Optmetry Register, June 1909 - Aug. 1940.
  Physicians' Records, Aug. 1889 - Oct. 1932; Feb. 1939 -
    July 1966.
  Quarterly Court Minutes, Apr. 1952 - July 1968.
  Ranger Book & Land Surveys, July 1868 - Dec. 1925.
  Death Records, 1881-83.
  Birth & Death Records, 1908-12.
  Wills, Sept. 1808 - July 1968.
  Deeds, Jan. 1808 - July 1968.
  Land Entries, Apr. 1824 - Feb. 1891.
  Military Discharges, Feb. 1944 - Sept. 1968.
  Oil & Gas Leases, Nov. 1911 - June 1924; Feb. 1947 - June
    1958.
  Plat Book, Nov. 1963 - Oct. 1967.
  Trust Deeds, Jan. 1872 - Aug. 1968.
  Board of Education Minutes, June 1949 - Oct. 1968.
  Cash Journals, Sept. 1927 - Oct. 1963.
  Tax Books, 1852-59; 1861-71; 1873-1966 (intermittantly).

MANUSCRIPT MATERIALS (available at the Tennessee State Library
    and Archives):
  Surveyor Books, 1814-1929, George Gray. (2 vols., 1 reel
    #171). Vol. 2 of these books consists of Gray's records
    of surveys completed, persons for whom they were done,
    and grant numbers.
  Collection of Mrs. Bernie Moore, 1833-1877, (2 vols., 1
    item, 1 reel #284). This collection consists of three
    seperate items: The daybook 1833-47, of the Reeves
    & Co. dry goods store in Winchester containing lists
    of materials sold, names of purchasers, etc. The records,
    1845-46, of the Winchester Polemick Society include
    the constitution, names of members, etc. The catalog,
    1876-77, of the Carrick Academy located in Winchester,
    contains the names of students and descriptions of
    courses.
  Church Records. Otey Memorial Parish and St. Mark's Mission,
    Sewanee, TN., 1873-1968, (7 vols, 1 reel #397). Five
    volumes of records for Otey Memorial Parish and two
    volumes for St. Mark's Mission, containing baptismal
    records, confimations, burials, marriages; and some
    records for St. Agnes' Mission in Cowan, TN.

FRANKLIN COUNTY
(continued)

MANUSCRIPT MATERIALS (continued)
  Church Records of the Baptist Church, Athens, 1834-1939,
  (reel #333). Records of membership, articles of faith,
  minutes of session, rules of order, church covenant,
  etc.

ADDITIONAL CHURCH RECORDS (may be purchased from the Historical
  Commission of the Southern Baptist Convention, 127 Ninth
  Ave. N., Nashville, TN 37234):
  Winchester. First Baptist Church, 1842-1937, (microfilm
  reel #1096).

GIBSON COUNTY

CREATED: 1823 from the Western District (Indian lands).
COUNTY SEAT: Trenton, TN 38382.

LIBRARY: Gibson County Memorial Library, 303 S. High St.,
Trenton, TN 38382.

HISTORICAL SOCIETY: Gibson County Historical Society, Trenton,
TN 38382.

PUBLISHED SOURCES:
  Carpenter, V. K. Gibson County, Tennessee 1850 Federal
    Census. [1970].
  Rose Hill Cemetery In Humbolt, Tennessee, 1868-1974.
    ClementScott Chapter, D.A.R., 1976-77.]
  Culp, F. M. & M. R. E. Ross. Gibson County, Past And Pre-
    sent, [Trenton: Gibson Co. Historical Society, 1961].
  Gossum, Mary Louise & Emily B. Walker. Gibson County,
    Tennessee Marriage Records; Vol. A, June, 1860 - Nov.,
    1870. [1984].
  History Of Tennessee. [Chicago & Nashville: Goodspeed
    Publishing Co., 1887]. (Gibson Co., pp. 797-816; 857-931.)
  Hargroves. The Honor Roll, U.S.A., 1917-1918-1919, [Eaton,
    TN, 1920].
  Whitley, E. R. Marriages Of Gibson County, Tennessee.
    [Baltimore: Genealogical Publishing Co., Inc., 1982].

W.P.A. TYPESCRIPT RECORDS (available at the Tennessee State
  Library and Archives):
  County Court Minute Book, A, 1824-28.
  Circuit Court Minute Book, A, 1824-32.

GIBSON COUNTY
(continued)

W.P.A. TYPESCRIPT RECORDS (continued)
Minute Book, A, Chancery Court, 1834-47, pts. I,II, & III.
Wills & Bonds, Book D, 1846-52.
Marriage Licenses & Bonds, 1824-60.
Captain King's Diary.

MICROFILMED RECORDS (available at the Tennessee State Library
    and Archives):
1830-80; & 1900-10 Federal Census.
Chancery Court Enrolling Books, May 1834 - Nov. 1876.
Clerk & Masters' Minutes, Mar. 1840 - Nov. 1900.
Circuit Court Minutes, May 1824 - July 1901.
Administrators' Bonds, Apr. 1860 - Dec. 1905.
Administrators' Books, May 1843 - July 1865.
Adminstrators' Settlements, May 1874 - Feb. 1903.
Administrators' & Executors' Accounts, Jan. 1852 - July
    1884.
County Court Enrolling Books, Dec. 1858 - Dec. 1868; Aug.
    1871 - Sept. 1874; Sept. 1886 - Feb. 1892.
Guardians' Book, May 1843 - May 1862; Jan. 1872 - Nov.
    1879.
Guardians' Bonds, May 1860 - Feb. 1922.
Guardians' Settlements, Apr. 1860 - Mar. 1900 (except 1872-78;
    & 1894).
Insolvent Estate Minutes, June 1876 - July 1909.
Claims against Estates, Oct. 1862 - Jan. 1917.
Estate Inventories, Nov. 1836 - June 1872.
Estate Settlements, Feb. 1870 - Aug. 1882.
Marriage Bonds, 1824-63; May 1888 - May 1912; May 1912
    - June 1917.
County Marriage Records, June 1860 - Dec. 1919.
County Court Minutes, Jan. 1824 - 1901.
Quarterly Court Minutes, Apr. 1891 - July 1900.
Road Book, July 1883; 1889 - Jan. 1891.
Accounts with Heirs, Dec. 1890 - Aug. 1905.
Auto Registers, June 1911 - Dec. 1919.
Births, 1881-82.
Births & Deaths, 1909-11.
Will Books, Jan. 1824 - Aug. 1908.
Deeds, Apr. 1819 - June 1900.
Trust Deeds, Apr. 1875 - July 1900.
Entry Book, May 1821 - Oct. 1845.
Grants, Sept. 1785 - Dec. 1793.
Survey Book, May 1821 - Apr. 1837.
Deed of Conveyance, Oct. 1827 - Mar. 1832.
Tax Duplicates, 1867 - 1900.
Marriage Record Books, 1824-63.

GIBSON COUNTY
(continued)

MANUSCRIPT MATERIAL (available at the Tennessee State
Library and Archives):
Church Records. Hopewell Presbytery of the Cumberland
Presbyterian Church, 1824-1892, (4 vols., 1 reel #176).
These records contain minutes, membership lists, lists
of ministers and elders, and a statistical report for
not only Gibson, but also, Carroll, Dyer, Obion, and
Weakley Counties.

GILES COUNTY

CREATED: 1809 from Maury County [1807 from Williamson Co.].
COUNTY SEAT: Pulaski, TN 38478.

SPECIAL NOTE: Courthouse burned in 1864-65.

LIBRARY: Giles County Public Library, Pulaski, TN 38478 (has
good collection of secondary sources books and manuscript
materials, which were inventoried in the Tennessee Genealogical Review Quarterly, Vol. 1, no. 9 (Nov. 1980), pp. 55-58.

HISTORICAL SOCIETY: Giles Co. Historical Society, 1225 2nd
St., Pulaski, TN 38478.
PUBLISHED SOURCES:
Brown, Erma L. S. Giles County, Tennessee Marriages, 1818-
1862. [1978].
Browning, Ruth B. Book B. Record Of Causes Decided In
Chancery Court At Pulaski, Giles County, Tennessee,
Sept. Term 1838 - March Term 1842. [1983].
Butler. Tall Tales & True Stories Of Giles Countains.
Butler. History Of First Methodist Church.
Cosby. Cemeteries, Giles Co., TN.
Cosby. Marriages & Deaths, Giles Co., Tenn.
Ensby, H. Index To Giles County, Tenn. Wills. [Nashville:
1960].
Giles County Lineage Book. [Giles Co. Historical Society,
1982].
History Of Tennessee. [Chicago & Nashville: Goodspeed
Publishing Co., 1887]. (Giles Co., pp. 749-66; 846-76.)
Lighfoot & Shackleford. Giles-Maury County Neighbors,
[Mt. Pleasant: 1967].
McCallum, James. Settlement And Early History Of Giles
County, [Pulaski: Pulaski Citizen, 1876]. Reprinted
1983.

GILES COUNTY
(continued)

PUBLISHED SOURCES (continued)
   Porch. U.S. Census Office, 7th Census 1850, [Nashville:
      1971].
   Smith. Marriages Of Giles County, Tennessee. [Elkmont,
      Ala.: 1952].
   Weddington. "Early Giles County Marriages," Ansearchin'
      News, v.6 (1959), no. 1: 1-2; no. 2:3-4; & no. 3:5-8.
   Williams & Beasley. History Of Giles County, Tennessee.
   Giles County, TN Sesequicentennial, 1809-1859.
   Bulletin, Giles Co. Historical Society, 1974-.
   Cemetery Records Of Giles County, Tennessee. (publication
      pending during preparation of this work; announced by
      the Giles Co. Hist. Soc.)

W.P.A. TYPESCRIPT RECORDS (available at the Tennessee State
      Library and Archives):
   General Index to Deeds, v.A, 1818-59.
   County Court Minutes, Books B & C, 1813-15; 1816-17.
   County Court Minutes, v.H, 1823-25, pts. I & II.
   Court of Pleas & Quarter Sessions Minute Book, v.1, 1825-27.
   County Court Minutes, 1833.
   Miscellaneous Wills, 1830-57.
   Marriage Records, v.2, 1865-70.
   First Presbyterian Church & Masonic Hall, Pulaski, 1828-30.
   Minutes of Trustees and Building Committee of Pisgah (Metho-
      dist) Church, 1867-69.

MICROFILMED RECORDS (available at the Tennessee State Library
      and Archives):
   1820-80; & 1900-10 Federal Census.
   Chancery Court Enrollment Books, Oct. 1860 - Sept. 1875.
   Chancery Court Minutes, Sept. 1838 - Feb. 1902.
   Sale Book, Oct. 1870 - Nov. 1921.
   Circuit Court Minutes, Apr. 1817 - Feb. 1902.
   Enrollment Books, Aug. 1866 - July 1876.
   Administrators' Bonds & Letters, Apr. 1865 - Oct. 1878.
   Guardians' Bonds & Letters, Apr. 1867 - Apr. 1872; May
      1883 - Aug. 1890.
   Administrators' Letters, July 1878 - July 1897.
   Guardians' Bonds, Aug. 1890 - Apr. 1899.
   Marriages, 1818-62; 1865 - Nov. 1913.
   Inventory of Estates, Apr. 1871 - Aug. 1906.
   County Court Minutes, Dec. 1810 - Apr. 1902.
   Administrators' Settlements, Apr. 1865 - Jan. 1903.
   Vital Statistics, 1908-1912.
   Wills & Inventories & Settlements, Apr. 1860 - June 1917.
   Deeds, June 1790 - Feb. 1900.

GILES COUNTY
(continued)

MICROFILMED RECORDS (continued)
Charter Books, Mar. 1875 - Mar. 1892.
Land Entries & Surveys, Apr. 1824 - Dec. 1889.
Trust Deeds, July 1868 - Aug. 1900.
Rehobeth Methodist Church Records, May 22, 1848.
Bee Springs Methodist Church Records, 1815.
Bee Springs Southern Presbyterian Church Records, 1937-1970.
Manual Brick Church Records.
Bethel Society Prospects.
Cemetery Records, Thomas Wilkerson, Mitchell.
Bible Records: Dowing, Randall, Abernathy, Comer, Yokely,
    Collins, Sands, Evans, Land, Walker, Coffman, Blasingim,
    Butler, Smith, Hamilton, Beazley, Pollard.
Miscellaneous Materials.

MANUSCRIPT MATERIALS (available at the Tennessee State Library
    and Archives):
Church Records. Roberson Fork Church of Christ, Lynnville,
    TN, 1830-68. (1 vol., 1 reel #334). Records consisting
    of minutes of sessions, membership lists for Blacks
    and Whites.
Cemeteries. South Carolina and Tennessee, ca. 1850 - 1956.
    (ca. 125 items, 1 reel #307). Alphabetical listing,
    by county, of tombstone inscriptions from 25 SC and
    48 TN cemeteries, including some from Giles Co.
Accounts and Account Books. Elkton General Store. Account
    Book, 1854-55. Account book listing customers' names,
    items purchased and prices. The first part contains
    clippings of obituaries and historical data.
County Records. Miscellaneous Records, 1750-1970. (150
    items, 12 vols., 2 reels #499). This collection consists
    of Bible, church, cemetery records, genealogical data,
    legal documents, scrapbooks, sketches, account books,
    and Civil War diaries of Louis L. Adams; and numerous
    early Giles County families are mentioned.
County Records. Lawrence County, Tennessee, ca. 1800-1940,
    (reel #566). Besides the assorted Lawrence County re-
    cords, there are Bible records and papers of the Alexander
    family of Giles County.
ADDITIONAL CHURCH RECORDS (may be purchased from the Historical
    Commission of the Southern Baptist Convention, 127 Ninth
    Ave., N., Nashville, TN 37234):
Prospect Baptist Church Records, July 1826 - 1862, (microfilm
    #526)

GRAINGER COUNTY

CREATED: 1796 from Hawkins [1786 from Sullivan Co.] and Knox County [1792 from Greene & Hawkins Cos.].
COUNTY SEAT: Rutledge, TN 37861.

LIBRARY: Grainger Co. Public Library, Rt. 4, Rutledge, TN 37861.

PUBLISHED SOURCES:
"Early East Tennessee Taxpayers; IV, Grainger County, 1799," by Creekmore; East Tennessee Historical Society Publications, no. 27 (1955), pp. 97-116.
History Of Tennessee. [Chicago & Nashville: Goodspeed Publishing Co., 1887]. (Grainger Co., pp. 853-56; 1152-60.)
"Index to grantee and locators in Grainger County, 1824-1860," by O'Hara; Ansearchin' News, v.10 (1963), no. 2, pp. 63-68; no. 3, pp. 119-124; & no. 4, pp. 173-178.
Roach, Thomas E. Gleanings From A Scrapbook. [1983]. Newspaper articles written over past 20 years, including historical articles on Grainger & Jefferson Cos.
_____ Gone But Not Forgotten. [1985]. Tombstone inscriptions from south of Clinch Mountain.
Sheffield, Ella L. Grainger County, Tennessee, Court Of Pleas And Quarter Sessions Record Book No.3, 1812-1816. [1983].
Lucas, Silas Emmett, Jr. Grainger County, Tennessee Records, Letters Of Administrations, 1842-1854. [1983].
Whitley, E. R. Marriages Of Grainger County, Tennessee, 1796-1837. [Baltimore: Genealogical Publishing Co., Inc., 1982].
Grainger County, Tennessee Cemetery Records, Volume 1. (details received incomplete - suggest contacting area libraries for this work.

W.P.A. TYPESCRIPT RECORDS (available at the Tennessee State Library and Archives):
County Court Minute Book, 1796-1802.
Minutes, Court of Pleas & Quarter Sessions, v.2, 1802-12, pts. I & II.
Record Book No. 3, 1812-16.
Marriage Records, 1796-1837.
Marriage Records, 1838-1857.
Polls & Taxable Property, 1814-1815.
Wills & Settlements, 1833-1841.
Letters of Administration, 1842-54.
Tombstone Records.
Merchants, Voters, Names, Scholastic Population, 1809-1848.
Guardian Bonds, 1796-1835.
Loose Wills.

GRAINGER COUNTY
(continued)

MICROFILMED RECORDS (available at the Tennessee State Library
   and Archives):
1830-80; & 1900-10 Federal Census.
Chancery Court Enrollment Books, Apr. 1872 - Apr. 1876.
Clerk & Master Minutes, June 1848 - Mar. 1904.
Circuit Court Enrollment Books, Oct. 1829 - Oct. 1834;
   Aug. 1852 - May 1853.
Equity Cases, 1826 - Oct. 1835.
Circuit Court Minutes, Aug. 1845 - Dec. 1904.
Administrators' & Executors' Settlements, Jan. 1899 - Oct.
   1914.
Executors' Bonds & Letters, Nov. 1856 - 1972.
Administrators' Bonds & Letters, May 1831 - Oct. 1910.
Guardian Bonds, 1856 - Sept. 1904.
Inventories of Estates, 1860-1901.
Insolvent Estates, Apr. 1885 - Nov. 1921.
Guardian Settlements, 1859 - Nov. 1900.
Marriages, 1796 - July 1916.
County Court Minutes, June 1796 - Dec. 1899.
Quarterly Minutes, Apr. 1890 - Apr. 1901.
Vital Statistics, 1908-1912.
Inventory of Estates & Wills, Nov. 1833 - Aug. 1892.
Wills, Nov. 1856 - Oct. 1917.
Deeds, Sept. 1796 - Dec. 1901.
Trust Deeds, June 1868 - Jan. 1905.
Entry Takers' Books, Feb. 1818 - Mar. 1921.
Land Entry Book, Mar. 1824 - May 1852.
Tax Duplicates, 1851-1900.

MANUSCRIPT MATERIAL (available at the Tennessee State Library
   and Archives):
Associations, Institutions, etc. Confederate Veterans
   Association of Upper East Tennessee, 1861 - ca. 1895,
   (microfilm #167). A roster containing name, county,
   state, date of enlistment, company and regiment, rank,
   wounds received, date and cause of discharge, and general
   remarks about members of the association living in Grainger County and other Tennessee Counties.
Cemeteries, 1800-1972. (45 items, 1 vol., 1 reel #505).
   Cemetery records for several church and family cemeteries
   in Grainger County and a few in Hawkins County. Also,
   the account book, 1850-53 for Marshall's Ferry general
   store giving names of customers, items purchased, etc.
Scrapbook Collection of Reuel B. Prichett, ca. 1820-1969,
   (microfilm #544). This includes newspaper clippings,
   photographs, and historical and biographical sketches
   concerning persons, places, and events in Jefferson
   Co., TN, and some information on Grainger Co.

GREENE COUNTY

CREATED: 1783 from Washington Co., NC.
COUNTY SEAT: Greeneville, TN 37743.

LIBRARY: Greeneville-Greene Co. Library, 210 North Main
St., Greeneville, TN 37743.

HISTORICAL SOCIETY: Greene County Heritage Trust, Box 108,
Greeneville, TN 37743.

PUBLISHED SOURCES:
Brown, Florence M. Greene County Court House Old Marriage
Bonds, 1791-1800.
Burgner, Goldene F. Greene County Minutes Of The Court
Of Common Pleas, 1783-1795. [1982].
_____ Green County, Tennessee Marriages, 1783-1868. [1981].
_____ Green County Tax Digests, 1809-1817. [1983].
_____ Greene County, Tennessee, Wills, 1783-1890. [1981].
_____ North Carolina Land Grants Recorded In Greene County,
Tennessee. [1981].
Burgner, Golden F., Marian K. Crosby, and A. C. Duggins.
St. James Lutheran Church, Greene Co., TN., "Kirchen
Boch" (Church Book). [Greeneville: 1964].
"Early East Tennessee Society Taxpayers, IX, Greene County,
1805," by Pollyanna Creekmore, East Tennessee Historical
Society Publications, no. 33 (1961), pp. 97-105.
"Early East Tennessee Taxpayers, XIV, Greene Co., 1783,"
by Pollyanna Creekmore, East Tennessee Historical Society
Publications, No. 39 (1967), pp. 118-130.
History Of Tennessee. [Chicago & Nashville: Goodspeed
Publishing Co., 1887] (Greene Co., pp. 881-890;
1239-1261).
Houston, Sandra Kelton. Greene County Minutes Of The Court
Of Common Pleas, 1797-1807. [1981].
_____ Greene County, Tennessee - Orphan's Court 1783-1870
And Greene County, Tennessee 1830 Tax List. [1983].
Index to Buford Reynolds' Greene County Cemeteries, by
McClung Collection, Lawson McGhee Library, Knoxville,
1973
Reynolds, Buford. Greene County Cemeteries. [1971]
Sodenberg, Gertrude L. Green County (original bonds and
licenses). [Knoxville: Clinchdale Press, 1965].

W.P.A. TYPESCRIPT RECORDS: (available at the Tennessee State
Library and Archives):
Wills & Inventories, 1802-10.
Inventories & Sales, 1828-43, pts. I, II, & III.
Tombstone Records.
Tax Book, 1809-1817.

GREENE COUNTY
(continued)

W.P.A. TYPESCRIPT RECORDS (continued)
  Minutes of the Court of Pleas & Quarter Sessions, 1783-96.
  County Court Records, 1802-04.
  County Court Minutes, 1805; 1806-07; 1807-09.
  Minutes of the Court of Pleas & Quarter Sessions, 1810-12;
     1812-14; 1815-16; 1817-19; 1820-22; 1826-27; 1828-29;
     & 1829-32.
  County Court Minutes, 1824-25; and v.13 1825-26.

MICROFILMED RECORDS (available at the Tennessee State Library
     and Archives):
  1830-80; & 1900-10 Federal Census.
  Delinquent Tax Docket, Sept. 1938 - Apr. 1972.
  Chancery Court Enrolling Dockets, Feb. 1828 - Nov. 1845.
  Land Sales, 1897-1920.
  Chancery Court Minutes, Nov. 1824 - Mar. 1973.
  Circuit Court Civil Minutes, Nov. 1809 - Mar. 1973.
  Circuit Court Criminal Minutes, Aug. 1815 - Feb. 1973.
  Privilege License Register, Mar. 1833 - Aug. 1856.
  Administrators' Bonds & Letters, Sept. 1882 - May 1973.
  Executors' Bonds and Letters, June 1883 - May 1973.
  Guardians' Bonds and Letters, Apr. 1882 - Jan. 1973.
  Claims against estates, Oct. 1921 - May 1973.
  Insanity Records, Jan. 1871 - Apr. 1959.
  Insolvent Estates, Accounts of, Jan 1843 - Aug. 1901.
  Marriages, Jan. 1870 - June 1973.
  County Court Minutes, Aug. 1783 - June 1973.
  Quarterly Court Minutes, Feb. 1935 - Apr. 1973.
  Road Commission Minutes, July 1834 - June 1973.
  Professional Licenses Register; Optometrists, Aug. 1909
     - July 1924.
  Administrators' & Executors' Settlements, Oct. 1802 - June
     1973.
  Guardians' Settlements, June 1872 - July 1973.
  Vital Statistics; Births, Nov. 1881 - Mar. 1939; Deaths,
     May 1881 - May 1939.
  Wills, Jan. 1828 - May 1973.
  Board of Education Minutes, July 1928 - Dec. 1972.
  Deeds, Mar. 1785 - May 1966.
  Land Entries, Apr. 1824 - Sept. 1905.
  Military Discharges, 1861-1865; 1918; May 1930 - Mar. 1973.
  Oil & Gas Leases, Jan. 1867 - Mar. 1973.
  Plat Books, Nov. 1915 - Mar. 1973.
  Surveyors' Book, May 1824 - June 1905.
  Trust Deeds, Aug. 1841 - Apr. 1954.
  Cash Journals, 1921-41.
  Tax Books, 1809 - 1913 (intermittantly).

GREENE COUNTY
(continued)

MANUSCRIPT MATERIALS (available at the Tennessee State Library
and Archives):
County Records, 1784-1831. (74 items). Original court
records covering the dates, 1784-1831, containing bonds,
cost and damage suits, indictments, summons, and two
land surveys.

GRUNDY COUNTY

CREATED: 1846 from Coffee [1846 from Warren, Franklin, &
Bedford Cos. (first Court met 1836)] and Warren County
[1807 from White].
COUNTY SEAT: Altamont, TN 37301].

LIBRARY: Altamont Public Library, Altamont, TN 37301.

PUBLISHED SOURCES:
Douthat, James L. Grundy County, Tennessee Marriages
1850-1874. [1982].
Sherrill, Charles A. Grundy County, Tennessee Marriage
Records 1844-1880. [1984].
_____ Tombstone Inscriptions Of Grundy County, Tennessee.
[Decorah, Iowa: Anundsen Pub., Co., 1977].

W.P.A. TYPESCRIPT RECORDS (available at the Tennessee State
Library and Archives):
Will Book, 1, 1838-74.
County Court Minute Book, 1, pts. I & II.
Marriage Record Book, A, 1850-74.
Estate Settlement Book, 1852-95.

MICROFILMED RECORDS (available at the Tennessee State Library
and Archives):
1850-80; & 1900-10 Federal Census.
Circuit Court Clerk Minutes, Apr. 1848 - Jan. 1854;
Jan. 1883 - Aug. 1968.
Clerk & Masters' Enrollment Books, Sept. 1872 - June 1913.
Chamber Minutes, June 1912 - 1928.
Land Sales, 1912-28.
Minutes, Sept. 1856 - Sept. 1968.
Administrators' & Guardians' Settlements, Jan. 1841 - Jan.
1860; June 1885 - Jan. 1968.
Administrators', Executors', & Guardians' Bonds & Letters,
Apr. 1902 - Sept. 1968.

GRUNDY COUNTY
(continued)

MICROFILMED RECORDS (continued)
  Board of Equalization Minutes, June 1912 - June 1953.
  Conservators' Bonds & Letters, Sept. 1961 - July 1968.
  Scholastic Population Enumeration, 1876-80.
  Insolvent Estates, May 1856 - Aug. 1954.
  Inventory Books, Feb. 1857 - Sept. 1968.
  Land Sales, June 1902 - Sept. 1906; Mar. 1909 - June 1911.
  Marriage Records, Apr. 1850 - Nov. 1968.
  Minutes, Aug. 1844 - Sept. 1968.
  Optometry Register, Nov. 1909 - Mar. 1930.
  Physicians' Register, May 1907 - Aug. 1956.
  Road Commissioner's Book, June 1891 - Oct. 1899.
  Vital Statistics: Births & Deaths, 1908-12.
  Wills, May 1838 - Mar. 1966.
  Deeds, Sept. 1852 - Feb. 1968.
  Land Entry Takers' Book, Jan. 1869 - Sept. 1898.
  Military Discharges, July 1919 - Nov. 1967.
  Miscellaneous Records, Sept. 1910 - May 1937; Feb. 1959
    - Oct. 1967.
  Oil & Gas Leases, Oct. 1946 - May 1958.
  Survey Book, Sept. 1844 - Oct. 1968.
  Trust Deeds, Oct. 1882 - May 1968.
  Board of Education Minutes, Sept. 1940 - Aug. 1968.
  Tax Books, 1850-77; 1880-89; 1892-96; 1899 - 1967.

HAMBLEN COUNTY

CREATED: 1870 from Grainger [1796 from Hawkins & Knox Cos.],
  Jefferson [1792 from Greene & Hawkins Cos.], and Hawkins
  Counties [1786 from Sullivan Co.].
  COUNTY SEAT: Morristown, TN 37814.

LIBRARIES:
  Morristown-Hamblen County Library, 417 West Main St., Morris-
    town, TN 37814.
  Nolichucky Regional Library, 315 McCrary Drive, Morristown,
    TN 37814.

HISTORICAL SOCIETY: Morristown-Hamblen Historical Commission,
  432 W. 2nd N. St., Morristown, TN 37814.

PUBLISHED SOURCES:
  Douthat, James L. Hamblen County, Tennessee Marriage Book
    1-5. [1984].

HAMBLEN COUNTY
(continued)

PUBLISHED SOURCES (continued)
History Of Tennessee. [Chicago & Nashville: Goodspeed
    Pub. Co., 1887]. (Hamblen Co., 868-71; 1200-1216.
Historic Hamblen 1870-1970. Hamblen County Historical
    Society. (Includes petition to form Hamblen Co. signed
    by 1,057 persons.)
Lane, Ernest O. Bent Creek Cemetery Inscriptions. [Whites-
    burg, TN: 1970].
Rudicil, R. K., F. Taylor, & W. H. Inman. Historic Hamblen.
    [Morristown, TN: Morristown Printing, 1970].

W.P.A. TYPESCRIPT RECORDS (available at the Tennessee State
    Library and Archives):
Marriage Records, Vol. I, 1870-73.
Marriage Records, Vol. II, 1873-76; Vol. III, 1877-82.
Bent Creek Church Minutes, 1785-1844.
History of Morristown, 1787-1936.
Record Books, A, B, & C, Westminister & St. Paul's Presby-
    terian Churches, 1818-75.
Minutes of Cincinnati, Cumberland Gap & Charleston Railroad,
    1854-60.
Diary of Kate Livingston, 1859-68.
Bible & Family Records.
Tombstone Records.
History of the King Family.

MICROFILMED RECORDS (available at the Tennessee State and
    Library):
1870-80; & 1900-10 Federal Census.
Chancery Court Minutes, Nov. 1870 - Aug. 1901.
Chancery Court Enrollment Books, May 1872 - Nov. 1874 (also
    contains Pleas & Answers, etc.).
Insolvent Estates, Jan. 1895 - Aug. 1918.
School District Records, May 1873 - July 1889.
Circuit Court Minutes, Dec. 1870 - Apr. 1893. (Civil and
    Criminal Minutes for Apr. 1893 - Feb. 1899 available
    in County Courthouse only.)
    Marriages, Jan. 1872 - Feb. 1916.
County Court Minutes, Jan. 1871 - Apr. 1901.
Probate of Deeds, Mar. 1890 - Sept. 1899.
Vital Statistics, Aug. 1909 - Aug. 1912.
Executors' Bonds & Letters, July 1880 - Dec. 1947.
Administrators' Bonds & Letters, July 1880 - Mar. 1912.
Wills, Aug. 1872 - Mar. 1929.
Insolvent Estates, Mar. 1871 - Mar. 1917.

HAMBLEN COUNTY
(continued)

MICROFILMED RECORDS (continued)
  Guardians' Settlements, Dec. 1870 - July 1914.
  Administrators' & Executors' Inventories, Apr. 1880 - Oct.
    1911.
  Administrators' Settlements, Mar. 1874 - Oct. 1912.
  Deeds, Nov. 1870 - Dec. 1892.
  Tax Books, 1877-1889.

MANUSCRIPT MATERIALS (available at the Tennessee State Library
    and Archives):
  Associations,   Institutions,   etc.   Confederate   Veterans
    Association of Upper East Tennessee, 1861 - ca. 1895,
    (microfilm #167). Roster containing name, county, state,
    date of enlistment, company and regiment, rank, wounds
    received, date and cause of discharge and remarks about
    the members of the association living in Hamblen as
    well as other east Tennessee counties.

CHURCH RECORDS (may be purchased from the Historical Commission
    of the Southern Baptist Convention, 127 Ninth Ave. N.,
    Nashville, TN 37234):
  Morristown, Bethel Baptist Church, Feb. 1874 - Aug. 1889;
    Apr. 1893 - Apr. 1896; Jan. 1938 - Sept. 1975, (microfilm
    reel #4806).
  Morristown, First Baptist Church, History, 1803 - 1964;
    minutes, 1912 - 1928, (microfilm reel #1892).
  Morristown, Laurel Fork Baptist Church, 1855-1909 (microfilm
    reel #2181).

HAMILTON COUNTY

CREATED: 1819 from Rhea County [1807 from Roane Co.].
COUNTY SEAT: Chattanooga, TN 37402.

LIBRARY: Chattanooga-Hamilton County Public Library, 1001
  Broad St., Chattanooga, TN 37402.

HISTORICAL SOCIETY: Chattanooga Area Historical Association,
  P. O. Box 1663, Chattanooga, TN 37401.

PUBLISHED SOURCES:
  Armstrong, Zella. History Of Hamilton County And Chatta-
    nooga. [Chattanooga: Lookout Publishing Co., 1931].

HAMILTON COUNTY
(continued)

PUBLISHED SOURCES (continued)
  Chattanooga City Directories, 1861-1881.
  Govan, G. E. & J. E. Lovingood. The Chattanooga Country.
    [Dutton, NY: 1952].
  History Of Tennessee. [Chicago & Nashville: Goodspeed
    Publishing Co., 1887].
  McGhee, Lucy K. Cherokee & Creek Indians, Returns of Property
    Left in Tennessee & Georgia, 1838, Book Vol. #64.
    [Washington: 1957].

W.P.A. TYPESCRIPT RECORDS (available at the Tennessee State
    Library and Archives):
  Deeds, v. A, B, C, 1796-1838.
  Deeds, v. 1, D, 1839-41.
  Deed Book, E, v. 1, 1841-43.
  Deed Book, F, v. 1, 1844-48.
  Entry Takers' Book, 1824-97.
  Chancery Court Minutes, 1864-66.
  Probate Records, No. 1, 1864-70, pts. I & II.
  Marriage Records, Book 1, 1857-64.
  Marriage Records, Book 2, 1864-74.
  Marriage Record Book, 1865-70.
  Interments in the National Cemetery, Chattanooga, 1863-1939.
  Mrs. Joseph H. Hooke's Diary, Cleveland Circuit, Holston
    Conference, 1874-75.
  Tombstone Inscriptions, Negro.
  Chattanooga Baptist Church Minutes, 1852-82.
  Concord Baptist Church Minutes, 1848-72.
  Good Spring Baptist Church Minutes, 1838 - .

MICROFILMED RECORDS (except for the census, all county records
    located in the courthouse in Chattanooga, TN):
  1830-80; & 1900-10 Federal Census.
  Birth records, 1908-12; Chattanooga births, 1881-1912.
  Death records, 1908-12; Chattanooga deaths, 1899-12.
  Administrators' Bonds & Letters, 1864 to present.
  Executors' Bonds & Letters, 1865 to present.
  Inventories of estates, 1864 to present.
  Estate settlements, 1864 to present.
  Chancery Court Minutes, 1864 to present.
  Wills, 1864 to present.
  Marriage Records, 1857 to present.
  Guardian records, 1864 to present.
  Deeds, 1819 to present.
  Land Grants, 1840-42.
  Circuit Court Minutes, 1858 to present.
  County Court Minutes, 1879 to present.
  Physicians' register, 1890 to present.
  Tax Rolls, 1836-37; 1881 to present)

HAMILTON COUNTY
(continued)

<u>MANUSCRIPT MATERIAL</u> (available at the Tennessee Library and
Archives):
Vine Street Orphan's Home, Chattanooga, TN, Records,
1889-1956, (#186); also, 1878-1905, (#352). [**Restricted**].
Records of the orphanage include the name, age, parents'
residence, and health of each child; financial status
of relatives; adoption information; and general remarks
for each child. 16 volumes.
Church Records. Second Presbyterian Church, Chattanooga,
1871-1969, (#278). Registers of pastors, elders, deacons,
communicants, baptisms 1871-1932, marriages 1876-1900,
deaths 1877-1900; chronological and alphabetical rolls
of communicants, index to communicants, minutes of direc-
tors, minutes of congregational meetings, a record book,
and minutes of session, etc.
Church Records. Church of the Good Shepherd, Lookout Mountain, 1946-1969, (#306). Lists of communicants, baptisms,
confirmations, marriages, and burials for this Hamilton
County Church which was founded in 1946.
Church Records. First Presbyterian Church, U. S., Chattanooga, 1840-1968. Registers of communicants, elders,
deacons, marriages, baptisms, deaths; and the personal
records, 1873-1924, of Rev. J. M. Bachman.
Church Records. St. Paul's Episcopal Church, Chattanooga,
1850-1900, (#503); also, 1900-50, (#350). Registers
of members, rectors, communicants, baptisms, confirmations,
marriages, and burials, etc.
Church Records. Centenary Methodist Episcopal Church, South,
Chattanooga, 1899-1966, (#454). Records consisting mainly
of rgisters of pastors, marriages, baptisms, and
membership. (Indexed).
Church Records. First Methodist Episcopal Church, Chattanooga, 1872-1954, (#455). Records of classes, proba-
tioners, full members, marriages, baptisms, removals,
statistics, and benevolences; alphabetized list of
baptisms, marriages, and deaths; historical record; and
list of pastors.
Church Records. Lookout Mountain Baptist Church, Lookout
Mountain, TN, 1945-60, (#328). Membership lists, lists
of officers, minutes, etc.
Church Records. Second Presbyterian Church, Chattanooga,
1881-1952, (#393). Minutes of session; roll of communicants; baptismals; & some newspaper clippings.
Church Records. Union Chapel of Walden's Ridge, Summertown,
1909-1967, (#474). Historical sketches, newspaper clippings; letters; pictures; programs; church minutes; etc.

HAMILTON COUNTY
(continued)

MANUSCRIPT MATERIAL (continued)
  Church Records. Chattanooga Primitive Baptist Church, 1910-
    1972, (#488). Membership register; minutes, correspon-
    dence; and records of the Sequatchie Valley Association
    of Primitive Baptists - constitution, articles of faith,
    delegates' names, and minutes.
  Church Records. Lookout Mountain Presbyterian Church, 1894-
    1975, (#493). Contains general records; minutes of ses-
    sion; lists of elders, deacons, and members; statistical
    reports; and some records for the church women's organiza-
    tion.

ADDITIONAL CHURCH RECORDS (may be purchased from the Historical
    Commission of the Southern Baptist Convention, 127 Ninth
    Ave., N., Nashville, TN 37234):
  Chattanooga. Concord Baptist Church, 1848-1872, (microfilm
    reel #891).
  Chattanooga. First Baptist Church, 1852-1967, (microfilm
    reel #3332).
  Chattanooga. Ridgedale Baptist Church, Oct. 1946 - 1956,
    (microfilm reel #3816).

HANCOCK COUNTY

CREATED: 1844 from Hawkins [1786 from Sullivan Co.] and
Claiborne County [1801 from Grainger and Hawkins Cos.].
COUNTY SEAT: Sneedville, TN 37869.

LIBRARY: Hancock County Public Library, Sneedville, TN 37869.

PUBLISHED SOURCES:
History Of Tennessee. [Chicago & Nashville: Goodspeed
Publishing Co., 1887]. (Hancock Co., pp. 871-72; 1216-25.)

MICROFILMED RECORDS (available at the Tennessee State Library
and Archives):
1850-80; & 1900-10 Federal Census.
1850 Census Index.
1860, 1870, & 1880 Federal Census partial index.
Church Records, Holston Presbyterian Association; Ready
Creek Presbyterian Church at Kingsport.
Obituaries, 1964-74.
Vital Statistics, 1964-74.
Vardy Church Records, 1921-25.

MANUSCRIPT MATERIAL (available at the Tennessee State Library
& Archives):
Associations, Institutions, etc. Confederate Veterans
Association of Upper East Tennessee, 1861 - ca. 1895,
(microfilm #167). Roster containing name, county, state,
date of enlistment, company and regiment, rank, wounds
received, date and cause of discharge, and general remarks
about members of the association living in Hancock County
and other East Tennessee Counties, and Fulton Co., GA.
Papers of Chris Davis Livesay from 1761-1973, (microfilm
#500). Collection consisting of correspondence, election
records, genealogical data, Civil War military records,
obituaries, biographical and historical sketches, legal
papers, photographs, etc. The names of numerous early
settlers are mentioned in this collection.
Papers of William Paul Grohse from 1610-1974, (microfilm
#501). Collection of cemetery, census, church, and
court records; correspondence, diaries, will and estate
papers, genealogical data, land records, scrapbooks,
maps, marriage records, memoirs, numerous obituaries,
photographs, sketches, tax records, etc. Data on numerous
families including several Melungeon families.

HARDEMAN COUNTY

CREATED: 1823 from the Western District (Indian lands).
COUNTY SEAT: Bolivar, TN 38008.

SPECIAL NOTE: The Courthouse burned during the Civil War with the loss of some records.

LIBRARY: Bolivar-Hardeman County Library, Bolivar, TN 38008.

PUBLISHED SOURCES:
  History Of Tennessee...History and Biography of Fayette and Hardeman Cos., TN. [Chicago & Nashville: Goodspeed Publishing Co., 1887].
  Armour, Quinnie. Hardeman County, Tennessee Marriage Records (ca. 1823-1860).
  Black, Roy W. Hardeman County, Cemetery Records. [Bolivar, TN: 1965].
  Clift, W. W. Early History Of Hardeman County, Dissertation, Peabody College, Nashville, TN, 1958.
  Owen, Fae Jacobs. The Cemetery Records Of Hardeman County, Tennessee.

W.P.A. TYPESCRIPT RECORDS (available at the Tennessee State Library and Archives):
  General Index to Deeds, No. 1, 1822-1876, pt. I.
  Minutes of the Circuit Court, v.1, 1823-1829.
  Minutes of the County Court, v.II, 1827-1829.
  Wills & Inventories, No. 1., 1823-38, pts. I & II.
  Marriage Records (loose), 1823-1838.
  Marriage Records, Book #1, 1838-1852.
  Marriage Records, 1860-1870.

MICROFILMED RECORDS (available at the Tennessee State Library and Archives):
  1830-80; & 1900-10 Federal Census.
  Clerk & Master Minutes, Oct. 1852 - Mar. 1901.
  Circuit Court Minutes, May 1833 - Apr. 1870.
  Circuit Court Minutes, 1877 - Jan. 1887; May 1887 - Jan. 1901.
  Guardian Settlements, Mar. 1850 - Jan. 1920.
  Administrators' Bonds, Oct. 1875 - Mar. 1908.
  Guardians' Bonds, Nov. 1854 - Sept. 1866.
  Executors' Bonds, Apr. 1860 - June 1866.
  Marriages, Oct. 1823 - Dec. 1859.
  License Records, Jan. 1860 - Dec. 1874.
  Marriage Bonds, Dec. 1874 - Feb. 1879.
  Freed Man Marriage Records, Nov. 1865 - Dec. 1870.

HARDEMAN COUNTY
(continued)

MICROFILMED RECORDS (continued)
Provost Marshall Marriages, June 1871 - June 3, 1871.
County Court Minutes, Oct. 1827 - Sept. 1900.
Wills, Feb. 1824 - June 1901.
Birth & Death Records, 1881 - 1927.
Deeds, Oct. 1822 - Jan. 1901.
Trust Deeds, July 1868 - Feb. 1901.
Survey and Entry Books, Feb. 1837 - May 1841.
Entry Book, Dec. 1820 - May 1846.
Tax Books, 1824-1880; 1881-1896.

HARDIN COUNTY

CREATED: 1819 from the Western District (Indian Lands).
COUNTY SEAT: Savannah, TN 38372.

LIBRARY: Hardin Co. Library, 1013 Main Street, Savannah,
TN 38372.

PUBLISHED SOURCES:
Brazelton, B. G. A History Of Hardin County. [Nashville:
Cumberland Presbyterian Publishing Co., 1885].
Curtis, Janet A. 1840 Census.
History Of Tennessee. [Chicago & Nashville: Goodspeed
Publishing Co., 1887]. (Hardin Co., pp. 829-41; 894-908.
Harbert, P. N. Early History Of Hardin County. [Memphis:
Tri-State Printing Co., 1968].

MICROFILMED RECORDS (available at the Tennessee State Library
and Archives):
1820-80; & 1900-10 Federal Census.
Clerk & Masters' Minutes, Mar. 1836 - Jan. 1903.
Enrolling Book, Feb. 1860 - Apr. 1876.
Circuit Court Minutes, Sept. 1840 - Sept. 1899.
Enrolling Book, Dec. 1870 - Dec. 1875.
Guardians' Bonds, Jan. 1875 - Sept. 1915.
Administrators' Bonds, Oct. 1895 - Dec. 1899.
Estates, Nov. 1865 - Apr. 1916 (except 1896 & 1897).
Guardians' Settlements, Mar. 1866 - Nov. 1913.
Bonds & Letters, Nov. 1874 - Dec. 1895.
Administrative Settlements, Mar. 1883 - Sept. 1916.
County Court Minutes, Jan. 1820 - May 1902.
Quarterly Court Minutes, Jan. 1899 - July 1908.

HARDIN COUNTY
(continued)

MICROFILMED RECORDS (continued)
  Merchants' Bonds, 1879-1897.
  Insolvent Estates, 1870-1896.
  Marriage Records, Oct. 1863 - Oct. 1914.
  Wills, Aug. 1836 - Nov. 1842.
  Settlements & Wills, Nov. 1842 - Sept. 1921.
  Deeds, Aug. 1835 - Oct. 1892; Aug. 1892 - July 1901.
  Trust Deeds, Sept. 1868 - July 1887; July 1887 - Nov. 1899.
  Survey Book, Feb. 1820 - Dec. 1853.
  Merchants' Bonds, Aug. 1878 - Sept. 1897.
  Tax Sales, 1896 - 1912.
  Receipts, 1889 - 1923.
  Physicians' Register, 1889 - 1931.
  Administrators' Minutes, 1873 - 1878.
  Circuit Court Case Files, 1840 - 1899.

W.P.A. TYPESCRIPT RECORDS (available at the Tennessee State
    Library and Archives):
  Record A, County Court Minutes, 1820-1825.
  General Administration Settlement B, 1836-1842.
  Record D Inventory Book, 1842-1849.
  Marriage Records, 1865-1868.

MANUSCRIPT MATERIALS (available at the Tennessee State Library
    and Archives):
  County Records. Miscellaneous Records, 1772-1911, (microfilm
    #539). Bible records; genealogical data; biographical
    sketches; letterbook, 1874-82, of Edmund D. Patterson;
    diaries 1866-1902; and many other items relating to
    Hardin County families.

HAWKINS COUNTY

CREATED: 1786 from Sullivan County [1779 from part of
  Washington District and area originally claimed by Virginia.]
COUNTY SEAT: Rogersville, TN 37857.

SPECIAL NOTE: Known as Spencer County, 1795-96, having been
  one of the four new counties created under the State of
  Franklin.

LIBRARY: Stamps Memorial Library, 415 Main Street,
  Rogersville, TN 37857.

HAWKINS COUNTY
(continued)

PUBLISHED SOURCES:
Bell. Record Of Wills, 1786-1851, Hawkins County, Tennessee.
[1932].
Burns. Record Of Wills, Hawkins County, Tennessee, 1786-1851.
[Wallings Creek, KY: 1932].
"Early East Tennessee Taxpayers, VII, Hawkins County, 1809-
1812," Pollyanna Creekmore; East Tennessee Historical
Society Publications, 1960, no. 32; pp. 117-31.
History Of Tennessee. [Chicago & Nashville: Goodspeed
Publishing Co., 1887]. (Hawkins Co. pp. 973-80; 1225-1239.)
Lucas, Silas Emmett, Jr. & Ella E. Lee Sheffield. The
Hawkins County Circuit Court Minutes, 1822-1825, And
Fragment For The Period, November 1827 - August 1828.
[1984].
Reber. Church Hill Tennessee Area History, 1754-1976.
[Church Hill, TN: 1977].

W.P.A. TYPESCRIPT RECORDS (available at the Tennessee State
Library and Archives):
Deed Book, No. 1, 1788-1800.
General Index to Deeds, v.1, 1787-1861.
Circuit Court Minutes, 1810-1821.
Minutes of the Circuit Court, 1817-1845.
Circuit Court Minutes, 1822-1825.
County Court Minutes, Nov. 1827 - Aug. 1828.
Marriage Records, v.1, 1820-1846.

MICROFILMED RECORDS (available at the Tennessee State Library
and Archives):
1830-80; & 1900-10 Federal Census.
Chancery Court Enrollment Books, May 1831 - Nov. 1833;
July 1862 - July 1874; Jan. 1865 - Aug. 1891.
Chancery Court Minutes, May 1825 - June 1894; Sept. 1894
- Mar. 1904 (intermittantly).
Circuit Court Minutes, 1810 - 1900 (intermittantly).
Administrators' & Guardians' Settlements, May 1874 - Aug.
1904.
Guardians' Bonds & Letters, Oct. 1879 - Feb. 1896.
Administrators' Settlements, Sept. 1869 - May 1873.
Executors' Bonds & Letters, Jan. 1880 - May 1917.
Administrators' Bonds & Letters, Oct. 1879 - Jan. 1918.
Insolvent Estates, Jan. 1875 - Sept. 1972.
Physicians' Register, Feb. 1895 - June 1970.
Marriages, June 1820 - Dec. 1912.
County Court Minutes, Nov. 1827 - Oct. 1902.
Wills, Nov. 1797 - June 1910.

HAWKINS COUNTY
(continued)

MICROFILMED RECORDS (continued)
Deeds, Oct. 1787 - Nov. 1907.
Entry Books, Apr. 1820 - Mar. 1902.
Survey Books, June 1824 - Feab. 1828; Feb. 1875 - Apr. 1868.
Trust Deeds, Dec. 1875 - Apr. 1901.
Tax Books, 1879 - 1893.
(Some plats and surveys may be found in the Clay Papers described subsequently in the manuscript section.

MANUSCRIPT MATERIALS (available at the Tennessee State Library and Archives):
Associations, Institutions, etc. Confederate Veterans' Association of Upper East Tennessee, 1861 - ca. 1895 (microfilm #167). Roster containing name, county, state, date of enlistment, company and regiment, rank, wounds received, date and cause of discharge, and general remarks about members of the association living in Hawkins County as well as other East Tennessee Counties, etc.
Cemeteries, Grainger County, Tennessee. 1800 - 1972, (microfilm #505). These cemetery records also include reports for Quarryville Methodist family and church cemeteries in Hawkins County.

CHURCH RECORDS (may be purchased from the Historical Commission of the Southern Baptist Convention, 127 Ninth Ave. N., Nashville, TN 37234):
Rogersville. Hickory Cove Baptist Church, 1835-1881, microfilm reel #1173.

HAYWOOD COUNTY

CREATED: 1823 from Western District (Indian lands).
COUNTY SEAT: Brownsville, TN 38012.

LIBRARY: Brownsville-Haywood Co. Public Library, 121 W. Main St., Brownsville, TN 38012.

PUBLISHED SOURCES:
Historical Records Survey. Tennessee. Inventory of the county archives of Tenn., no. 38, [Nashville: The Survey, 1939].
Carpenter, V. K. Haywood County, Tennessee 1850 Federal Census. [1970].

HAYWOOD COUNTY
(continued)

PUBLISHED SOURCES (continued)
  History Of Tennessee. [Chicago & Nashville: Goodspeed
    Publishing Co., 1887]. (Haywood Co., pp. 818-29; 921-47.)

W.P.A. TYPESCRIPT RECORDS (available at the Tennessee State
    Library and Archives):
  County Court Minutes, 1823-30; 1826-30; 1831.
  Minutes of the County Court, 1837-40.
  Court of Pleas & Quarter Sessions Journal, C, 1834-40.
  Deed Book, A, 1823-30.
  Will Book No. 1, 1826-39.
  Marriage Docket, 1859-66.
  Bradford Family Record.
  Brownsville City Directory, 1872-73.

MICROFILMED RECORDS (available at the Tennessee State Library
    and Archives):
  1830-80; & 1900-10 Federal Census.
  Clerk & Master Enrollments, July 1869 - Jan. 1877.
  Clerk & Master Minutes, May 1842 - Sept. 1901.
  Administrators' Bonds, Jan. 1869 - Sept. 1904.
  Administrators' Settlements, May 1870 - Dec. 1896.
  Executors' Bonds & Letters, Jan. 1876 - Dec. 1926.
  Guardians' Bonds, Apr. 1852 - Jan. 1857.
  Guardians' Bonds & Letters, Aug. 1870 - Nov. 1908.
  Guardians' Minute Books, Apr. 1875 - Jan. 1912.
  Guardians' Settlements, Apr. 1856 - Feb. 1936.
  Enrollments, Dec. 1868 - Jan. 1876.
  Inventories, Guardians', Administrators', and Executors',
    Apr. 1856 - May 1926.
  Insolvent Estates, June 1870 - Aug. 1962.
  Vital Statistics, 1881-82; 1908-12.
  Widows and Orphans, May 1873 - Apr. 1925.
  Marriage Licenses and Bonds, Mar. 1859 - Apr. 1901.
  Marriage Record Book, Apr. 1901 - May 1915.
  County Court Minutes, Mar. 1823 - June 1902.
  Wills, Dec. 1826 - Aug. 1918.
  Deeds, Aug. 1823 - May 1900.
  Trust Deeds, June 1868 - Feb. 1901.
  Grants, Dec. 1820 - June 1834.
  Land Entries, Nov. 1793 - Feb. 1821; Dec. 1842 - Sept.
    1902.
  World War I Records.
  Tax Books, 1887-1900.

HAYWOOD COUNTY
(continued)

MANUSCRIPT MATERIALS (available at the Tennessee State Library Archives):
Church Records of Brownsville Station Methodist Episcopal Church, South, 1824-1957, (microfilm #527). Records consisting of historical sketch of the church for 1824-1900, and registers of members, 1893-1909; 1919-1957.
Church Records of Harmony Baptist Church, 1837-1973, (microfilm #533). Records consisting of minutes of meetings and membership rolls, list of charter members.

ADDITIONAL CHURCH RECORDS (may be purchased from the Historical Commission of the Southern Baptist Convention, 127 Ninth Ave. N., Nashville, TN 37234.
Woodland Baptist Church, 1835-1881, formerly Browns' Creek. (Microfilm reel #862).

HENDERSON COUNTY

CREATED: 1821 from the Western District (Indian lands).
COUNTY SEAT: Lexington, TN 38351.

LIBRARY: Lexington-Henderson Co. Public Library, Louis St., Lexington, TN 38351.

PUBLISHED SOURCES:
Carpenter, V. K. Henderson County, Tennessee 1850 Federal Census. [1971].
History Of Tennessee. [Chicago & Nashville: Goodspeed Publishing Co., 1887]. (Henderson Co., pp. 798-906; 841-947.)
Harris, R. H. Henderson County, Tennessee Cemetery Inscriptions. [Memphis: 1976].
Powers, A. History Of Henderson County. [Lexington, TN: The Arthur, 1930].
Stewart, G. T. Henderson County. [Memphis: Memphis State University Press, 1979].

W.P.A. TYPESCRIPT RECORDS (available at the Tennessee State Library and Archives):
Will Book, No. 3, 1895-1932.
County Court Minutes, 1860-66.
Bible Records & Tombstone Inscriptions.

HENDERSON COUNTY
(continued)

MICROFILMED RECORDS (available at the Tennessee State Library
and Archives):
1830-80; & 1900-10 Federal Census.
Clerk & Masters' Minutes, Mar. 1880 - Oct. 1902.
Circuit Court Minutes, Nov. 1895 - Oct. 1902.
Quarterly Court Minutes, Sept. 1860 - June 1866.
Guardians' Bonds, Jan. 1861 - Apr. 1919.
Wills & Inventories, Nov. 1893 - Nov. 1906.
Executors' Bonds, Jan. 1861 - Oct. 1900.
Insolvent Estates, Jan. 1867 -Jan. 1896.
County Court Minutes, Apr. 1891 - Apr. 1901.
Administrators' Bonds, Jan. 1861 - May 1899.
Insolvent Estates, Feb. 1879 - Jan. 1940.
Guardians' & Administrators' Settlements, Apr. 1893 -July
1896.
Marriage Records, June 1893 - Nov. 1909.
Administrators' & Executors' Settlements, Oct. 1866 - Mar.
1906.
Guardians' & Administrators' Settlements, Apr. 1887 - Mar.
1915.
Wills, Feb. 1895 - 1932.
Deeds, Jan. 1856 - May 1900.
Trust Deeds, May 1890 - Apr. 1901.
Tax Books, 1895-99.

MANUSCRIPT MATERIALS (available at the Tennessee State Library
and Archives):
County Records, Miscellaneous, 1789-1953, (microfilm #521).
    Collection consisting of account books, advertisments,
    Bible records, church records, genealogical data, 1836
    assignment of civil districts, etc.
Church Records. Mt. Gilead Cumberland Presbyterian, 1830-
    1892; Jack's Creek Church, 1831 - 1888; 1888 - 1913;
    Baptist Church of Lexington, 1864 - 1937; Marl Bluff
    Church Minutes, Reagen, TN, 1853 - 1953; Bible Records,
    miscellaneous. (Included in the County Record microfilm
    in the State Library and Archives.)
Church Records. Christian Chapel Church of Christ, 1860
    - 1943, (microfilm #550). Records consisting of member-
    ship lists with information on births, baptisms, mar-
    riages, deaths, dismissals; minutes of meetings; and
    records of pastors.

ADDITIONAL CHURCH RECORDS (may be purchased from the Historical
    Commission of the Southern Baptist Convention, 127 Ninth
    Ave. N., Nashville, TN 37234):
Chesterfield. Union Baptist Church, 1842 - 1978. (Microfilm
    reel #4813).

HENRY COUNTY

CREATED: 1821 from the Western District (Indian lands).
COUNTY SEAT: Paris, TN 38242.

LIBRARY: Paris-Henry County Library, Paris, TN 38242.

HISTORICAL/GENEALOGICAL SOCIETIES:
Paris Area Genealogical Society, P. O. Box 726, Paris,
TN 38242.
Henry County Historical Society, P. O. Box 356, Paris,
TN 38242.

PUBLISHED SOURCES:
"Henry County, Tennessee Marriage Bonds, 1838-1842,"
Ansearchin' News, v.8 (1961), no. 2:57-61.
"Henry County, Tennessee Marriage Records, 1843-1845,"
Ansearchin' News, v.9 (1962), no. 2:47-50, and 3:85-87.
"Calloway County, Kentucky Cemetery Records," (includes
some from Henry Co., TN), Calloway County Genealogical
Society, 1965, Murry, KY.
History Of Tennessee. [Chicago & Nashville: Goodspeed
Publishing Co., 1887]. (Henry Co., pp. 813-32; 888-935.)
Greene, W. P. The City Of Paris And Henry County, Tennessee.
[Paris, TN: Paris Publishing Co., 1900].
Inman, W. O. Henry County, Tennessee Marriages, 1838-1880.
Whitley, E. R. Henry County "Old Time Stuff". [Nashville:
1968].

W.P.A. TYPESCRIPT RECORDS (available at the Tennessee State
Library and Archives):
General Index to Deeds, Grantor, No. 1, 1822-83.
Minute Book, A, 1824-25.
Tax Book, 1827-35, pts. I, II.
Wills & Inventories, 1844-56, pts. I, II, & III.
Minutes of the County Court, 1825-28, pts, I & II; 1836-49,
pts. I & II.
County Court Minute Book C, 1832-36, pts. I & II.
Tombstone Records.

MICROFILMED RECORDS (available at the Tennessee State Library
and Archives):
1830-80; & 1900-10 Federal Census.
Circuit Court Minutes, May 1834 - July 1968.
Clerk & Masters' Enrollment Books, Feb. 1835 - Jan. 1934.
Clerk & Masters' Minute Books, June 1846 - July 1908.
Administrators', Executors', & Guardians' Bonds & Letters,
June 1856 - May 1968.
Administrators', Executors', & Guardians Settlements, July
1844 - Aug. 1968.

HENRY COUNTY
(continued)

MICROFILMED RECORDS (continued)
Guardians' Minute Book, Oct. 1867 - Nov. 1925.
Guardians' Settlements & Reports, June 1888 - Aug. 1968.
Inventories & Accounts Sales Records, Dec. 1886 - Aug. 1928.
Marriage Books, Jan. 1868 - June 1929.
Marriage Records, Jan. 1838 - Aug. 1968.
County Court Minutes, Mar. 1824 - June 1968.
Physcians' Register, 1889-1950.
Quarterly Court Minutes, July 1908 - July 1968.
Ranger Book Road Minutes, July 1856 - Dec. 1927.
Vital Statistics, Births & Deaths: 1881-82; 1908-12; 1925-35.
Will Books, May 1822 - Nov. 1865.
Deeds, Mar. 1822 - June 1968.
Highway Deed Book, June 1968 - Oct. 1968.
Land Entry Books, Nov. 1820 - Apr. 1886.
Military Discharges, Dec. 1864 - Oct. 1968.
Oil & Gas Leases, Sept. 1918 - Oct. 1968.
Plat Book, May 1956 - Sept. 1968.
Index of Plats, (prior to 1856).
Plat of Paris, 1909.
Surveyors' Reports Books, Dec. 1836 - June 1905.
Trust Deeds, Oct. 1872 - July 1968.
Board of Education Minutes, July 1907 - Jan. 1968.
Cash Journals, Mar. 1860 - Oct. 1968.
Tax Books, 1827 - 1967.

MANUSCRIPT MATERIALS (available at the Tennessee State Library and Archives):
Church Records. Walnut Fork Primitive Baptist Church, Cottage Grove, TN., 1821-1860, (microfilm #280). Records consisting of minutes of church meetings and membership lists which include baptismal records, death dates, and dismissals for this church.
Church Records. Blood River Church of Christ, 1867 - 1885, (microfilm #281). Records consisting of membership list with some information on baptisms, deaths, and dismissals.
Church Records. North Fork Baptist Church, 1827 - 1976, (microfilm #529). Records consisting mainly of membership rolls; minutes of business meetings; rules of order; some statistical data; etc.

ADDITIONAL CHURCH RECORDS (may be purchased from the Historical Commission of the Southern Baptist Convention, 127 Ninth Ave. N., Nashville, TN 37234):
Point Pleasant Baptist Church, 1843-1854, (microfilm reel #4209).

HICKMAN COUNTY

CREATED: 1807 from Dickson County [1803 from Montgomery Co.].
COUNTY SEAT: Centerville, TN 37033.

SPECIAL NOTE: Courthouse burned in 1865 with loss of some records.

LIBRARY: Hickman County Public Library, Centerville, TN 37033.

PUBLISHED SOURCES:
Dotson. Hickman County, Tennessee Court Records 1814-1829. [Columbia, TN: P-Vine Press, 1981].
Old Marriage Records Of Hickman County, Tennessee. [Duck River Chapter D.A.R., 1979].
Garrett, Jill K. & Catherine Kelly Gilliam. 1850 Census Of Hickman County, Tennessee. [Columbia, TN: 1967].
Garrett, J. K. & I. H. McClain. Sacred To The Memory, Hickman Co. Cemetery Records. [Columbia, TN: 1966].
Hickman County, Tennessee Cemetery Records, Part II, C. G. Lynn editon. [Centerville, TN: Lynn, 1976]. (A continuation of Sacred To The Memory, by Garrett.)
History Of Tennessee. [Chicago & Nashville: Goodspeed Publishing Co., 1887]. (Hickman Co., pp. 788-801; 910-23)
Leeper, Kate D. Family And Military Records From Spence's History Of Hickman County, Tennessee. [Nashville: 1965].
Leeper, Kate and Paul. Court Records Of Hickman County, Tennessee, 1833-1856. [Nashville: 1968].
Marsh, Helen C. Name Index To History Of Tennessee, Goodspeed. [Shelbyville, TN: 1972].
Spence, J. D. & D. L. A History Of Hickman County, Tennessee. [Nashville: Gospel Advocate Publishing Co., 1900].

W.P.A. TYPESCRIPT RECORDS (available at the Tennessee State Library and Archives):
Deed Book, A, 1808-11.
Deed Book, B, 1811-13.
Guardian & Administration Settlement, 1844-46.
Guardian & Administration Settlement, v.D, 1847-52.
Minute Book, 1844-1855.
Bible, Family, and Tombstone Records.
Account of Negro Sunday Time at Aetna Furnace, 1854-63.

MICROFILMED RECORDS (available at the Tennessee State Library and Archives):
1820-80; & 1900-10 Federal Census.
Clerk & Master Enrollment Books, June 1855 - May 1875.

HICKMAN COUNTY
(continued)

MICROFILMED RECORDS (continued)
   Circuit Court Minutes, Nov. 1841 - Mar. 1848; Jan. 1847
      - June 1895.
   Chancery Court Minutes, Sept. 1854 - Mar. 1893; Mar. 1895
      - 1902.
   Marriages, Feb. 1868 - Mar. 1883.
   County Court Minutes, Apr. 1866 - June 1900.
   Guardians' Bonds, June 1866 - Jan. 1915.
   Administrators' Settlements, 1847-52; 1852-1902.
   Road Book, 1896-1898.
   Merchants' Bonds & Licenses, Jan. 1887 - Aug. 1902.
   Inventory of Estates, Apr. 1897 - Apr. 1913.
   Claims against Estates, Feb. 1883 - Jan. 1938.
   Deeds, July 1808 - Apr. 1901.
   Trust Deeds, Oct. 1876 - Apr. 1909.
   Surveyors' Book, Apr. 1827 - Oct. 1901.
   Tax Duplicates, 1867-86; 1887-98.

MANUSCRIPT MATERIALS (available at the Tennessee State Library
      and Archives):
   Cemeteries. South Carolina and Tennessee, ca. 1850 - ca.
      1956, (microfilm #307). Alphabetically listing, by
      county, of tombstone inscriptions from 25 South Carolina
      and 48 Tennessee cemeteries including some in Hickman
      County.
   Sketches - Places. "The Rise of Christianity in Southwestern
      Hickman County," by Chessor, 1920, (microfilm #426).
   Church Records. Bethabara Primitive Baptist Church, 1885-
      1931, (microfilm #525).
   Church Records. Willow Springs Primitive Baptist Church,
      1883-1942, (microfilm #512).

HOUSTON COUNTY

CREATED: 1871 from Dickson [1803 from Robertson & Montgomery
   Cos.], Humphreys [1809 from Stewart Co.], and Stewart County
   [1803 from Montgomery Co.].
COUNTY SEAT: Erin, TN 37061.

LIBRARY: Houston Co. Public Library, Courthouse, Erin, TN
   37061.

PUBLISHED SOURCES:
   History Of Tennessee. [Chicago & Nashville: Goodspeed
      Publishing Co., 1887]. (Houston Co., pp. 974-98; 1388-
      1402.)

HOUSTON COUNTY
(continued)

PUBLISHED SOURCES (continued)
McClain, I. H. A History Of Houston County. [Columbia,
  TN: Garrett-McClain, 1966].

MICROFILMED RECORDS (available at the Tennessee State Library
  and Archives):
1880; & 1900-10 Federal Census.
General Sessions Minutes, Aug. 1960 - Sept. 1962.
Circuit Court Minutes, May 1871 - Mar. 1967.
Clerk & Masters' Minutes, May 1871 - June 1967.
Administrators' Bonds & Letters, Dec. 1926 - July 1967.
Administrators' Settlements, Sept. 1914 - Nov. 1953.
Appropriation Book, Mar. 1889 - Dec. 1889.
Guardians' Bonds, June 1888 - Dec. 1946.
Guardianship, Letters of, Apr. 1947 - June 1965.
Guardians' Settlements, June 1871 - Feb. 1967.
Physicians' Register, Feb. 1865 - June 1911.
Probate Deed Book, Apr. 1871 - Aug. 1954.
Road Overseers' Book, July 1883 - Jan. 1891.
Tipplers' Bond, Aug. 1875 - Feb. 1901.
Birth Records, 1881-82.
Wills & Inventories, Aug. 1869 - Mar. 1966.
Charter Books, Aug. 1897 - May 1967.
County Officials' Bond Book, Oct. 1942 - Sept. 1966,
Deed Book, Apr. 1871 - Apr. 1967.
Military Discharges, Oct. 1945 - July 1967.
Plat Book, Mar. 1953 - May 1967.
Trust Deeds, Sept. 1822 - Nov. 1967.
Board of Education Minutes, July 1907 - Sept. 1967.
Tax Books, 1873 - 1965.

HUMPHREYS COUNTY

CREATED: 1809 from Steward [1803 from Montgomery Co.].
COUNTY SEAT: Waverly, TN 37185.

SPECIAL NOTE: Fires in 1876 and 1898 destroyed some of the
county records.

LIBRARY: Humphreys County Public Library, Waverly, TN 37185.

HISTORICAL SOCIETY: Humphreys County Historical Society,
  Court Square, Waverly, TN 37185.

HUMPHREYS COUNTY
(continued)

PUBLISHED SOURCES:
  Anderson, Gladys, et al. Humphreys County Burials, 1969-1975.
    [Humphreys County Historical Society, 1976]. (These
    burials taken from newspaper accounts beginning Jan.
    1, 1969 - Dec. 31, 1975.)
  Anderson, G. P. & J. K. Garrett. Humphreys County, Tennessee
    Cemetery Records. [Columbia: 1969].
  Burns, Ruth Blake, et. al. Humphreys County, Tennessee
    Marriage Records 1861-1888. [1984]. (Complete details
    as to co-compiler unavailable to this compiler at time
    of publication of this work).
  Garrett, Jill K. A History Of Humphreys County, Tennessee.
    [Columbia: 1963]. Revised & reprinted 1984].
  History Of Tennessee. [Chicago & Nashville: Goodspeed
    Publishing Co., 1887]. (Humphreys Co., pp. 868-94;
    1205-1288.
  Histories Of The Churches Of Humphreys County, Tennessee.
    [Humphreys Co. Historical Society, 1970-71].
  Humphreys County Physicians, 1800-1895. [Waverly, TN:
    Old Reynoldsburg Chapter, D.A.R., 1975].
  Rowe, Imogene. Humphreys County, Tennessee 1820 Federal
    Census. [1974].

W.P.A. TYPESCRIPT RECORDS (available at the Tennessee State
    Library and Archives):
  Deed Book, A, 1810-16.
  Wills & Inventories, 1838-44, pts. I & II.
  County Court Minute Book, Vol. 1, 1842-50.
  Marriage Records, Vol. A, 1864-68.
  Minutes of Sycamore Landing Church of Christ, 1917-37.
  History of the Shannon Family, 1822 and Bible, Family,
    and Tombstone Records.

MICROFILMED RECORDS (available at the Tennessee State Library
    and Archives):
  1820-80; & 1900-10 Federal Census.
  Administrators' Bonds, Mar. 1882 - Mar. 1913.
  Claims against estates, July 1870 - Apr. 1902.
  Guardians' Settlements, Aug. 1868 - May 1924.
  Abstract of Conveyances, 1899.
  Scholastic Record, 1885-97.
  Land sold for taxes, 1899-1909.
  Marriage Records, Sept. 1864 - Oct. 1915.
  County Court Minutes, Jan. 1842 - Nov. 1850; Oct. 1897
    - July 1900.
  Minutes of Insolvent Estates, June 1886 - Oct. 1962.

HUMPHREYS COUNTY
(continued)

MICROFILMED RECORDS (continued)
Minutes, Mar. 1883 - Mar. 1887; Sept. 1894 - Sept. 1897.
Wills & Inventories, Apr. 1837 - Dec. 1843; Dec. 1847 -
Mar. 1852; May 1852 - 1857; July 1868 - Jan. 1888; Mar.
1889 - Mar. 1904.
Vital Statistics, July 1908 - Aug. 1912.
Guardians' Settlement Records, Aug. 1856 - Oct. 1868.
Guardians' Bonds, May 1886 - Sept. 1974.
Deeds, July 1810 - Aug. 1889; 1889 - May 1900.
Trust Deeds, Sept. 1880 - July 1901.
Revenue Dockets, Nov. 1832 - Mar. 1886.
Tax Records, to 1897 intermittantly.

CHURCH RECORDS (may be purchased from the Historical Commission of the Southern Baptist Convention, 127 Ninth Ave.
N., Nashville, TN 37234):
Denver. Trace Creek Baptist Church, 1847-1967, (microfilm
reel #2070).

JACKSON COUNTY

CREATED: 1801 from Smith County [1799 from Sumner Co.].
COUNTY SEAT: Gainesboro, TN 38562.

SPECIAL NOTE: Courthouse fire in 1872 destroyed most records.

LIBRARY: Charles Ralph Holland Memorial Library, Gainesboro,
TN 38562.

PUBLISHED SOURCES:
"Early History of Jackson County," by R. C. Draper, Jackson
County Sentinel articles, Gainesboro, TN, 1928-29.
"Taxpayers in Jackson County, Tennessee," by Richard C.
Fulcher, Tennessee Genealogical Review, Vol. 2, no.
3 (July 1981), p. 49. (List compiled from early newspa-
pers, ca. 1800.).
Jackson County, TN Records. [W.P.A.] reprinted 1977.
Lee, Ramona Hudson. Jackson County, Tennessee 1840 United
States Census. [1984].

W.P.A. TYPESCRIPT RECORDS (available at the Tennessee State
Library and Archives):
Miscellaneous Records, 1810-1909.
Cumberland Presbyterian Church Minute Book, 1811-1935.

JACKSON COUNTY
(continued)

W.P.A. TYPESCRIPT RECORDS (continued)
Ranger Book, 1817-60.
Register of Church of Christ at Bagdad, 1844-1936.
Wills, Gainesboro, Tennessee.

MICROFILMED RECORDS (available at the Tennessee State Library
and Archives):
1820-80; & 1900-10 Federal Census.
Clerk & Masters' Minutes, Nov. 1840 - Mar. 1886; Feb. 1891
- Apr. 1901.
Clerk Enrollments, June 1859 - Sept. 1889; Mar. 1888 -
Aug. 1892.
Minutes, Sept. 1872 - Mar. 1893; July 1893 - July 1902.
County Court Minutes, Sept. 1872 - Dec. 1892; Jan. 1893
- Jan. 1900.
Administrators' Bonds & Letters, Oct. 1878 - July 1907.
Insolvent Estates, Mar. 1872 - Mar. 1932.
Guardians' Settlements, Oct. 1872 - May 1904.
Enrollment Book, Jan. 1872 - Jan. 1899.
Wills, Inventories, and Administrators' Settlements, Sept.
1872 - Aug. 1914.
Death Records, 1881-83; 1909-12.
Marriages, Jan. 1870 - Sept. 1918.
Land Deeds, Sept. 1872 - Apr. 1905.
Trust Deeds, Aug. 1872 - June 1902.
Land Entries, 1873 - 1901.
Tax Books, 1872-84; 1855-99.
1890 Federal Census.
Miscellaneous Book, microfilm reel #547.
Court Transcripts, 1839-1915.

MANUSCRIPT MATERIALS (available at the Tennessee State Library
and Archives):
County Records. Miscellaneous Records, 1841-1952, (microfilm
#547). Including account book, 1841, 1866; indexed
legal case record 1853-60; census notes of 1890; and
scrapbook.
Church Records of Spring Creek Baptist Church, 1845-1968,
(microfilm #270). Contains membership lists; minutes
of session; financial records, etc.

JAMES COUNTY

CREATED: 1871 from Bradley [1835 from Indian lands] and
Hamilton County [1819 from Rhea Co.].
COUNTY SEAT: Ooltewah, TN.

SPECIAL NOTE: This county was abolished in 1919 and absorbed
by Hamilton County where its records are now held.

PUBLISHED SOURCES:
History Of Tennessee...(East TN. edition). [Chicago &
Nashville: Goodspeed Publishing Co., 1887]. (James
Co., pp. 797-98; 955-62.)

MANUSCRIPT MATERIALS (available at the Tennessee State Library
and Archives):
County Records. Bradley County, Tennessee. Miscellaneous
Records, ca. 1835 - 1960, (microfilm #561). Various
records concerning the history and growth of Bradley
County, including store account books; scrapbooks concerning Bradley, McMinn, Polk, and James counties in Tennessee, etc.

JEFFERSON COUNTY

CREATED: 1792 from Greene [1783 from Washington Co., NC]
and Hawkins County [1786 from Sullivan Co.].
COUNTY SEAT: Dandridge, TN 37725.

LIBRARY: Dandridge Public Library, Dandridge, TN 37725.

PUBLISHED SOURCES:
d'Armand, Virginia C. Jefferson County, Tennessee Marriages
1792 Thru 1870.
"Early East Tennessee Taxpayers, V, Jefferson County, 1801,"
by Creekmore; East TN Historical Society Publications,
no. 28, 1956, pp. 146-64.
Douthat, James L. Jefferson County, Tennessee Grants Book
1, 1792-1794. [1980].
          . Jefferson County, Tennessee Will Book 1, 1792
- 1810. [1981].
History Of Tennessee. [Chicago & Nashville: Goodspeed
Publishing Co., 1887]. (Jefferson Co., 856-64; 1160-1193.)
Roach, Thomas E. Gleanings From A Scrapbook. [1983].
(Newspaper articles from past 20 years, including historical articles on Grainger and Jefferson Cos., TN.)

JEFFERSON COUNTY
(continued)

PUBLISHED SOURCES (continued)
Whitley, E. R. Marriages Of Jefferson County, Tennessee,
1792-1836. [Baltimore: Genealogical Publishing Co.,
Inc., 1983].
Historical Records Of Tennessee, Jefferson County, Dandridge
Ed., 1954. (marriage records, v.1, 1792-1851; v.2,
Abstracts of Wills, 1792-1851.)
Shunen Church And Cemetery Speak, 1824-1965. [Gatlinburg,
TN: Brazor Press, 1965]. (Strawberry Plains, Jefferson
Co., TN.)

W.P.A. TYPESCRIPT RECORDS (available at the Tennessee State
Library and Archives):
French Broad River Baptist Church Minutes, 1786-1859.
Hopewell Presbyterian Church Minutes, 1788-1860.
Antioch Baptist Church Minutes, 1839-1870.
Bible Records.
Church and Family Records.
Dumplin Baptist Church Minutes, 1797-1860.
Tombstone Records.
Minutes of Maury Academy, 1818-1860.
Boundary of School District, 1840.
Scholastic Population, 1841-1861.
General Index to Deeds, 1792-1846.
Will Book No. 1, 1792-1810.
Will Book No. 2, 1811-1826.
Sales and Will Book, Vol. 3, 1826-1840.
Will Books 4-10, 1841-44.
Guardian Report Book No. 1, 1805-32.
Tax List, 1822-30.
Records of Monies Received by County Court Clerk, 1827-60.
Order Book of Court Pleas & Quarter Sessions, 1801-07.
Grant Book No. 1, 1792-94.
Quorum Minutes, V.1, 1792-1802.
Marriage License and Bond Book, 1792-1840.
Marriage Records No. 2, 1840-60; 1870.
County Court Record Book No. 1, 1792-98.
Court of Pleas and Quarter Sessions Minute Book No. 4,
1807-10.
Court of Pleas and Quarter Sessions Minute Books 5 and
6, 1810-18.
Court of Pleas and Quarter Sessions Minute Books 7 and
8, 1818-31, pts. I & II.
Minute Book, Circuit Court, 1810-16; 1817-31.
Chancery Court Minutes, V.1, 1836-46.

JEFFERSON COUNTY
(continued)

MICROFILMED RECORDS (available at the Tennessee State Library
    and Archives):
1830-80; & 1900-10 Federal Census.
Chancery Court Minutes, Apr. 1836 - Jan. 1890; July 1890
    - July 1904.
Circuit Court Minutes, Nov. 1809 - Jan. 1816.
Circuit Court Civil Minutes, Apr. 1844 - Aug. 1889; Aug.
    1889 - Nov. 1903.
Circuit Court Minutes, Jan. 1826 - Dec. 1889.
Administrators' Bonds, Oct. 1886 - Dec. 1907.
Insolvent Estates, Minutes of, Mar. 1876 - July 1960.
Administrators', Executors' and Guardians' Bonds, Jan.
    1871 - Oct. 1886.
Executors' Bonds & Letters, Nov. 1886 - July 1938.
Executors' Settlements, May 1895 - Jan. 1901.
Guardians' Bonds & Letters, 1856-70; Oct. 1880 - May 1905.
Guardians' Settlements, Oct. 1805 - Feb. 1900.
Marriages, Dec. 1792 - Oct. 1910.
County Court Minutes, July 1792 - May 1896; Oct. 1896 -
    Oct. 1904.
Probate Deeds, Sept. 1874 - Mr. 1893.
Deeds of Conveyance, Jan. 1840 - May 1844.
Guardians' Minutes, July 1871 - Oct. 1887.
Settlements of Estates, Dec. 1891 - Apr. 1898.
Physicians' Register, 1889-91.
Account Books of Maury Academy.
Vital Statistics, Nov. 1908-09.
Wills & Settlements, Apr. 1792 - Oct. 1891.
Deeds, Sept. 1792 - Mar. 1892; Mar. 1892 - Mar. 1900.
Civil War Mustering Out Book, Nov. 1860 - Oct. 1872.
Land Entry Book, Apr. 1824 - Mar. 1918.
Surveyors' Entry Book, Jan. 1831 - Mar. 1891.
Tax Books, 1822-87; 1888-99.

MANUSCRIPT MATERIALS (available at the Tennessee State Library
    and Archives):
Associations, Institutions, etc. Confederate Veterans
    Association of Upper East Tennessee, 1861 - ca. 1895,
    (microfilm #167). Roster containing name, county, state,
    date of enlistment, company and regiment, rank, wounds
    received, date and cause of discharge, and general remarks
    about members of the association living in Jefferson
    County as well as other East Tennessee Counties, etc.
Cemeteries. South Carolina and Tennessee, ca. 1850 - ca.
    1956, (microfilm #307). Alphabetical listing, by county,
    of tombstone inscriptions from 25 South Carolina and
    48 Tennessee cemeteries, including some from Jefferson Co.

JEFFERSON COUNTY
(continued)

MANUSCRIPT MATERIALS (continued)
Reuel B. Pritchett Collection, ca. 1820 - 1969, (microfilm
#544). Scrapbooks compiled by Rev. Pritchett for Jeffer-
son County Historical Museum, including newspaper clippings, photographs, and historical and biographical
sketches concerning persons, places, and events.
Church Records. Westminster and St. Paul's Presbyterian
Churches, 1804; 1819-77, (microfilm #162) [see microfilm
#174 for years 1878-1947]. Church records consisting
of minutes of session; baptismal, marriage, and death
records; registers of deacons, elders, and communicants,
and a brief church history.
Church Records of White Pine Presbyterian Church, 1873-1901,
(microfilm #177). Consists of minutes of session and
financial records; registers of deacons, elders, and
communicants. Was called Westminster Presbyterian Church,
then Long Creek Presbyterian Church; and present name
in 1880.

ADDITIONAL CHURCH RECORDS (may be purchased from the Historical
Commission of the Southern Baptist Convention, 127 Ninth
Ave. N., Nashville, TN 37234):
Dandridge Baptist Church, 1786-1966, (microfilm reel #2050).
Dumplin Creek Baptist Church, 1797-1938, (microfilm reel
#2049).
Friendship Baptist Church, Mar. 12, 1819 - 1897, (microfilm
reel #1396).
Nolachucky Association. Friendship Baptist Church, 1858-1902,
(microfilm reel #1400).
First Baptist Church, Apr. 1834 - Mar. 1891, (microfilm
reel #5273). Formerly called Blackoak Grove Church;
merged with Oakland Church to form Mossy Creek, May
8, 1841; name changed to First Baptist Church, Jan.
8, 1902.
Materials for a History of First Baptist Church, 1841-1941,
(microfilm reel #1357).

JOHNSON COUNTY

CREATED: 1836 from Carter County [1796 from Washington Co.].
COUNTY SEAT: Mountain City, TN 37683.

LIBRARY: Johnson City Public Library, 211 N. Church St.,
Mountain City, TN 37683.

JOHNSON COUNTY
(continued)

PUBLISHED SOURCES:
Douthat, James L. Johnson County, Tennessee Marriages, 1838-1857. [1982].
_____. Johnson County, Tennessee Will Book 1, 1827-1860. [Signal Mtn., TN: 1982].
Gentry, Thomas W. Johnson County, Tennessee 1870 Census. [1982].
History Of Tennessee. [Chicago & Nashville: Goodspeed Publishing Co., 1887]. (Johnson Co., pp. 922-25; 1312-1317.)
Johnson, Georgia Marie & Della Hawkins. Marriage Records Of Johnson County, Tennessee 1796-1880. 3 vols. Vol. I & II, 1796-1880. [1979]. Vol. III, 1881-1905. [1980].
Neal, C. B. The Wills Of Johnson County, Tennessee. [Olympia, Washington: 1960].
Wilson, Walter W. Johnson County, Tennessee 1840 And 1850 Census Records. [1974].
_____. Johnson County, Tennessee 1860 Census Records. [1979].

W.P.A. TYPESCRIPT RECORDS (available at the Tennessee State Library and Archives):
Wills & Letters of Administration, Vol. 1, Book 1, 1827-1867.
Tax Lists, Vol. 1, 1836-1839.
County Court Minute Book 1, Vol. 1, 1836-1854.
Marriage Record Book 1, 1838-1857.
Marriage Records, 1857-1860.
Bible & Tombstone Records.

MICROFILMED RECORDS (available at the Tennessee State Library and Archives):
1840-80; & 1900-10 Federal Census.
Circuit Court Civil Minutes, Nov. 1846 - Sept. 1912.
Circuit Court Enrollment Books, July 1841 - Nov. 1873.
Criminal Minutes, Mar. 1848 - Sept. 1903.
Minute Books, Mar. 1836 - Nov. 1897.
Chancery Court Enrollment Books, Aug. 1871 - Feb. 1898.
Chancery Court Minutes, Apr. 1856 - Oct. 1908.
Administrators' Letters and Bonds, June 1839 - May 1900.
Guardians', Executors', & Administrators' Bonds, Oct. 1856 - Apr. 1899.
Administrators' & Guardians' Settlements, July 1879 - Dec. 1907.
Claims against estates, Jan. 1872 - Aug. 1932.
Administrators' Settlements, Jan. 1848 - Sept. 1874.
Insolvent Estates, Oct. 1874 - Nov. 1937.
Marriages, 1838 - 1909.
County Court Minutes, May 1836 - Sept. 1905.

JOHNSON COUNTY
(continued)

MICROFILMED RECORDS (continued)
Settlements, Sept. 1837 - Apr. 1862; 1867-1884.
Physicians' Register, Sept. 1889 - Feb. 1928.
Wills, 1836-1872; Mar. 1882 - July 1932.
Vital Statistics, 1908 - 1912.
Deeds, May 1836 - June 1900.
Surveys, Aug. 1836 - Dec. 1905.
Land Entries, May 1836 - Mar. 1888.
Entry Takers' Book, Aug. 1836 - Mar. 1851.
Trust Deeds, Mar. 1889 - Mar. 1905.
Tax Books, 1836 - 1889; 1890 - 1900.

MANUSCRIPT HOLDINGS (available at the Tennessee State Library
    and Archives):
Associations, Institutions, etc. Confederate Veterans
    Association of Upper East Tennessee, 1861 - ca. 1895,
    #167. Roster containing name, county, state, date of
    enlistment, company and regiment, rank, wounds received,
    date and cause of discharge, and general remarks about
    members of the association living in Johnson County
    as well as other East Tennessee counties, etc.

KNOX COUNTY

CREATED: 1792 from Greene [1783 from Washington Co.] and
    Hawkins County [1786 from Sullivan Co.].
COUNTY SEAT: Knoxville, TN 37901.

LIBRARIES:
    Lawson-McGhee Library, 500 W. Church St., Knoxville, TN
        37902.
    McClung Library, University of Tennessee, Knoxville, TN
        37916.
    Branch Genealogical Library, Church of Jesus Christ of
        Latter Day Saints, 400 Kendall Road, Knoxville, TN 37919.

HISTORICAL SOCIETY: East Tennessee Historical Society, 500
    W. Church St., Knoxville, TN 37902.

PUBLISHED SOURCES:
    "Early East Tennessee Taxpayers, III, Knox County, 1806,"
        by Pollyanna Creekmore; East TN Historical Society
        Publications, no. 26 (1954), pp. 67-109.
    d'Armand, R. C. Knox County, Tennessee Marriage Records,
        1792-1900. [Knoxville: Family Record Society, 1970].

PUBLISHED SOURCES (continued)
 Grady. <u>Tombstone</u> <u>Inscriptions</u> <u>And</u> <u>Death</u> <u>Records,</u> <u>Calvary</u>
  <u>Cemetery,</u> <u>Knoxville,</u> <u>Tenn.,</u> <u>1869-1967</u>. [Knoxville:
  1967].
 <u>History</u> <u>Of</u> <u>Tennessee</u>...(East TN edition). [Chicago & Nashville: Goodspeed Publishing Co., 1887] (Knox Co.,
  pp. 925-93; 1072.
 <u>Historical</u> <u>Records</u> <u>Survey</u>. Minutes of the county court
  of Knox County, Book O, 1792-95. [Nashville: The Survey,
  1941].
 <u>Knox</u> <u>County</u> <u>In</u> <u>The</u> <u>World</u> <u>War,</u> <u>1917-1918-1919</u>. [Knoxville:
  Knox Lithography Co., 1919].
 Rothrock, M. H. <u>The</u> <u>French</u> <u>Broad</u> - <u>Holston</u> <u>Country</u>: A
  History of Knox County. [Knoxville: East TN Historical
  Society, 1946].
 "Marriage Records of Knox County, Tennessee, 1792-1837,"
  by Kate White; <u>Tennessee</u> <u>Historical</u> <u>Magazine</u>, v.6 (1920),
  pp. 10-17; 58-68; & 187-199.
 Tennessee Historical Society. <u>Knoxville's</u> <u>First</u> <u>Graveyard</u>
  ...Tombstone Inscriptions in the First Presbyterian
  Church Cemetery. [1979].

W.P.A. TYPESCRIPT RECORDS (available at the Tennessee State
  Library and Archives):
 County Court Minutes, Book O, 1792-95.
 District - Superior Court, 1793-98.
 Superior Court Minute Book, v.C, 1798-1803.
 Superior Court Minute Book, no. 3, 1793-1809.
 Court of Pleas and Quarter Sessions Minute Books 2 & 3,
  1799-1802.
 Superior Court Record Book B., 1797-1804, pts. I & II.
 Superior Court of Law & Equity Minute Book, No. 1, 1793
  - 1808.
 Minutes of the Circuit Court, 1799-1851.
 Circuit Court Minute Book 3-A, 1810-1817.
 County Court Minute Books nos. 6 thru 25, 1809-1872.
 Estate Books, vols. 2, 3, & 4, 1812-1830.
 A List of Taxable Property, 1844-1845.
 Tombstone Records of Old Gray Cemetery.
 Tombstone Records.
 Pleasant Forest Presbyterian Church Minute Book, 1833-1891.
 Beaver Creek Church Records, 1833-1879.
 Marriage License Records, Books 1 & 2, 1838-1864.
 Will Book, 1792-1803.
 Guardian Book, 1792-1821, v.O.
 Record Books, Nos. 1, 1795-99, pts. I & II; No. 4, 1802-05;
  No. 5, 1805-06.

KNOX COUNTY
(continued)

MICROFILMED MATERIALS (available at the Tennessee State Library
    and Archives):
1830-80; & 1900-10 Federal Census.
Charter Book, 1887-1927.
Deeds, 1788-1965.
Entry Book, 1806-1904.
Lien Book, 1931.
Map Book, 1877; 1883; 1902; 1906; 1919; 1924-26; and
    intermittantly until 1965.
Power of Attorney, 1898-1962.
Release Book, 1931-1965.
Quit Claim Deed Book, 1896, 1912, 1920.
Trust Deeds, 1868-1966.
Court Records, Knox County, 1797 (filmed with Hancock County
Records and available at TSLA).

MANUSCRIPT MATERIALS (available at the Tennessee State Library
    and Archives):
Association, Institutions, etc. Confederate Veterans
    Association of Upper East Tennessee, 1861 - ca. 1895.
    #167. Roster containing name, county, state, date of
    enlistment, company and regiment, rank, wounds received,
    date and cause of discharge, and general remarks about
    members of the association living in Knox and other
    East Tennessee counties, etc.
Church Records. First Baptist Church, Knoxville, 1843-1952,
    (microfilm #195). Records consisting of minutes; member-
    ship lists; records of baptisms, deaths, marriages,
    dismissals, new members, and records of other church
    activities.
Church Records. First Presbyterian Church, Knoxville,
    1816-1941, (microfilm #338). Consists of minutes of
    session; register of pastors, elders, deacons, communi-
    cants, slaves, baptisms, marriages, and deaths, 1816-1931.
Church Records. First Presbyterian Church, Knoxville,
    1816-1837, (microfilm #355). Records include annual
    membership list; annual report, 1832-33, which contains
    records of baptisms, deaths, suspensions, and communi-
    cants; register of admittances and removals.
Church Records. St. John's Episcopal Church, Knoxville,
    1844-1971, (microfilm #356). Historical sketch; baptisms,
    marriages, families, deaths, burials, etc.
Church Records. Second Presbyterian Church, Knoxville,
    1819-1972, (microfilm #423). Minutes of session; baptis-
    mal records, marriages, infant members, deaths, pastors,
    communicants, etc.

KNOX COUNTY
(continued)

MANUSCRIPT MATERIALS (continued)
    Church Records. Mt. Hebron Primitive Baptist Church, Knox-
        ville, 1824-1942, (microfilm #450). Lists of members,
        deaths, and dismissals; minutes; etc.
    Cemeteries. South Carolina and Tennessee, ca. 1850 - ca.
        1956, (microfilm #307). Alphabetical listing, by county,
        of tombstone inscriptions from 25 South Carolina and
        48 Tennessee cemeteries including information from Knox
        Co.
    Cemeteries. First Presbyterian Church Cemetery, Knoxville,
        1793 - ca. 1942, (microfilm #340). Cemetery records
        with short biographical sketches and genealogical notes
        for many of those interred. Indexed.
    Cemeteries for Anderson County, Tennessee, (microfilm #506).
        Included are some cemetery records for Knox County.
    Genealogical Data of Frost and Allied Families, ca. 1500
        - 1973, (microfilm #452). Data on the Frost and related
        families; also included are church, cemetery, and military
        service records for the Revolutionary War, War of 1812,
        Civil War, and World War I.

MANUSCRIPT MATERIALS (available at the Tennessee State Library
        and Archives):
    Sneed Papers, ca. 1000 items. 1786-1860. Composed of court
        records, sheriff records, deeds, land grants, wills,
        account book for store at Estellville, correspondence,
        bills, notes, receipts, genealogical data, sketches,
        church records, and school records; for the area around
        Knoxville, primarily, for the Sneed family.

ADDITIONAL CHURCH RECORDS (may be purchased from the Historical
        Commission of the Southern Baptist Convention, 127 Ninth
        Ave. N., Nashville, TN 37234):

    Fountain City. Beaver Dam Baptist Church, 1802-1959; Sunday
        School Records, Jan. 1900-12, (microfilm reel #1058).
    Fountain City. Beaver Dam Baptist Church, History of,
        by Mary Sue Beggs, 1959, (microfilm reel #1059).
    Ball Camp Baptist Church, 1818 - Apr. 1966, (microfilm
        reel #1938).
    Knoxville. First Baptist Church, 1843-1952, (microfilm
        reel #224).

19th CENTURY LAND OWNERSHIP MAP (available from the Library
        of Congress, Washington, D.C.):
    Knox County, 1877, D. G. Beers Co., Surveyor & Publisher;
        scale 1:50,688; Map No. 873.

LAKE COUNTY

CREATED: 1870 from Obion County [1823 from Western District (Indian Lands)].
COUNTY SEAT: Tiptonville, TN 38079.

LIBRARY: Tiptonville Public Library, 126 Tipton St., Tiptonville, TN 38079.

PUBLISHED SOURCES:
Callis, Ruby. Ridgeby Panorama. [1967].
History Of Tennessee. [Chicago & Nashville: Goodspeed Publishing Co., 1887]. (Lake Co., pp. 852-57; 1073-87.)
Humphries, C. C. "The History of the Reelfoot Lake Region," Thesis, University of Tennessee, Knoxville, TN, 1938.

MICROFILMED RECORDS (available at the Tennessee State Library and Archives):
1870-80; & 1900-10 Federal Census.
Chancery Court Minutes, Nov. 1896 - Oct. 1913.
Rule Docket, Jan. 1871 - Mar. 1931.
Circuit Court Minutes, Mar. 1892 - Mar. 1902.
Administrators' Bonds and Letters, Sept. 1896 - Apr. 1963.
Guardians' Bonds & Letters, Sept. 1898 - Apr. 1963.
Marriage Bonds, Nov. 1883 - Mar. 1930.
County Court Minutes, Sept. 1870 - Jan. 1902.
Administrators', Guardians' and Executors' Settlements, Jan. 1872 - Jan. 1916.
Will Book, Apr. 1871 - Oct. 1943.
Deeds, Sept. 1870 - Nov. 1914.
Trust Deeds, Sept. 1870 - Jan. 1901.
Entry Book, Oct. 1893 - Jan. 1929.
Tax Book, 1878-79.

LAUDERDALE COUNTY

CREATED: 1835 from Dyer, Haywood, and Tipton Counties [all created 1832 from the Western District (Indian lands)].
COUNTY SEAT: Ripley, TN 38063.

LIBRARY: Sugar Hill - Lauderdale County Library, Ripley, TN 38063.

PUBLISHED SOURCES:
"1840 Census of Lauderdale County, Tennessee," Ansearchin' News, v.16 (1969), no. 4:161-62; & 171.

LAUDERDALE COUNTY
(continued)

PUBLISHED SOURCES (continued)
"Lauderdale County Marriage Records, Book A, 1838-1850,"
Ansearchin News, v.16 (1969), no. 4:163-68.
History Of Tennessee. [Chicago & Nashville: Goodspeed
Publishing Co., 1887]. (Lauderdale Co., pp. 797-808;
842-85.
Peters, K. J. Lauderdale County From Earliest Times. [1957].
Williams, Joseph S. Old Times In West Tennessee. [Memphis:
W. G. Cheeney, 1873]. Reminiscences - semi historic
- of pioneer life and the early emigrant settlers in
the Big Hatchie country.

W.P.A. TYPESCRIPT RECORDS (available at the Tennessee State
Library and Archives):
County Court Minute Books, A, B, C, D, 1836-1861.
Inventories, Sales Bills & Wills, 1837-44 and Wills,
Inventories & Sales Bills, 1844-49.
Inventories, Sales, Bills & Wills, 1849-55.
Marriage Register, v.A, 1838-57; & B, 1857-66.
Key Corner, the Birthplace of Civilization in West Tennessee.
Family Records.

MICROFILMED RECORDS (available at the Tennessee State Library
and Archives):
1840-80; & 1900-10 Federal Census.
Clerk & Master Minutes, Jan. 1856 - May 1905.
Clerk & Master Enrollment Dockets, Jan. 1872 - Dec. 1913.
Circuit Court Minutes, June 1836 - July 1889; Nov. 1889
- Mar. 1902.
Vital Statistics: Births & Deaths, 1881-1882.
Probate of Deeds, Wills, Inventories, June 1836 - Feb.
1847.
Physicians' Register, 1889.
Widows' Pension, Sept. 1866 - Nov. 1928.
Insolvent Estates, July 1849 - Nov. 1905.
Marriage Bonds, Mar. 1838 - Oct. 1918.
County Court Minutes, May 1836 - July 1901.
Administrators' Receipts, May 1884 - nov. 1896.
Guardians' Minutes, Apr. 1878 - July 1903.
Administrators' Bonds, July 1854 - Sept. 1913.
Guardians' Letters, Jan. 1882 - Apr. 1885.
Guardians' Bonds, Jan. 1846 - May 1905.
Administrators' & Guardians' Settlements, Jan. 1847 - June
1902.
Wills, Sept. 1837 - Sept. 1904.

LAUDERDALE COUNTY
(continued)

MICROFILMED RECORDS (continued)
Deeds, Dec. 1835 - July 1900 (except Aug. 1891 - Dec. 1899).
Survey Books, May 1822 - Oct. 1957.
Mortgages, May 1868 - Jan. 1874.
Road Books, Oct. 1838 - Jan. 1889.
Tax Books, 1852 - 1897.
License Register, 1844 - 1860.
Ripley Presbyterian Church Record Ledger, 1890-1898.
Lauderdale County Funeral Home Records, 1894-1902.
St. Paul's Methodist Church, 1881.
St. Paul's Methodist Church Record & Roll Book, 1881-1887.
St. Paul's Annual Record, 1896.
Clipping from the Enterprise, Mar. 1904.
Woodville Baptist, 1800, 1863, 1884.

MANUSCRIPT MATERIALS (available at the Tennessee State Library
    and Archives):
County Records. Miscellaneous Records, 1840-1973, (microfilm
    #554).   Assorted   records   reflecting   the   history   and
    growth of Lauderdale County, including church records;
    papers collected by Robert C. Johnston; reminiscences
    of S. O. Rice (1840-1924), a Confederate Soldier; and
    diaries, 1861-67, of Cornelia A. Watkins.

LAWRENCE COUNTY

CREATED: 1817 from Hickman [1807 from Dickson Co.] and Maury
    County [1807 from Williamson Co.].

LIBRARY: Lawrence County Public Library, 519 E. Gaines St.,
    Lawrenceburg, TN 38464.

HISTORICAL   SOCIETY: Lawrence   County   Historical   Society,
    P. O. Box 431, Lawrenceburg, TN 38464.

PUBLISHED SOURCES:
    Alexander, I. M. B. & C. H. Gresham. At Rest: Cemetery
        Records of Lawrence County, Tennessee. [Lawrenceburg:
        1968].
    Annals Of Lawrence County, Vol. 1, July, Aug, Sept. 1970;
        Lawrence County Historical Society Quarterly.
    Carpenter, V. H. & M. K. Carter. Lawrence County, Tennessee
        1860-1840 [sic] Census, Private Acts, Miscellaneous.
        [Columbia, TN: P-Vine Press, 1977].

LAWRENCE COUNTY
(continued)

PUBLISHED SOURCES (continued)
  Carter, M. K. & Joan Coffey Hudgins. 1850 Census Lawrence
    County, Tennessee. [1972]. (Includes some other records.)
  History Of Tennessee. [Chicago & Nashville: Goodspeed
    Publishing Co., 1887] (Lawrence Co., pp. 749-63; 807-49.)
  Court Of Pleas And Quarter Sessions Lawrence County, Tennes-
    see 1818-1822. [1977].
  Lawrence County, Tennessee 1880 Census.
  Lawrence County, Tennessee Court Of Pleas & Quarter Sessions,
    July 1822-Oct. 1826. [Lawrenceburg: 1977]. (Compiler's
    name unavailable to this author at the time of publication
    of this work.)
  Lawrence County, Tennessee Historical Society Bulletin,
    Nos. 1-55, Apr. 1953 - Nov. 1967.
  Marsh, Helen C. Name Index To Goodspeed's History Of Tennes-
    see.
  Moore, L. E. Glimpses Of Lawrence County History. [Colum-
    bia, TN: Columbia State College, 1970].
  Morrison, J. F., Jr. A Brief History Of Early Lawrence
    County, Tennessee. [1968]. (Includes 1820 Federal
    Census.)
  Reeves, C. E. Loretto In The Happy Long Ago, 1800-1954.
    [Lawrenceburg, TN: 1954].
  Whitley, E. R. Marriages Of Lawrence County, Tennessee,
    1818-1854. [Baltimore: Genealogical Publishing Co.,
    Inc., 1982].

W.P.A. TYPESCRIPT RECORDS (available at the Tennessee State
    Library and Archives):
  County Court Minutes, v.1, 1818-1823.
  General Index to Deed Books, A-P, 1819-1871.
  Wills, Inventories, etc., Book B, 1829-1847.
  Marriage Records, 1838-1860.
  Marriage Records, 1861-1866.
  Rule Docket-Chancery Court, 1848-1871.
  Road Record Book, 1853-1883.
  Bible, Family & Tombstone Records.

MICROFILMED RECORDS (available at the Tennessee State Library
    and Archives):
  1820-80; & 1900-10 Federal Census.
  Clerk & Masters' Enrollments, Mar. 1871 - Mar. 1925.
  Claims, 1874, 1894, 1935.
  Clerk & Master Minutes, May 1840 - Dec. 1901.
  Circuit Court Minutes, Feb. 1832 - Dec. 1902.
  Administrative Bonds, Mar. 1861 - Dec. 1894.
  Insolvent Estates, Jan. 1874 - Jan. 1942.

LAWRENCE COUNTY
(continued)

MICROFILMED RECORDS (continued)
  Settlements, June 1880 - Nov. 1907.
  Index to Marriages, 1838 - 1923.
  Marriages, Feb. 1838 - Mar. 1915.
  Marriage Bonds, 1818 - 1909.
  County Court Minutes, 1818-22; 1827 - May 1890; June 1890
    - Mar. 1902.
  Howard's Chapel Presbyterian Church, 1886-1895.
  Second Creek Associate Primitive Baptist Church.
  W.P.A. Project Index.
  Lawrence 11 District Tax Book, 1872.
  Circuit Court Decision Book, 1825.
  County State Docket, 1830.
  Partial list of registered voters, 1906.
  Post Office Applicants.
  Minutes of Presbyterian, 1877 - 1903.
  Guardians' Minutes, Jan. 1873 - Apr. 1901.
  Guardians' & Administrators' Settlements, Feb. 1874 - June
    1880.
  Road Book, Dec. 1885 - Feb. 1890.
  Probate Deeds, Sept. 1854 - Oct. 1901.
  Claims against estates, Mar. 1874 - Nov. 1903.
  Vital Statistics: Birth Records, 1908-1910.
  Wills, Jan. 1829 - Feb. 1919.
  Deeds, Aug. 1819 - Feb. 1900.
  Surveyors' Book, May 1820 - Apr. 1929.
  Entry Taker, Oct. 1820 - Sept. 1849.
  Trust Deeds, May 1868 - Apr. 1900.
  Plat Book, 1820-1885.
  Tax Books, 1859-1886; & intermittantly 1887-1900.

MANUSCRIPT MATERIALS (available at the Tennessee State Library
    and Archives):
  Cemeteries.   South Carolina and Tennessee, ca. 1850 - ca.
    1956, (microfilm #307).   Alphabetical listing, by county,
    of tombstone inscriptions from 48 Tennessee cemeteries
    including some from Lawrence Co.
  Church Records.   St. Joseph Methodist Episcopal Church,
    1918-1972, (microfilm #476).   Registers of baptisms,
    marriages, members, and pastors.
  Church Records.   Loretto United Methodist Church, Loretto,
    TN, 1918-1971, (microfilm #481).   Registers of baptisms,
    marriages, members, and pastors; and historical sketch
    of the church.
  Church Records.   Second Creek Primitive Baptist Church,
    1830-1973, (microfilm #462).   Minutes, 1929 membership
    list, etc.

LAWRENCE COUNTY
(continued)

MANUSCRIPT MATERIALS (continued)
Church Records. Cumberland Presbyterian Church, 1904-1973,
(microfilm #463). Registers of pastors, elders, deacons,
and communicants; and minutes.
Church Records. First Presbyterian Church, 1938-1973,
(microfilm #464). Registers of pastors, elders, deacons,
communicants, minutes, and historical sketch.
County Records. Misc. Records, ca. 1800-1940, (microfilm
#566). Various records concerning history and growth
of Lawrence County, including papers of the Lawrence
Co. Historical Society; scrapbooks; W.P.A. Project Index
for the county; various court and church records; and
Bible records and papers of the Alexander family of
Giles Co., TN.

LEWIS COUNTY

CREATED: 1843 from Hickman [1807 from Dickson Co.], Lawrence
[1817 from Hickman and Maury Cos.], Maury [1807 from Williamson Co.], and Wayne County [1817 from Hickman and Humphreys
Cos..]
COUNTY SEAT: Hohenwald, TN 38462.

LIBRARY: Lewis County Public Library, Hohenwald, TN 38462.

PUBLISHED SOURCES:
History Of Tennessee. [Chicago & Nashville: Goodspeed
Publishing Co., 1887] (Lewis Co., pp. 801-07; 923-24.)
Graves, Marjorie B. Lewis County, Tennessee Cemetery Re-
cords. [Columbia, TN: P-Vine Press].
_____. First Fifty Years Of Lewis County Marriage Records,
1844-1894. [Hohenwald, TN: Table Top Press].
Graves, Marjorie B. & Betty Glenn. 1880 Lewis County,
Tennessee Federal Census. [Hohenwald: P-Vine Press].
Lightfoot, M. P. & Evelyn B. Shackelford. Maury County
Neighbors: Records of Giles, Lewis, and Marshall Coun-
ties, TN. [Mt. Pleasant, TN: 1967].

W.P.A. TYPESCRIPT RECORDS (available at the Tennessee State
Library and Archives):
Minutes of the County Court, 1846-1870.
Guardian Bonds, 1846-1874.
Union Church of Christ, 1871-1884.
The Mormon Massacre, 1884.
Early Days in Lewis County.

LEWIS COUNTY
(continued)

MICROFILMED RECORDS (available at the Tennessee State Library
and Archives):
1850-80; & 1900-10 Federal Census.
Clerk & Master, Apr. 1871 - Dec. 1904.
Enrollment Book, Mar. 1844 - July 1904.
Minutes, Mar. 1846 - Feb. 1906.
Marriage Records, Nov. 1847 - Oct. 1909.
Marriage Bonds, Mar. 1903 - Oct. 1920.
Wills, Nov. 1846 - 1936.
Inventories, Nov. 1846 - Jan. 1874.
Administrators' Settlements, Feb. 1875 - Feb. 1926.
County Court Minutes, Mar. 1848 - Nov. 1903.
Vital Statistics, 1908-1912.
Deeds, Mar. 1844 - Sept. 1902.
Trust Deeds, Jan. 1895 - Mar. 1905.
Land Surveys, 1827-1883.
Land Entries, Feb. 1827 - Feb. 1859.
Tax Duplicates, 1887-1900.

LINCOLN COUNTY

CREATED: 1809 from Bedford County [1807 from Rutherford
Co.].
COUNTY SEAT: Fayetteville, TN 37334.

LIBRARY: Fayetteville - Lincoln County Public Library, Fayetteville, TN 37334. (Substantial genealogical collection
and lineage chart collection of the Lincoln Co. Historical
Society.)

HISTORICAL SOCIETY: Lincoln County Historical Society, 202
E. Washington St., Fayetteville, TN 37334.

PUBLISHED SOURCES:
History Of Tennessee. [Chicago & Nashville: Goodspeed
Publishing Co., 1887] (Lincoln Co., pp. 767-84; 876-924.)
Jones, K. P. & P. J. Gandrud. Records Of Lincoln County,
Tennessee. [Fayetteville: 1932].
"Lincoln County News Supplement, Fayetteville, Tennessee,
May 4, 1904," Lincoln Co. Historical Society, 1971.
Marsh, H. C. & T. R. Abstracts Of Wills, Lincoln County,
Tennessee, 1810-1895. [Shelbyville, TN: 1977].
_____. Lincoln County, Tennessee Official Marriage Records,
1838-1880. [Shelbyville, TN: 1974].

LINCOLN COUNTY
(continued)

PUBLISHED SOURCES (continued)
Marsh. Cemetery Records, Lincoln County, Tennessee. [Shelbyville, TN: 1972].
Porch, Miss Deane. U.S. Census Office, 7th Census, 1850. [Nashville: 1970].
Taylor, H. L. & C. G. Some Early Settlers; Lincoln County, Tennessee. [Northport, Ala.: 1970].
Tucker, M. A. & J. W. Waller. Lincoln County Bible Records. 6 volumes. [Batavia, Ill.: 1971].
Waller. Lincoln County, Tennessee Pioneers, Vol. 1, Sept. 1970, Batavia, Illinois.

W.P.A. TYPESCRIPT RECORDS (available at the Tennessee State Library and Archives):
Court of Pleas & Quarter Sessions, 1814-1817.
County Court of Pleas & Quarter Sessions, 1810.
Church Records.
Minute Docket Book I, 1811-1812.
Marriages, 1823-28; & 1838-66.
Wills & Inventories, 1810-1824.
Will Book, 1827-1850.

MICROFILMED RECORDS (available at the Tennessee State Library and Archives):
1820-80; & 1900-10 Federal Census.
Delinquent Tax Dockets, 1898-99; 1920-33; & 1936-1966.
Chancery Court Enrolling Dockets, Mar. 1870 - 1894.
Chancery Court Minutes, Mar. 1838 - Jan. 1844; July 1847 - Sept. 1892; Mar. 1893 - Nov. 1969.
Circuit Court Enrolling Dockets, July 1856 - July 1877.
Circuit Court Equity Records, Oct. 1819 - Mar. 1828.
Circuit Court Minutes, Civil & Criminal, July 1849 - Oct. 1969.
Administrators' Bonds & Letters, May 1872 - Dec. 1969.
Executors' Bonds & Letters, July 1872 - Aug. 1951; Oct. 1951 - Dec. 1969.
Guardians' Bonds & Letters, May 1872 - Dec. 1969.
Claims against estates, June 1927 - Ma. 1929.
Committment Records, July 1951 - Dec. 1969.
County Court Enrolling Docket, Apr. 1868 - Dec. 1874.
Estate Sales, Accounts of, Oct. 1847 - Jan. 1914.
Insolvent Estates, Accounts of, Jan. 1895 - May 1923.
Insolvent Estates, Minutes of, Dec. 1861 - Jan. 1895.
Inventories of Estates, Oct. 1840 - Feb. 1854; Jan. 1907 - Sept. 1969.

LINCOLN COUNTY
(continued)

MICROFILMED RECORDS (continued)
  Marriage Bonds, May 1888 - Oct. 1898.
  Marriages, 1838 - 1969.
  County Court Minutes, Feb. 1810 - Dec. 1810 (found in Deed
    Book C, pp. 1-43); Feb. 1811 - July 1823; Jan. 1826
    - Jan. 1970.
  Minutes, Corp. of Fayetteville, Jan. 1892 - Sept. 1899.
  Minutes, Quarterly Court, Nov. 1897 - Oct. 1902.
  Road Commission Minutes, Sept. 1871 - July 1880; 1889.
  Settlements, Administrators', & Executors', Dec. 1842 -
    Oct. 1847; Aug. 1858 - Dec. 1907.
  Guardians' Settlements, Dec. 1836 - Dec. 1846; Oct. 1861
    - Nov. 1902.
  Vital Statistics, Deaths, May 1881 - Feb. 1883.
  Wills, Mar. 1809 - Nov. 1861; Feb. 1864 - Dec. 1921 (indexed
    from Sept. 1826).
  Deeds, Feb. 1810 - Oct. 1819; Jan. 1824 - Mar. 1852; Apr.
    1855 - Jan. 1860; Apr. 1864 - Oct. 1900.
  Land Entries, Jan. 1855 - Dec. 1874.
  Land Surveys, Apr. 1824 - Jan. 1876.
  Trust Deeds, July 1868 - May 1899.
  Tax Books, 1846-50; 1865-67; 1870-72; 1875-97.
  Miscellaneous Records.
  Mt. Carmel Baptist Church, May 1812 - June 1921.
  Shiloh Methodist church, 1881-1912; History of, 1842-1923.
  Buckeye Primitive Baptist, 1871-1886.
  Miscellaneous Papers.
  Oakhill Missionary Baptist Church, 1883-1946, Belleville.
  Mt. Hebron Presbyterian Church, Belleville, TN (formerly
    Norris Creek) 1829 - 1869.
    Book II, 1892-1912; Book 4, 1931-1957; Book 3, 1926-1931.
    Sunday School Record, 1890-1906.
  Bible Record, primarily Stewart.
  Buckeye Primitive Baptist, 1848-1926.
  Prosperity Reformed Associates Church from 1866 (Yukon, TN).
  Lincoln Memorial Association Reformed Presbyterian, Fayette-
    ville, TN, 1900-1929.
  Shiloh-Taft, Methodist, Taft, TN.
  Shiloh Primitive Baptist, 1830-1952.
  Providence Methodist Episcopal.
  Dick White College, Fayetteville, 1899-1900.
  New Salem Congregation, Elk Presbyterian Church.
  Presbyterian Church, Fayetteville.
  Fayetteville Baptist.
  First Presbyterian Church of Fayetteville (history of), 1941.
  Petersburg Methodist, history of.
  New Lebanon Presbyterian, Kelso, Tennessee.

LINCOLN COUNTY
(continued)

MANUSCRIPT MATERIALS (available at the Tennessee State Library
and Archives):
Church Records. Mt. Moriah Primitive Baptist, Fayetteville,
1833-1904; 1925-1941, (microfilm #331). List of members,
baptisms, deaths, ministers, church minutes, etc.
Church Records. Hannah's Gap Baptist Church of Christ,
1854-1911, (microfilm #396). Minutes, membership list;
deaths; date of reception, etc.
Church Records. Buckeye Primitive Baptist Church, 1871-1969,
(microfilm #322). Minutes of session and membership
lists.
Church Records. Boiling Fork Baptist, 1808-1861, (microfilm
#330). Minutes of church conferences with names of
new members, members dismissed, ministers.
Church Records. Mt. Olivet Primitive Baptist, 1826-1963,
(microfilm #335). Minutes of session, membership lists
for Negroes and whites, etc.
Church Records. Baptist Church of Christ at Concord and
Elk River Association of Primitive Baptists, Fayetteville,
1808-1941.
Church Records. Boiling Fork Baptist, 1808-1861, (microfilm
#574; see also, above, #330).
County Records. Miscellaneous, 1800-1973, (microfilm #513).
Account books, Bible records, correspondence, genealogical
data, newspapers, some church records, etc.

ADDITIONAL CHURCH RECORDS (may be purchased from the Historical
Commission of the Southern Baptist Convention, 127 Ninth
Ave., N., Nashville, TN 37234):
Fayetteville. Mulberry Baptist Church, 1818-1869. Formerly
Ball Fork Baptist Church, name changed in 1869. (Micro-
film reel #1443).

LOUDON COUNTY

CREATED: 1870 from Roane [1801 from Knox Co.], Monroe [1819
from the Hiwassee Purchase (Indian lands)], and Blount
County [1795 from Knox Co.].
COUNTY SEAT: Loudon, TN 37774

LIBRARY: Loudon City Library, Loudon, TN 37774.

LOUDON COUNTY
(continued)

PUBLISHED SOURCES:
History Of Tennessee...(East TN edition). [Chicago & Nashville: Goodspeed Publishing Co., 1887]. (Loudon Co., pp. 825-28; 1081-1088.)
Historical Records Survey. Inventory of the county archives of Tennessee, no. 53, Loudon Co. [Nashville: The Survey, 1941].
Beloved Landmarks Of Loudon Co., Tennessee. Hiwassee Chapter D.A.R. [Loudon: 1902].
Abstract Of Headstones And Markings In Steeke Cemetery, Loudon, Tennessee. Hiwassee Chapter D.A.R. [Loudon: 1957].

W.P.A. TYPESCRIPT RECORDS (available at the Tennessee State Library and Archives):
Tombstone Records.

MICROFILMED RECORDS (available at the Tennessee State Library and Archives):
1870-80; & 1900-10 Federal Census.
Circuit Court General Sessions Minutes, Aug. 1963 - July 1968.
Circuit Court Civil & Criminal Minutes, Sept. 1870 - Feb. 1927.
Circuit Court Civil Minutes, Feb. 1927 - July 1968.
Clerk & Masters' Enrolled Cases, July 1870 - July 1876.
Clerk & Masters' Minutes, Nov. 1870 - July 1968.
Administrators' Bonds & Letters, Dec. 1879 - July 1968.
Minutes, Final Decree - Appeals, May 1836 - Mar. 1968.
Administrators' Settlements & Inventories, Oct. 1870 - May 1968.
Dentist Register, July 1919 - July 1964.
Executors' Bonds & Letters, July 1880 - Aug. 1960.
Executors' Settlements, Aug. 1950 - Jan. 1968.
Guardians' Bonds & Letters, Nov. 1879 - July 1968.
Guardians' Settlements, Aug. 1870 - Oct. 1912; Jan. 1913 - Sept. 1967.
Marriage Records, Aug. 1870 - Aug. 1968.
County Court Minutes, June 1870 - May 1968.
Nurses' Register, Dec. 1940 - June 1955.
Optometry Records, Jan. 1910 - Feb. 1951.
Physicians' Register, Apr. 1907 - Feb. 1950.
County Court Quorum Minutes, Jan. 1917 - July 1968.
Tax Sales, 1894-1911; Mar. 1912 - Mar. 1918; Nov. 1919 - Mar. 1920.
Vital Statistics; Births & Deaths, 1908-1936.
Will Books, Nov. 1870 - July 1943; Aug. 1948 - Dec. 1966.

LOUDON COUNTY
(continued)

MICROFILMED RECORDS (continued)
Deeds, Sept. 1870 - Aug. 1968.
Land Entry Takers' Book, Apr. 1891 - Mar. 1898.
Military Discharges, Jan. 1920 - Aug. 1968.
Plat Books, Dec. 1942 - Oct. 1967.
Trust Deeds, June 1874 - Sept. 1968.
Board of Education Minutes, July 1907 - Mar. 1943; Feb. 1950 - Aug. 1958.
Cash Journals, Sept. 1898 - Sept. 1909; Jan. 1910 - June 1916; Sept. 1916 - Feb. 1920.
Tax Books, 1870 - 1967 (intermittantly).

MANUSCRIPT MATERIALS (available at the Tennessee State Library and Archives):
Church Records. Cedar Fork Baptist Church, Philadelphia, TN, 1844-1968, (microfilm #263). Minutes; membership rolls; baptisms; lists of those received and dismissed by letter; historical sketch; lists of pastors; etc. (This church is in an area which was once part of Roane County.)
Cemeteries. Anderson County, Tennessee, 1800-1974, (microfilm #506). In addition to cemetery records for Anderson County, some cemetery records are listed for Loudon County and other counties. Also included are records for Valley View Methodist Church, Clinton, TN, including a church history and registers of pastors, infant baptisms, marriages, and members.

McMINN COUNTY

CREATED: 1819 from Cherokee lands ceded to the United States that year.
COUNTY SEAT: Athens, TN 37303.

LIBRARIES: E. G. Fisher Public Library, 106 Hornsby St., Athens, TN 37303.
Fort Loudon Regional Library Center, 718 George St., Athens, TN 37303.

HISTORICAL SOCIETY: McMinn County Historical Society, P. O. Box 416, Athens, TN 37303.

McMINN COUNTY
(continued)

PUBLISHED SOURCES:
 Boyer, Reba Bayless. Wills And Estate Records Of McMinn
  Co., Tennessee, 1820-1870. [Athens, TN: 1966].
  _____. Population Schedule Of The U.S. Census Of 1850
  (7th Census) For McMinn County, Tennessee. [Athens,
  TN: McMinn Co. Chapter, East Tennessee Historical Society,
  1961].
  _____. Chancery Court Records Of McMinn County, Tennessee,
  1844-1894. [1980].
  _____. McMinn County, Tennessee, Marriages, 1820-1870.
  [1964].
 Boyer & Duncan. A History Of Marr Hill Presbyterian Church.
  [Athens, TN: 1973].
 History Of Tennessee...(East TN edition). [Chicago & Nash-
  ville: Goodspeed Publishing Co., 1887]. (McMinn Co.,
  pp. 811-15; 1012-1032.

 Whitley, E. R. Marriages Of McMinn County, Tennessee,
  1821-1864. [Baltimore: Genealogical Publishing Co.,
  Inc., 1983].

W.P.A. TYPESCRIPT RECORDS (available at the Tennessee State
  Library and Archives):
 Court Proceedings, 1819-29, v.1, pt. 1.
 Court Proceedings, 1819-29, v.1, pt. 2.
 Eastern Cherokee Claims, 1797-1909.
 Wills & Inventories, v.2, 1828-34.
 Wills & Inventories, 1838-41.
 Will Book D, 1841-48, pts. I & II.
 Loose Marriage Bonds, 1821-38.
 Marriage Records, 1838-1848.
 Marriage Records, 1848-59; 1859-64.
 Tombstone Inscriptions, v.I.
 Tombstone Inscriptions, v.II, pts. I & II.
 Tennessee Negro Cemetery Records (McMinn Co.).

MICROFILMED RECORDS (available at the Tennessee State Library
  and Archives):
 1830-80; & 1900-10 Federal Census.
 Chancery Court Delinquent Tax Dockets, Feb. 1930 - 1968.
 Chancery Court Minutes, Mar. 1844 - Aug. 1853; Feb. 1854
  - Feb. 1862; Aug. 1862 - May 1868; Nov. 1868 - Nov.
  1875; May 1876 - nov. 1879; May 1880 - Nov. 1883; Feb.
  1884 - Aug. 1887; Feb. 1888 - June 1894; Nov. 1894 -
  Dec. 1898; May 1899 - Sept. 1906; Feb. 1907 - Apr. 1931;
  June 1931 - Sept. 1969.

McMINN COUNTY
(continued)

MICROFILMED RECORDS (continued)

Chamber Minutes, Mar. 1929 - Aug. 1958.
Inventories & Estate Settlements, Nov. 1958 - Nov. 1969.
Circuit Court Civil Minutes, Dec. 1915 - Dec. 1918; July
  1927 - Nov. 1969.
Circuit, Civil & Criminal Minutes, Apr. 1919 - Apr. 1927.
Circuit Court Civil & Criminal Minutes, Dec. 1860 - Dec.
  1872; Apr. 1873 - Dec. 1877; Apr. 1878 - Apr. 1884;
  Aug. 1884 - Feb. 1887; Dec. 1887 - Apr. 1892; Aug. 1892
  - Dec. 1904; Apr. 1905 - Dec. 1918.
Circuit Court Criminal Minutes, May 1925 - Feb. 1933; June
  1933 - Oct. 1945; Feb. 1946 - Nov. 1968; Dec. 1968 -
  Dec. 1969.
Probate Court Minutes, Sept. 1958 - Nov. 1969.
Will Books, Sept. 1958 - Nov. 1969.
Administrators' & Executors' Bonds, Jan. 1874 - Mar. 1910;
  May 1910 - June 1942; Sept. 1942 - Feb. 1955; Oct. 1955
  - May 1961.
Conservators' Bonds & Letters, Apr. 1961 - Ocat. 1969.
Guardians' Bonds & Letters, Dec. 1873 - Feb. 1946; Mar.
  1948 - Jan. 1961; Mar. 1961 - Dec. 1967; Feb. 1968 -
  Sept. 1969.
Claims against estates, May 1921 - Aug. 1942.
Insanity Records, Oct. 1922 - Oct. 1969.
Insolvent Estates, Accounts of, Jan. 1917 - Apr. 1931.
Insolvent Estates, Minutes, Mar. 1879 - Mar. 1942.
Estate Inventories & Settlements, July 1873 - Dec. 1879;
  Feb. 1879 - Nov. 1894; Feb. 1895 - July 1912; Sept.
  1912 - May 1962.
Loose Marriage Records, 1838.
Marriage Records, Feb. 1838 - Apr. 1859; July 1859 - Dec.
  1969.
County Court Minutes, Nov. 1819 - July 1863; Sept. 1868
  - Jan. 1970.
County Court Quarterly Minutes, Jan. 1926 - Oct. 1943;
  Jan. 1944 - Nov. 1969.
Road Commission Minutes, Jan. 1846 - May 1863.
Professional License Registers, Feb. 1904 - July 1966.
Administrators' & Executors' Settlements, Mar. 1876 - Apr.
  1943.
Guardians' Settlements, Jan. 1878 - Oct. 1892; Jan. 1893
  - Jan. 1970.
Birth & Death Records, 1908 - 1912.
Wills, Dec. 1819 - Mar. 1838; June 1838 - Aug. 1958.
Board of Education Minutes, May 1913 - Apr. 1926; Jan.
  1931 - Apr. 1943; June 1943 - Dec. 1951; Aug. 1951 -
  Oct. 1969.

McMINN COUNTY
(continued)

MICROFILMED RECORDS (continued)
Deeds, Mar. 1820 - Jan. 1970.
Land Entries, Nov. 1820 - Aug. 1836; Apr. 1827 - Aug. 1849.
Military Discharges, July 1919 - Feb. 1970.
Miscellaneous Records, Sept. 1921 - Jan. 1968.
Plats, Apr. 1927 - Apr. 1970.
Trust Deeds, Jan. 1877 - Jan. 1970.
Cash Journals, Jan. 1950 - Mar. 1970.
Tax Books, 1829-32; 1872; 1875-90; 1892-95; 1897-1902; 1904; 1906; 1915; 1918; 1923; 1928; 1933; 1939; 1943; 1948; 1953; 1958-67 (intermittantly).

MANUSCRIPT MATERIALS (available at the Tennessee State Library and Archives):
Church Records. First Baptist Church of Niota, 1885-1967, and Niota Methodist Episcopal Church, 1919-1956, (microfilm #247). Minutes, membership rolls, etc. for First Baptist; and membership rolls, baptisms, marriages, and funeral records of Niota Methodist Episcopal Church.
Church Records. Mars Hill Presbyterian Church, Athens, 1832-1967, (microfilm #466). Baptisms, communicants, deacons, marriages, pastors, minutes, etc.
Church Records. First Baptist Church, McMinnville, 1838-1916, (microfilm #261). Minutes, membership rolls, etc.
Church Records. McMinn County Baptist Association, 1924-1868, (microfilm #283). Records of annual meetings contained names of ordained and licensed ministers and church delegates; minutes, etc.
Church Records. Shellsford Missionary Baptist, McMinnville, 1855-1960, (microfilm #286).
Church Records. First Baptist Church of Englewood, 1900-1969, (microfilm #308). (Known earlier as Cross Grove Baptist Church and Englewood Baptist Church.)
Church Records. Athens Methodist Episcopal Church, 1865-1929, (microfilm #369).
Church Records. Trinity Methodist Church, Athens, 1949-1969, (microfilm #387).
County Records. Bradley County, TN, (miscellaneous records), ca. 1835-1960, (microfilm #561). Scrapbooks concerning McMinn County are also included in these records.
Cemeteries. Anderson County, TN, 1800-1974, (microfilm #506). Some records for McMinn County included in this collection.

McNAIRY COUNTY

CREATED: 1823 from Hardin County [1819 from the Western District (Indian lands).]
COUNTY SEAT: Selmer, TN 38375.

SPECIAL NOTE: (Courthouse fire during Civil War destroyed most records.)

LIBRARY: Selmer Public Library, Selmer, TN 38375.

PUBLISHED SOURCES:
  "Old Purdy Cemetery, Purdy, Tennessee," contributed by James L. Borrum, Ansearchin' News, v.9 (1962), no. 1, pp. 20-25.
  History Of Tennessee. [Chicago & Nashville: Goodspeed Publishing Co., 1887]. (McNairy Co., pp. 819-28; 870-80.
  Wright, M. J. Reminiscences Of The Early Settlement And Early Settlers Of McNairy County, Tennessee. [Washington, D.C.: Commercial Publishing Co., 1882]. (Reprinted 1956).

W.P.A. TYPESCRIPT RECORDS (available at the Tennessee State Library and Archives):
  Deed Books, A & B, 1823-1845.
  Marriage Books, B,C, & D, 1861-1869.
  Church Minutes of Pleasant Ridge, Tennessee, Mar. 21, 1869 - Sept. 15, 1899.

MICROFILMED RECORDS (available at the Tennessee State Library and Archives):
  1830-80; 1900-10 Federal Census.
  Clerk & Master, Feb. 1866 - Apr. 1889; Oct. 1889 - Feb. 1903.
  Circuit Court Minutes, July 1856 - June 1900.
  County Court Minutes, Jan. 1858 - Nov. 1873; Sept. 1878 - Nov. 1879; Jan. 1884 - Jan. 1902.
  Marriages, Mar. 1861 - Dec. 1920.
  Wills, Feb. 1872 - Oct. 1936.
  Guardians' Bonds, Jan. 1861 - Oct. 1947.
  Birth Records, Apr. 1881 - Nov. 1882.
  Guardians' Settlements, July 1866 - July 1902.
  Insolvent Estates, Oct. 1878 - Apr. 1941.
  Administrators' Bonds & Letters, Dec. 1865 - July 1932.
  Administrators' Settlements, Oct. 1865 - Mar. 1936.
  Inventories of Estates, Nov. 1865 - Dec. 1931.
  Deeds, Dec. 1823 - Jan. 1903.
  Land Grants, 1828 - 1852; (Roll 36 of Deeds).
  Tax Books, 1867 - 1900.

McNAIRY COUNTY
(continued)

MANUSCRIPT MATERIALS (available at the Tennessee State Library and Archives):
Scrapbooks, Florence (Abernathy) Hockaday, fl. 1890-1910; Scrapbook ca. 1880 - ca. 1910, (mf. #194). Consists mainly of newspaper clippings on members of the Abernathy & Hockaday families; local politicians; records of official votes; hand bills, wedding announcements; photographs, etc.

MACON COUNTY

CREATED: 1842 from Smith [1799 from Sumner Co.] and Sumner County [1786 from Davidson Co.].

COUNTY SEAT: Lafayette, TN 37083

SPECIAL NOTE: (1901 Courthouse fire destroyed early records.)

LIBRARY: Macon County Library, 371 Church Street, Lafayette, TN 37083.

PUBLISHED SOURCES:
History of Tennessee. [Chicago & Nashville: Goodspeed Publishing Co., 1887]. (Macon Co., pp. 834-42; 971-88.)

W.P.A. TYPESCRIPT RECORDS (available at the Tennessee State Library and Archives):
Chancery Court Records - Minutes, 1844-60.
Execution Dockets, 1846-55.
Trial Dockets, 1854-74.
Bible Records and Cemetery Records.

MICROFILMED RECORDS: (available at the Tennessee State Library and Archives or the courthouse in Lafayette, TN if marked with (*):
1850-80; & 1900-10 Federal Census.
Chancery Court Minutes, Mar. 1844 - Mar. 1904. (Rolls, 1,2,3.)
*Birth records, 1902-1912.
*Circuit Court Minutes, 1901 to present.
*Deeds, 1901 to present.
*Marriages, 1901 to present.
*Wills, 1901 to present.

MANUSCRIPT MATERIALS (available at the Tennessee State Library and Archives):
Church Records of Hillsdale Baptist Church, 1831-1928, (mf. #215). Minutes; some correspondence; and misc. items. (Organized in 1817, as East Fork of Goose Creek Baptist Church in Smith Co.; was reorganized, renamed, and moved to present location in 1870.)

MACON COUNTY
(continued)

CHURCH RECORDS (may be purchased from the Historical Commission of the Southern Baptist Convention, 127 Ninth Ave. N., Nashville, TN 37234):
Lafayette. Lafayette Baptist Church, 1849-1958. (Microfilm reel #941)

MADISON COUNTY

CREATED: 1821 from the Western District (Indian lands).
COUNTY SEAT: Jackson, TN 38301.

LIBRARIES: Jackson-Madison County Library, 433 E. Lafayette, Jackson, TN 38301. (The Tennessee Room in this library houses an extensive and excellent collection of genealogical secondary sources.)
Shiloh Regional Library, Hamilton Mills South Center, Jackson, TN 38301.

GENEALOGICAL SOCIETY: Mid-West Tennessee Genealogical Society, P.O. Box 3343, Jackson, TN 38301.

PUBLISHED SOURCES:
Carpenter, V. K. Madison County, Tennessee 1850 Federal Census. [1971].
History Of Tennessee. [Chicago & Nashville: Goodspeed Publishing Co., 1887].
"Index to 1840 Census, Madison County, Tennessee," compiled by T. P. Hughes, Jr., Ansearchin' News, v.17 (1970), no. 1, pp. 5-12.
Sistler, Byron & Barbara. Madison County, TN Marriages, 1838-1871. [1984].
Williams, E. I. Historic Madison. [Jackson, TN: Madison Co. Historical Society, 1946].
"Index to Wills, Settlements, Inventories, Madison County, Tennessee, Will Book A, 1820-1835," Ansearchin' News, v.17 (1970), no. 1, pp. 18-20, 37.

W.P.A. TYPESCRIPT RECORDS (available at the Tennessee State Library and Archives):
County Court Minute Books, I & II, 1821-1825.
County Court Minutes, v.4, 1833-40, pts. I & II.
County Court Minutes, v.5, 1840-48, pts. I & II.
Circuit Court Minute Book 1, 1821-28; & Book 2, July 1828 - Dec. 1836, pts. I & II.
Chancery Court Minute Book 1, 1846-54.

MADISON COUNTY
(continued)

W.P.A. TYPESCRIPT RECORDS (continued)
Tax Book, 1822-1832.
Loose Marriage Bonds, 1846-1866; and Deed Record, v.1, 1822-28.
Marriage Records, 1866-68; 1868-71.
Wills & Inventories, v.1, 1822-35, pts. I & II.
Wills & Inventories, 1835-39, pts. I & II.
Wills & Inventories, 1835-39, pts. III & IV.
Marriage License Book, v.II, 1838-1847.
Guardian Renewal Bonds, 1868-1879.
Tombstone Inscriptions.
County Court Minutes, v.3, 1828-33, pts. I & II; and v.6, 1849-53, pts. I & II.
Marriage Records (Colored), 1868-1871.
Directory, Jackson, Tennessee.
Tennessee Negro Cemetery Records (Madison Co.).

MICROFILMED RECORDS (available at the Tennessee State Library and Archives):
1830-80; & 1900-10 Federal Census.
Deeds, 1821-1964.
Trust Deeds, 1821-1964.
Mortgage Books, 1869-73; 1895-1964.
Chancery Court Clerk Minute Book, 1846-1963.
Rule Dockets, 1852-1963.
Circuit Court Civil & Criminal Minutes, 1821-28; 1840-44; 1848-50; 1869-1961.
Marriage Records, 1838-1963.
Will Books, 1825-62; 1862-1963.
Juvenile Court Minutes, 1912-1962.
Guardian Settlements, 1874-1960.
Vital Statistics, 1908-1912.
Birth Records, 1925-1939.
Death Records, 1925-1939.
Administrators' & Executors' Settlements, 1865-1961.
Administrators' & Executors' Inventories, 1878-1942.
Rule Dockets, 1950-63.
Executors' Dockets, 1821-44; 1860-88.
Rule & Execution Dockets, 1902-1953.
Drainage Book, 1913-1943.

CHURCH RECORDS (may be purchased from the Historical Commission of the Southern Baptist Convention, 127 Ninth Ave. N., Nashville, TN 37234):
Medon. Clover Creek Baptist Church, Sept. 1848-1899; 1937-1967. (Microfilm reel #2205)

MADISON COUNTY
(continued)

19TH CENTURY LAND OWNERSHIP MAP: (available from the Library of Congress, Washington, D.C.):
Madison County, 1877. D. G. Beers Co. Surveyors & Publishers. Scale: 1:50,688, #874.

MARION COUNTY

CREATED: 1817 from Cherokee lands.
COUNTY SEAT: Jasper, TN 37347.

SPECIAL NOTE: (Courthouse fire in 1922 destroyed many records.)

LIBRARY: Jasper Public Library, Betsy Pack Drive, Jasper, TN 37347.

PUBLISHED SOURCES:
Carpenter, V. K. Marion County, Tennessee 1850 Federal Census. [1971].
Douthat, James L. 1840 Sequatchie Valley Census. [1982].
Kelly, M. C. A History Of South Pittsburg, Tennessee. [1973].
Link G. B. A History Of Marion County, Thesis, Middle TN State College, Murfreesboro, TN, 1953.

W.P.A. TYPESCRIPT RECORDS (available at the Tennessee State Library and Archives):
Deed Books, A & B, 1819-1830.
Ebenezer Cumberland Presbyterian Register, 1889-1918; and Register of Sulphur Spring Methodist Episcopal Church, South, 1887-1928; and a family record of the Hall's, 1794-1933, (Hall family in manuscript unit.)

MICROFILMED RECORDS (available at the Tennessee State Library and Archives):
1830-80; & 1900-10 Federal Census.
Clerk & Masters' Chambers Minutes, Oct. 1926 - Mar. 1969.
Clerk & Masters' Minutes, Sept. 1922 - July 1969.
Circuit Court Clerk Minutes, Aug. 1922 - Oct. 1968.
County Court Minute Books, Jan. 1842 - Oct. 1847; Apr. 1890 - Oct. 1900; July 1911 - Aug. 1969.
Administrators' Bonds & Letters, Nov. 1912 - July 1969.
Equalization Minutes, June 1923 - July 1937.

MARION COUNTY
(continued)

MICROFILMED RECORDS (continued)
Claims against estates, Jan. 1922 - Aug. 1940.
Conservators' Bonds & Letters, Mar. 1919 - Oct. 1968.
Executors' Bonds & Letters, Mar. 1919 - Oct. 1968.
Guardians' Bonds & Letters, Jan. 1913 - July 1956.
Insanity Records, Aug. 1934 - Feb. 1969.
Insolvent estates, Sept. 1885 - Aug. 1907.
Minutes & Accounts of Inventory Books, Mar. 1878 - Nov. 1968.
Marriage Records, May 1881 - Apr. 1888; Aug. 1919 - Aug. 1969.
Physcians' Records, Mar. 1889 - Jan. 1913.
Quorum Minutes, Dec. 1910 - Aug. 1969.
Road Book, July 1883 - Jan. 1891.
Administrators' & Executors' & Guardians' Settlements, Sept. 1877 - July 1968.
Vital Statistics: Births & Deaths, 1908-1912.
Will Books, Nov. 1875 - Apr. 1968.
Deed Books, Oct. 1819 - Apr. 1968.
Land Entry Takers' Book, Nov. 1823 - Aug. 1895.
Military Discharges, July 1919 - Mar. 1953; Sept. 1943 - Aug. 1969.
Plat Books, Jan. 1946 - Apr. 1968.
Surveyors' Books, Apr. 1824 - Jan. 1903.
Trust Deeds, May 1963 - Apr. 1968.
School Board Minutes, Sept. 1954 - Aug. 1968.
Tax Books, 1875; 1903-04; 1923; 1928; 1933; 1938; 1943; 1948; 1953; 1958; 1959-1968.

MARSHALL COUNTY

CREATED: 1836 from Bedford [1807 from Rutherford], Lincoln [1809 from Bedford], and Maury County [1807 from Williamson Co.]
COUNTY SEAT: Lewisburg, TN 37091.

LIBRARY: Marshall County Memorial Library, 310 Farmington Pike, Lewisburg, TN 37091. (The library's substantial genealogical collection was inventoried in the Tennessee Genealogical Review, Vol. 1, no. 3 (Apr. 1980), pp. 14-17.
HISTORICAL SOCIETY: Marshall County Historical Society, Lewisburg, TN 37091.

MARSHALL COUNTY
(continued)

PUBLISHED SOURCES:
Alford, J. W. Revolutionary War Patriots Of Marshall County,
Tennessee. [Lewisburg?: Robert Lewis Chapter D.A.R.,
1976].
History Of Tennessee. [Nashville: Goodspeed Publishing
Co., 1886]. (Marshall Co., pp.884-903; 1190-1232.)
Lightfoot, M. P. & E. B. Shackelford. Maury County Neighbors:
Records of Giles, Lewis, and Marshall Counties, TN.
[Mt. Pleasant, TN: 1967].
Marsh, H. C. Name Index To Goodspeed's History Of Tennesee
...Marshall Co.
Porch, Deane. Marshall County, Tennessee Tax Records,
1839-1841. [Nashville: 1966].
Veterans Of Foreign Wars Of The U.S., by Bill Wheatley
Post No. 5109, Lewisburg, TN. Service Records of World
Wars I & II, [1948].
Whitsell, Ralph. Tombstone Inscriptions Of Marshall County,
Tennessee. [Nashville: Porch, 1968].
"A History of Marshall County, Tennessee," by Mitchell
Wright. Marshall County Historical Society Quarterly,
Vol. 1, no. 1, Aug. 1970.

W.P.A. TYPESCRIPT RECORDS (available at the Tennessee State
Library and Archives):
County Court Minutes, v.A, 1836-40, pts. I & II.
Will Book, v.A, 1835-55.
Marriage Bonds, v.1, 1838-49.
Marriage Bonds, v.2, 1849-65.

MICROFILMED RECORDS (available at the Tennessee State Library
and Archives):
1840-80; & 1900-10 Federal Census.
Chancery Court Enrollment Books, Jan. 1872 - May 1881.
Chancery Court Minutes, Aug. 1840 - Dec. 1900.
Circuit Court Minutes, Nov. 1836 - Oct. 1853; June 1865
- June 1867.
Administrators' Letters, Nov. 1859 - Aug. 1904.
Administrators' & Executors' Settlements, 1839 - Mar. 1917.
Administrators' & Executors' Settlement Minutes, 1842-57.
Administrators' & Guardians' Bonds, 1842-57; Nov. 1859
- May 1905.
Inventories of Estates, 1839-1913.
Petitions to sell land, Mar. 1872 - Mar. 1877.
Insolvent Estates, 1869-97.
Merchants' Bond Book, 1869-72.
Guardians' Settlements, 1836 - Nov. 1907.
Marriages, Aug. 1836 - Oct. 1916.
County Court Minutes, Oct. 1836 - Aug. 1901.
Wills, Nov. 1835 - Feb. 1912.
Deeds, Oct. 1836 - Aug. 1900.
Trust Deeds, May 1868 - Dec. 1901.

MARSHALL COUNTY
(continued)

<u>MICROFILMED RECORDS</u> (continued)
Civil War Muster Rolls, 1861-65.
Tax Books, 1839-1901.
Miscellaneous Material - Agriculture Census, 1857.

<u>MANUSCRIPT MATERIALS</u> (available at the Tennessee State Library
and Archives):
Cemeteries for South Carolina and Tennessee, ca. 1850-1956,
(microfilm #307). Alphabetical listing, by county,
of tombstone inscriptions from South Carolina and
Tennessee cemeteries including some from Marshall Co.
Church Records. Bear Creek Cumberland Presbyterian Church,
1902-1938, (microfilm #203). Minutes of session; registers of pastors, elders, deacons, communicants, adult
baptisms, marriages, and deaths.
Church Records. Pleasant Grove Cumberland Presbyterian
Church, Chapel Hill, TN, 1840-99, (microfilm #345).
Lists of elders; membership lists, births, marriages,
dismissals, baptisms, deaths, minutes of session, etc.
Church Records. Bethbirei Presbyterian Church, 1810-1975,
(microfilm #548 & #24). Minutes of session & congregational meetings; treasurer's reports; registers of death,
marriages, and baptisms; registers of pastors, elders,
deacons, communicants, etc.
Church Records. Rock Creek Primitive Baptist Church, 1814-
1851, (microfilm #386). Minutes, and membersship list.
Organized in 1810 on Rock Creek and was later known
as Shiloh Baptist Church; was moved to Silver Creek
in Marshall Co.
County Records. Miscellaneous Records, 1841-57, (microfilm
#556). Various papers relating to the history & growth
of Marshall Co., including an agricultual census of
1857; genealogy for the William Thomas family; and a
diary, 1841, kept by an unnamed student.

MAURY COUNTY

<u>CREATED</u>: 1807 from Williamson Co. [1799 from Davidson Co.].
<u>COUNTY SEAT</u>: Columbia, TN 38401.

<u>LIBRARIES</u>: Maury Co. Public Library, 211 W. 8th St., Columbia,
TN 38401. (This library has a substantial genealogical
collection inventoried in the <u>Tennessee Genealogical
Review</u>, Vol. 1, no. 5 (June 1980), pp. 24-29.
Columbia State Community College Library, Columbia, TN
37401.
Bluegrass Regional Library, 104 W. 5th St., Columbia, TN
38401.
<u>HISTORICAL SOCIETY</u>: Maury Co. Historical Society, P.O. Box
127, Culleoka, TN 38451.

MAURY COUNTY
(continued)

PUBLISHED SOURCES:
Alexander, Virginia Wood & C. C. Alexander. Historic
   Ebenezer (Reese's Chapel) Presbyterian Church And
   Cemetery, Maury County, Columbia, Tennessee. [Columbia,
   TN: 1968].
Alexander, V. H. & J. K. Garrett. Maury County, Tennessee
   Marriage Records, 1838-1852. [Columbia, TN: 1963].
Alexander, V. H., J. K. Garrett, & R. H. Priest. Maury
   County, Tennessee Marriage Records, 1807-1837. [Columbia,
   TN: 1962].
Alexander, V. H. & R. H. Priest. Maury County, Tennessee
   Deed Abstracts, 1807-1817. [Columbia, TN: 1965].
Cole, E. & M. Glenn. Ancestor Charts. [Huntsville, Ala.:
   1976].
Dobbins, D. P., compiler. Century Review, 1805-1905.
   [Columbia, TN: 1905]. (250 pages of biographical informa-
   tion, and approximate 40,000 name index.)
Garrett, Jill K. Maury County, Tennessee Newspapers (ab-
   stacts) 1810-1844. [Columbia, TN: 1965].
_____. Maury County, Tennessee Newspapers (abstracts)
   1846-1850. [Columbia, TN: 1965].
_____. Maury County, Tennessee Court Minutes, 1807-1809.
   [Columbia, TN: 1965].
_____. The Maury Genealogist, V.1-3, Feb. 1972 - Nov.
   1974.
_____. Footprints In Stone; Historical Sketches.
   [Columbia, TN: First Farmers & Merchants Nat'l Bank,
   1966?]
_____. Maury County, Tennessee Historical Sketches.
   [Columbia, TN: 1967].
_____. Confederate Soldiers & Patriots Of Maury County,
   Tennessee. [Columbia, TN: Capt. James Madison Sparkman
   Chapter U.D.C., 1985].
_____. War Of 1812 Soldiers Of Maury County, Tennessee.
   [Columbia, TN: Jane Knox Chapter D.A.R., 1975].
Garrett, J. K. & M. P. Lightfoot. Maury County, Tennessee
   Chancery Court Records. [Columbia, TN, 1965].
_____. Maury County, Tennessee Wills & Settlements,
   1807-1824, And 1820 Census. [Columbia, TN: 1964].
History Of Tennessee. [Chicago & Nashville: Goodspeed
   Publishing Co., 1887] (Maury Co., pp. 749-87; 904-65.)
Hendrix, D. K. The History Of Hunter Meeting House And
   Its Cemetery Records. [Mt. Pleasant, TN: 1983].
"Ebenezer Presbyterian Church, Maury County, Tennessee
   (Records of), 1805-1921," copied by Mrs. W. L. Jackson,
   Nashville, 1939.

MAURY COUNTY
(continued)

PUBLISHED SOURCES (continued)
Lightfoot, M. P. Let The Drums Roll: Veterans and Patriots
of the Revolutionary War who settled in Maury County,
Tennessee. [Columbia: Maury County Historical Society,
1976].
Lightfoot, M. P. & E. P. Shackelford. They Passed This
Way: Maury County, Tennessee Cemetery Records. [1964].
_____. Maury County Neighbors: Records of Giles, Lewis,
& Marshall Counties, Tennessee. [Mt. Pleasant, TN:
1967].
Maury County Cousins. [Columbia, TN: Maury County Historical
Society, 1967]. (Bible & family records.)
Frank H. Smith's History Of Maury County, Tennessee.
[Columbia, TN: Maury Co. Historical Society, 1969].
Historic Maury, Vol. 1, no. 1, May, 1965; Maury County
Historical Society.
Sistler, Byron & Barbara. 1880 Census, Maury County,
Tennessee. [1979].
Turner, W. B. History Of Maury County. [Nashville:
Parthenon Press, 1955].
Whitley, E. R. Marriages Of Maury County, Tennessee
1808-1852. [Baltimore: Genealogical Publishing Co.,
Inc., 1982.]

W.P.A. TYPESCRIPT RECORDS (available at the Tennessee State
Library and Archives):
General Index to Deeds, v.1, Bargainee, 1807-1843.
General Index to Deed Book, v.1, Bargainor, 1807-1843.
County Court Minute Book 1, 1808-1809.
Circuit Court Minute Book, 1817-1821.
Circuit Court Minute Book, A, 1810-1815.
Chancery Court Minutes, 1823-1829.
Wills and County Court Minutes, v.1, Book B, 1810-1825,
index.
History of Zion (Presbyterian Church), 1805-1858.
St. Peter's Episcopal Church History, and
St. Peter's Church Records, 1828-90; and
St. Peter's Church Minutes, 1914-19.
Bible, Family, & Tombstone Records.

MICROFILMED RECORDS (available at the Tennessee State Library
and Archives):
1820-80; & 1900-10 Federal Census.
Circuit Court Civil & Criminal Minutes, Apr. 1810 - Aug.
1871.

MAURY COUNTY
(continued)

MICROFILMED RECORDS (continued)
Circuit Court Civil Minutes, Sept. 1871 - Apr. 1967.
Circuit Court Criminal Minutes, Dec. 1899 - Apr. 1967 (County).
Circuit Court Criminal Minutes, Mar. 1872 - Apr. 1967.
Clerk & Masters' Enrollment Books, Dec. 1818 - 1841; Dec. 1849 - Apr. 1877.
Clerk & Masters' Minutes, Mar. 1822 - Apr. 1967.
Administrators' Bonds & Letters, Apr. 1856 -Mar. 1863; Aug. 1868 - May 1967.
Equalization Minutes, June 1915 - .
Conservators' Bonds, Sept. 1956 - Apr. 1967.
County Officials' Revenue & Tax Book, Oct. 1808 - Oct. 1848.
Dentists' Register, Sept. 1919 - Feb. 1955.
Optometry Register, July 1909 - Nov. 1950.
Physicians' Register, May 1891 - June 1957.
Estate Settlements, Feb. 1853 - Dec. 1872; Nov. 1875 - Mar. 1967.
Executors' Bonds & Letters, May 1852 - July 1869; July 1872 - May 1967.
Guardians' Bonds & Letters, Apr. 1856 - Oct. 1860; Sept. 1868 - May 1967.
Guardians' Minutes, Nov. 1874 -May 1891.
Guardians' Receipts, Oct. 1852 - Apr. 1874.
Guardians Settlements, Jan. 1851 - Aug. 1854; June 1875 - Apr. 1879; Mar. 1885 - Mar. 1967.
Insane Patients, Apr. 1872 - Aug. 1962.
Insolvent Estates Claims, May 1866 - May 1958.
Insolvent Estates Minutes, May 1852 - Mar. 1958.
Inventories & Settlements, Apr. 1854 - Jan. 1967.
Marriages (Negro), May 1865 - June 1967.
Marriages, Sept. 1808 - July 1967.
Marriage Bonds, June 1809 - July 1823; Dec. 1825 - Feb. 1833; July 1835 - Dec. 1838.
County Court Minutes, Dec. 1807 - July 1967.
Notary Bonds, Aug. 1900 - July 1918; Sept. 1918 - May 1935; July 1935 - July 1967.
Minutes of County Agriculture, Mechanical, Horticulture, and Live Stock Society, May 1867 - Oct. 1878.
Probate Deeds, Mar. 1833 - June 1922.
County Court Quarterly Minutes, July 1915 - July 1967.
Road Minutes, Apr. 1889 - Jan. 1891.
Road Commissioners' Minutes, Feb. 1917 - Dec. 1920.
Ex-Soldiers' Settlements and Beneficiaries, Feb. 1957 - May 1967.
Surveyors' Book, 1824-1838.

MAURY COUNTY
(continued)

MICROFILMED RECORDS (continued)
Wills, Nov. 1806 - July 1967.
Affidavit of Releases, Jan. 1932 - Mar. 1957.
Charter Books, Sept. 1879 - Aug. 1967.
Deeds, Jan. 1808 - Dec. 1966.
Land Entries, Oct. 1820 - Nov. 1919.
Lien Books, Jan. 1932 - Nov. 1967.
Military Discharges, July 1943 - Oct. 1967.
Oil & Gas Leases, Apr. 1947 - May 1948.
Plat Books, Apr. 1924 - May 1942; Feb. 1946 - Oct. 1967.
County Officials' Bonds, Sept. 1942 - July 1967.
Record of Judgement, Apr. 1927 - Feb. 1964.
Trust Deeds, Dec. 1884 - Dec. 1966.
Board of Education Minutes, July 1925 - Feb. 1968; Mar. 1936 - May 1966.
Tax Books, (Early tax book; no date.)
Tax Books, 1811-18; 1825-26; 1830-31; 1833-38; 1840-41; 1843; 1854-57; 1859-62; 1865-78; 1883-90; 1892-1960.

MANUSCRIPT MATERIALS (available at the Tennessee State Library and Archives):
Vaught Collection, Ac. No. 1521. Memoirs of Nathan Vaught, 1799-1880, containing much valuable information about early settlers and happenings in this county.
Church Records. Zion Presbyterian Church, Columbia, 1805-1939, (microfilm #125). Minutes of Session, 1808-1939; register of births, deaths, baptisms, marriages, and communicants, 1838-1939; history of church, etc.
Church Records. McCains Cumberland Presbyterian Church, McCains, Tennessee, 1848-1954, (microfilm #347). Minutes of Session; lists of communicants, elders, deacons, and pastors; registers of baptisms, marriages, and deaths.
Church Records. St. Mark's Episcopal Church, 1838-1883, (microfilm #437). Lists of baptisms, burials, communicants, confirmations, marriages, and rectors; etc.
Church Records. St. Peter's Episcopal Church, Columbia, 1828-1973, (microfilm #438). Lists of assistant ministers, baptisms, burials, communicants, confirmations, families, marriages, members, rectors, etc.
Church Records. Holy Cross Episcopal Church, Mt. Pleasant, 1900-1969, (microfilm #439). Lists of baptisms, burials, communicants, confirmations, families, marriages, and rectors. (Indexed)
Church Records. Advent Chapel Episcopal, 1874-1927, (microfilm #440). Lists of baptisms, burials, communicants, confirmations, marriages, and members; and a Sunday School Roll Book.

MAURY COUNTY
(continued)

MANUSCRIPT MATERIALS (continued)
    Church Records. Grace Chapel Episcopal, Spring Hill, 1878-
        1969, (microfilm #441). Lists of baptisms, burials,
        communicants, confirmations, families, marriages, and
        rectors; historical data; and newspaper clippings.
    Church Records. United Methodist Church, Spring Hill,
        1840-1965, (microfilm #448). Registers of members,
        pastors, baptisms, deaths, and dismissals; some quarterly
        and annual minutes.
    Church Records. Pleasant Mount Cumberland Presbyterian
        Church, Columbia, 1888-1956, (microfilm #188). Lists
        of communicants, deacons, elders, ministers; minutes,
        etc.

MEIGS COUNTY

CREATED: 1836 from Rhea [1807 from Roane], Roane [1801 from
    Knox], Hamilton [1819 from Rhea], and McMinn County [1819
    from lands ceded by Cherokees to the U.S. in that year].
COUNTY SEAT: Decatur, TN 37322.

SPECIAL NOTE: (Courthouse fire in 1904 destroyed some records.)

LIBRARY: Meigs County Public Library, Decatur, TN 37322.

PUBLISHED SOURCES:
    Allen, V. C. Rhea And Meigs Counties In The Confederate
        War. [1908].
    History Of Tennessee...(East TN Edition). [Chicago & Nash-
        ville: Goodspeed Publishing Co., 1887]. (Meigs Co.,
        pp. 815-17; 1032-46.)
    Lillard, Steward. Meigs County, Tennessee: a documented
        account of its European settlement and growth. [Sewanee,
        TN: Tennessee University Press, University of the South,
        1975].

W.P.A. TYPESCRIPT RECORDS (available at the Tennessee State
        Library and Archives):
    County Court Minutes, v.1, 1836-41.
    County Court Minutes, v.2, 1841-46.
    School Book, v.1, 1838-48.
    Wills, Inventories, & Sales, v.1, 1836-50.

MEIGS COUNTY
(continued)

W.P.A. TYPESCRIPT RECORDS (continued)
  Marriage Records, v.1, 1838-46
    v.2, 1846-59.
    v.3, 1857-81.
    v.4, 1881-95.
    v.5, 1895-1902.
  County Commissioners, 1836-40.

MICROFILMED RECORDS (available at the Tennessee State Library
    and Archives):
  1840-80; 1900-10 Federal Census.
  Chancery Court Common School Records, July 1838 - Aug.
    1878.
  Delinquent Tax Dockets, Feb. 1950 - Sept. 1968.
  Enrolling Dockets, June 1871 - Mar. 1877.
  Land Sales Records, Apr. 1906 - June 1920.
  Chancery Court Minutes, Sept. 1854 - July 1969.
  Circuit Court Jury List, Aug. 1844 - Apr. 1866.
  Circuit Court Civil & Criminal Minutes, Mar. 1902 - Aug.
    1969.
  Administrators' Bonds & Letters, Oct. 1897 - July 1969.
  Executors' Bonds & Letters, Oct. 1897 - July 1969.
  Guardians' Bonds & Letters, Aug. 1897 - July 1969.
  Insanity Records, Nov. 1919 - June 1945.
  Insolvent Estates, Apr. 1859 - June 1929.
  Marriages, Mar. 1838 - May 1846; Apr. 1857 - Sept. 1969.
  County Court Minutes, May 1836 - May 1969.
  Quorum Minutes, Sept. 1950 - July 1969.
  Probate Records, Oct. 1836 - Nov. 1847; Sept. 1857 - Mar.
    1962.
  Road Books, Apr. 1854 - Apr. 1885; Apr. 1889 - Oct. 1889.
  Guardians' Settlements, Jan. 1839 - Dec. 1850; Mar. 1859
    - Mar. 1938.
  Vital Statistics: Births & Deaths, 1908-1912.
    Deaths, 1925-1937.
  Wills, Inventories, & Settlements, June 1836 - July 1969.
  Board of Education Minutes, Mar. 1938 - July 1969.
  Deeds, Dec. 1879 - Apr. 1969.
  Land Abstracts, May 1836 - Apr. 1844; Mar. 1845 - Aug.
    1856; Jan. 1857 - Dec. 1872.
  Military Discharges, Aug. 1919 - Mar. 1969.
  Plats, Dec. 1931 - Sept. 1942.
  Liens, Releases, Charters, Chattel Mortgages, Apr. 1940
    - June 1969.
  Trust Deeds, Mar. 1902 - Feb. 1969.
  Tax Books, 1839-83; 1886; 1890-91; 1896-98; 1901-1915;
    1918; 1924; 1928; 1933; 1938; 1940-68.

MEIGS COUNTY
(continued)

MANUSCRIPT MATERIALS (available at the Tennessee State Library
    and Archives):
  Sketches - Places. Notes On History Of Meigs County, Tennes-
    see, by Jasper Worth Lillard, 1866-1947, (microfilm
    #158). An extensive history of Meigs County for the
    period 1836 - ca. 1940, containing detailed information
    of the formation and naming of the county in 1836; early
    settlers; developement of schools and churches; and
    growth of towns. Also included are lists of soldiers
    from the Revolutionary, Mexican, and Civil Wars; and
    some genealogical data on some families. Indexed.
  Lillard Family Papers, 1806-1913, (microfilm #117). Along
    with correspondence, accounts, deeds, land grants, and
    biographical and genealogical data on the Lillard family,
    there are also church and school records, poll lists,
    militia records, and Confederate muster rolls.
  Church Records. Shiloh Missionary Baptist Church, 1840-1895,
    (microfilm #275). Volume 1 contains membership lists,
    minutes of session and records of deaths and dismissals.
    Volume 2 contains church school records, 1892-95, includ-
    ing a list of names of teachers and pupils.
  Church Records. Good Hope Baptist Church, 1898-1969, (micro-
    film #277). Minutes of session and membership lists
    giving death dates.
  Church Records. Hiwassee Baptist Association, Kingston,
    TN, 1878-1967, (microfilm #319). Session minutes which
    include names and addresses of ordained and licensed
    ministers; list of church clerk; obituaries; and general
    news relating to members.
  Church Records. Walnut Grove Baptist Church, Decatur,
    1910-1963, (microfilm #321). Membership lists, etc.

MONROE COUNTY

CREATED: 1819 from the Hiwassee Purchase (Indian lands).
COUNTY SEAT: Madisonville, TN 37354.

SPECIAL NOTE: (Fire and war activities in 1864, caused
    destruction of some county records.)

LIBRARY: Madisonville Public Library, Madisonville, TN 37354.

MONROE COUNTY
(continued)

PUBLISHED SOURCES:
"Members of Pond Creek Baptist Church, Monroe County, Tennes-
see," 1824-1860,"Ansearchin' News, v.11, 1964, no. 2,
pp. 69-78.
Boyer, Reba Bayless. Monroe County, Tennessee Records,
1820-1870. [Athens, TN: 1970].
_____. Monroe County, Tennessee Records, Vol. 1, Marriages
1838-1870; Marriage Notices from Newspapers; Deeds,
1820-1870. [1969].
_____. Monroe County, Tennessee, Records, Vol 2, Wills;
Estate records, County Circuit & Chancery Court Records;
Newspaper notices, etc. [1983].
Fort Loudon Newsletter, Fort Loudon Association. v.1, July
1, 1955 - Mar. 1963.
History Of Tennessee...(East TN Edition). [Chicago & Nash-
ville: Goodspeed Publishing Co., 1887]. (Monroe Co.,
pp. 807-11; 994-1012.)
Lenoir, W. B. History Of Sweetwater Valley. [Sweetwater,
TN: 1916].
McConkey, Lynn. Marriages Of Monroe County, Tennessee
1868-1880. [1983].
Sands, S. G. C. History Of Monroe County. [Baltimore,
MD: Gateway Press, 1980].
Stickley, W. S. Early Days In Monroe County, Tennessee.
[Austin, TX: 1943?].

W.P.A. TYPESCRIPT RECORDS (available at the Tennessee State
Library and Archives):
Chancery Court Minute Book, 1832-42.
Circuit Court Minute Book, 1827-34, pts. I & II.
Will Book A, 1825-69.
Marriage Records Book I, 1838-43.
  Book II, 1843-45.
  Book III, 1847-52.
  Book IV, 1856-68.
Christianburg Baptist Church Minutes, v.I-V, 1828-1917.
Tennessee Negro Cemetery Records (Monroe Co.)

MICROFILMED RECORDS (available at the Tennessee State Library
and Archives):
1830-80; & 1900-10 Federal Census.
Chancery Court Minutes, Apr. 1832 - Dec. 1901.
Chancery Court Enrollment Books, Jan. 1872 - Mar. 1886.
Circuit Court Enrollment Books, 1820 - July 1829; May 1830
  - Nov. 1831; May 1852 - Jan. 1866.
Circuit Court Minutes, Nov. 1827 - Jan. 1904.
Administrators' Bonds & Letters, Nov. 1864 - Dec. 1901.
Insolvent Estates, Jan. 1872 - May 1895.

MONROE COUNTY
(continued)

MICROFILMED RECORDS (continued)
  Claims against estates, Oct. 1892 - Jan. 1904.
  Inventories of estates, Jan. 1853 - Oct. 1902.
  Executors' Bonds & Letters, July 1872 - Mar. 1921.
  Administrators' & Guardians' Settlements, July 1968 - Aug.
    1885.
  Guardians' Bonds & Letters, Nov. 1877 - Sept. 1903.
  Guardians' Settlements, Dec. 1864 - Jan. 1909.
  County Court Minutes, Sept. 1858 - Oct. 1903.
  Marriages, Jan. 1838 - Nov. 1852; Mar. 1856 - Dec. 1915.
  Road Book, July 1881 - Jan. 1891.
  Insolvent Estates, Jan. 1872 - Apr. 1941.
  Vital Statistics: Births, Sept. 1881 - Oct. 1889.
  Vital Statistics: Deaths, 1911-1942.
  Vital Statistics: Births & Deaths, Aug. 1909 - Dec. 1911.
  Wills, July 1833 - Oct. 1922.
  Deeds, June 1820 - June 1902.
  Trust Deeds, July 1868 - June 1902.
  Tax Books, 1868; 1874; 1899; 1900.
  Chancery Court Depositions, 1832-1863. Roll 55. (Some cases
    up to 1890 in index.)

MANUSCRIPT MATERIALS (available at the Tennessee State Library
    and Archives):
  Church Records. Notchey Creek Baptist Church, Madisonville,
    TN, 1908-1930, (microfilm #25). See microfilm #428
    for years 1853-1972. Records consist of membership
    list and minutes.
  Cemetery Records. Manuscript, Madisonville High School.

ADDITIONAL CHURCH RECORDS (may be purchased from the Historical
    Commission of the Southern Baptist Convention, 127 Ninth
    Ave. N., Nashville, TN 37234):
  Monroe County. Ponds Creek Baptist Church, 1824 - Oct.
    1860.

MONTGOMERY COUNTY

CREATED: 1796 from Tennessee County [1788 from Davidson Co.].
COUNTY SEAT: Clarksville, TN 37040.

LIBRARIES: Clarksville - Montgomery Co. Public Library, Clarksville, TN 37040. (This library contains a substantial genealogical collection.)
Warioto Regional Library Center, 827 N. Franklin St., Clarksville, TN 37040.
Austin Peay State University Library, Clarksville, TN 37040. (This library houses an extensive genealogical collection.)

GENEALOGICAL SOCIETY: Montgomery County Genealogical Society, Rt. 1, Box 70, Adams, TN 37010.

HISTORICAL SOCIETY: Montgomery Co. Historical Society, 512 Madison St., Clarksville, TN 37040.

19TH CENTURY LAND OWNERSHIP MAP: (available from the Library of Congress, Washington, D.C.):
Montgomery Co., 1877: D. G. Beers Co. Surveyor & Publisher; scale 1:42,240, #877.

PUBLISHED SOURCES:
Alley, Ann E., pub. The Montgomery County Genealogical Journal, (Quarterly), v.1, Sept. 1971.
Alley & Beach. 1798 Property Tax List And 1820 Census Of Montgomery County, Tennessee. [Clarksville, TN: 1961].
_____. 1850 Federal Census Of Montgomery County, Tennessee. [1971].
Beach, Ursula S. Along The Warioto, A History Of Montgomery County, Tennessee. [Nashville: TN Historical Commission, 1965].
Darnell, A. W. Abstracts Of Wills And Records Recorded In Books A And B 1796-1818. [1976].
Darnell, A. W. & M. L. R. Jones. Cemetery Records Of Fort Campbell, Kentucky. [Clarksville: 1970].
Darnell, A. W., M. L. R. Jones, & A. A. Allen. Cemetery Records Of Montgomery County, Tennessee. [Clarksville: 1968].
History Of Tennessee. [Chicago & Nashville: Goodspeed Publishing Co., 1886]. (Montgomery Co., pp. 749-827; 999-1124.)
Marsh, H. C. Name Index To Goodspeed's History Of Tennessee...Montgomery Co. [1971].

MONTGOMERY COUNTY
(continued)

PUBLISHED SOURCES (continued)
Titus, W. P. Picturesque Clarksville, Past And Present.
[Clarksville: 1887].
Williams' Clarksville Directory, City Guide And Business
Mirror 1859-1860, v.1, [Clarksville: C. O. Faxon, 1859].

W.P.A. TYPESCRIPT RECORDS (available at the Tennessee State
Library and Archives):
Wills & Inventories, Guardian & Bond Books, v.A, 1797-1810.
Wills & Inventories, v.B, 1811-1818.
Court of Pleas & Quarter Sessions, Minute Book, v.1, 1805-08.
County Court Minute Books, Vols. 2 through 13, 1808-1825.
Marriage Records, v.I, 1838-45; & v.II, 1845-54.
Minutes of the Board of Stewards of the Methodist Episcopal
Church of Clarksville, 1893-1925.
Bible and Family Records, Tombstone Inscriptions.

MICROFILMED RECORDS (available at the Tennessee State Library
and Archives):
1820-80; & 1900-10 Federal Census.
Circuit Court Civil Minutes, Sept. 1896 - Oct. 1961.
Circuit Court Criminal Minutes, Aug. 1916 - Apr. 1960.
Clerk and Masters' Minutes, Sept. 1840 - May 1962.
County Court Clerk Minutes, Dec. 1805 - Apr. 1961.
Insanity Records, Sept. 1919 - Oct. 1950.
Inventories & Settlements, Jan. 1871 - Apr. 1961.
Marriage Records, Feb. 1838 - Aug. 1961.
Quarterly Court Minutes, Jan. 1905 - July 1956.
Wills, Apr. 1796 - Feb. 1939.
Charter Books, Jan. 1895 - Apr. 1962.
Deeds, May 1789 - Dec. 1962.
Registers' Note Books, Mar. 1891 - Jan. 1962.
Oil & Gas Leases, May 1919 - Apr. 1960.
Trust Deeds, Aug. 1871 - Nov. 1962.
Tax Books, 1949 - 1959.
Circuit Court Civil Minutes, Jan. 1962 - May 1967.
Circuit Court Criminal Minutes, Nov. 1907 - Feb. 1967.
Clerk & Masters' Chambers Minutes, Apr. 1953 - Aug. 1965.
Chancery Court Enrollment Books, Jan. 1872 - Feb. 1879.
Clerk & Masters' Minutes, July 1951 - Oct. 1955; May 1962
- Mar. 1967.
Administrators' Bonds, June 1928 - June 1966.
Conservators' Bonds, Dec. 1955 - May 1967.
Executors' Bonds & Letters, July 1913 - Apr. 1967.

MONTGOMERY COUNTY
(continued)

MICROFILMED RECORDS (continued)
Guardians' Bonds, Feb. 1942 - May 1967.
Inventories & Settlements, Apr. 1961 - Dec. 1965.
Marriage Records, Aug. 1961 - June 1967.
Quarterly Court Minutes, July 1956 - Apr. 1967.
Wills, May 1850 - Jan. 1853; Mar. 1914 - Dec. 1966.
Health Board Minutes, Mar. 1958 - Sept. 1966.
Juvenile Court Minutes, Mar. 1937 - Aug. 1953; Sept. 1955
    - Oct. 1966.
Registers' Charter Books, Apr. 1962 - May 1967.
Deeds, Dec. 1962 - Aug. 1966.
Military Discharges, June 1919 - May 1967.
Oil & Gas Leases, Mar. 1960 - Mar. 1964.
Plats, 1792-1895; 1860 - Apr. 1967.
Trust Deeds, Oct. 1962 - June 1965.
School Board Minutes, Dec. 1906 - Apr. 1967 (City). County,
    Sept. 1822 - Apr. 1967. Joint, Apr. 1910 - Dec. 1953.
Tax Books, 1960-1966.

MANUSCRIPT MATERIALS (available at the Tennessee State Library
    and Archives):
Church Records. Indian Mound Methodist Church of Stewart
    County, and Hopewell Methodist Church of Montgomery
    County, 1842 - 1962, (microfilm #128). Records for
    Hopewell Methodist Church include a list of pastors
    appointed, 1894-1935; membership list, 1861-1961; and
    a partial list of baptisms and marriages, 1896-1912.
Church Records. Trinity Episcopal Church, Clarksville,
    1832-1965, (microfilm #400). Church history; membership
    and vestryman lists; minutes of the vestry; baptism,
    communion, a list of marriages, burials, list of rectors,
    etc.
Church Records. First and Second Presbyterian Churches,
    Clarksville, 1822-1972, (microfilm #401). Minutes of
    session, membership lists; lists of baptisms, marriages,
    deaths, dismissals; and church business records.
Church Records. New Providence Baptist Church, New Provi-
    dence, TN, 1851-1921, (microfilm #497). Membership
    register and minutes, and some death, baptism, and dismis-
    sals notes.
Vital Statistics. T. E. Reynolds & Sons, Clarksville,
    1898-1923, (microfilm #552). Records for the Reynolds
    family funeral home contain information on name, age,
    cause and date of death, and date and place of burial.
Diaries, Memoirs, etc., John Nick Barker; 1843-1868, (micro-
    film #126). Diaries of a plantation owner, including
    daily activities, local church news, Civil War events,
    and deaths of friends and family. Resided near Clarksville.

MOORE COUNTY

CREATED: 1871 from Bedford [1807 from Rutherford Co.], Coffee [1846 from Warren, Franklin, & Bedford Cos.], Franklin [1807 from Warren & Bedford Cos.], and Lincoln County [1809 from Bedford Co.]
COUNTY SEAT: Lynchburg, TN 37352.

LIBRARY: Moore County Public Library, Main St., Lynchburg, TN 37352.

PUBLISHED SOURCES:
History Of Tennessee. [Chicago & Nashville: Goodspeed Publishing Co., 1886]. (Moore Co., pp. 804-19; 924-34).
Marsh, H. C. Name Index To Goodspeed's History Of Tennessee ...Moore Co. [1971].
Marsh, H. C. & T. R. Moore County, Tennessee Cemetery Records. [Shelbyville, TN: 1975].

MICROFILMED RECORDS (available at the Tennessee State Library and Archives):
1880; 1900-1910 Federal Census.
Circuit Court Clerk Minutes, June 1872 - Oct. 1966.
Clerk & Master Minutes, July 1872 - Oct. 1966.
Administrators' & Executors' Bonds, July 1872 - Aug. 1966.
Guardians' & Administrators' Settlements, Oct. 1871 - Oct. 1966.
Guardians' Bonds, July 1897 - Aug. 1966.
Guardians' Minutes, Jan. 1874 - Apr. 1874.
License Book, Aug. 1897 - May 1899.
Marriage Records, June 1872 - Nov. 1966.
Merchants' Bonds, Sept. 1900 - Nov. 1937.
Minute Books, June 1872 - July 1966.
Optometry Register, July 1909 - Oct. 1923.
Physicians' Register, Sept. 1889 - Apr. 1942.
Probate Deeds, Nov. 1887 - July 1966.
Vital Statistics: Births & Deaths, 1881-82; 1908-12.
Wills, Dec. 1872 - May 1966.
Board of Health Minutes, May 1961 - Aug. 1966.
Charter Books, July 1832 - June 1966.
Deeds, July 1872 - Nov. 1966.
Military Discharges, Dec. 1918 - .
Note Books, Dec. 1872 - Nov. 1963.
Trust Deeds, June 1872 - Dec. 1966.
School Board Minutes, May 1929 - Dec. 1966.
Tax Books, 1872 - 1966.

MORGAN COUNTY

CREATED: 1817 from Roane County [1801 from Knox Co.].
COUNTY SEAT: Wartburg, TN 37887.

LIBRARY: Wartburg Public Library, Wartburg, TN 37887.

HISTORICAL SOCIETY: Morgan Co. Historical Society, Wartburg, TN. 37887.

PUBLISHED SOURCES:
Centennial Committee of Morgan Co., TN. Centennial History Of Morgan County. [1976].
Cross, L. M. Morgan County, Tennessee 1850 Census. [1985].
Freytag, E. & G. K. Ott. A History Of Morgan County. [Wartburg, TN: Specialty, 1971].
History Of Tennessee...(East TN Edition). [Chicago & Nashville: Goodspeed Publishing Co., 1887]. (Morgan Co., pp. 841-43; 1123-1125).
Report about and from America given first-hand observation in the years 1848 and 1849 and published for emigrants by J. G. Hacklin.
Hughes, Thomas. Rugby, Tennessee: Being some account of the settlement founded on the Cumberland Plateau by the Board of Administration to Land Ownership, Ltd. [1891].

W.P.A. TYPESCRIPT RECORDS (available at the Tennessee State Library and Archives):
County Court Minutes, 1824-1827.
Marriage Records, 1862-1887.
Rugby, Tennessee: An Attempted Utopia by Kathleen Brock Stott.

MICROFILMED RECORDS (available at the Tennessee State Library and Archives):
1830-80; & 1900-10 Federal Census.
Circuit Court Minutes, Nov. 1840 - Aug. 1905.
Clerk & Master Minutes, Apr. 1865 - Aug. 1904.
Insolvent Estates Minutes, 1890-1913.
Enrollments, Mar. 1880 - Dec. 1910.
Circuit Court Minutes, May 1848 - Oct. 1861; Mar. 1874 - Jan. 1904.
Probate Deeds, Mar. 1886 - Jan. 1912.
Marriages, 1862 - Dec. 1914.
Vital Statistics, 1908-1912.
Administrators', Guardians', & Executors' Settlements, Mar. 1878 - Oct. 1925.
Guardians' Settlements, Oct. 1886 - May 1926.

MORGAN COUNTY
(continued)

<u>MICROFILMED RECORDS</u> (continued)
  Wills, Sept. 1866 - Apr. 1935.
  Inventory of Estates, Mar. 1887 - Sept. 1947.
  Insolvent Estates, 1887 - 1934.
  Deeds, Jan. 1818 - Nov. 1901.
  Trust Deeds, Jan. 1877 - June 1903.
  Entry Takers' Book, Apr. 1824 - Jan. 1887.
  Index to Surveys, 1824-1836.
  Surveyors' Book, June 1824 - Mar. 1893.
  Tax Duplicates, 1881-1900.

<u>MANUSCRIPT MATERIALS</u> (available at the Tennessee State Library
    and Archives):
  Rugby Colony Papers, 1880-1934, (microfilm #253). An
    extensive collection consisting primarily of account
    books and business records, 1880-1908, of Rugby Colony,
    founded by Thomas Hughes in 1880. Included are records
    for payment of sawmill, labor, etc., letterbooks, guest
    register, and various land records such as deeds,
    indentures, leases, maps, grants, and court cases about
    land.
  Cemeteries. Anderson County, 1800-1974, (microfilm #506).
    Includes some cemetery records from Morgan County.
  County - Church Records, ca. 1800-1974. Assorted papers
    including records of the First Baptist Church in Wartburg;
    records of St. Paul's Lutheran Church in Wartburg; record
    book of Congregational Wartburg (the Reformed Swiss
    Church); papers reflecting the history and growth of
    the county.

<u>ADDITIONAL CHURCH RECORD</u> (may be purchased from the Historical
    Commission of the Southern Baptist Convention, 127 Ninth
    Ave. N., Nashville, TN 37234.
  Pleasant Grove Baptist Church, 1866 - , (Microfilm reel
    #2328).

OBION COUNTY

<u>CREATED</u>: 1823 from the Western District (Indian lands).
<u>COUNTY SEAT</u>: Union City, TN 38261.

<u>LIBRARIES</u>: Obion Co. Public Library, 701 S. 1st St., Union
    City, TN 38261.
  Forked Deer Regional Library Center, Trimble, TN 38259.

OBION COUNTY
(continued)

GENEALOGICAL SOCIETY: Obion County Genealogical Society, Union City, TN 38261.

PUBLISHED SOURCES:
Cavanaugh, J. Historical Sketch Of Obion. Avalanche Co. H, Ninth Tennessee Infantry C.S.A. [Union City, TN: 1922].
History Of Tennessee. [Chicago & Nashville: Goodspeed Publishing Co., 1887]. (Obion Co., pp. 816-31; 923-83.)
Marshall, E. H. History of Obion County. [Union City, TN: 1941].
Obion Co. Genealogical Society. Cemetery Records of Obion County - in progress.

W.P.A. TYPESCRIPT RECORDS (available at the Tennessee State Library and Archives):
County Court Minute Book, 1824-48, and index.
Circuit Court 1st Minute Book, 1825-32 and #2, 1832-34.
Circuit Court Journal, May 1835 - June 1939.
Minutes of the Court of Pleas & Quarter Sessions, 1834-35.
Will Book, v.1 or A, 1833-61.
Marriage Records (loose), 1824-60; and
Marriage Book, 1838-45.

MICROFILMED RECORDS (available at the Tennessee State Library & Archives):
1830-80; & 1900-10 Federal Census.
Chancery Enrolling Dockets, Dec. 1871 - Mar. 1895.
Chancery Minutes, May 1854 - Mar . 1873; Apr. 1893 - Nov. 1902.
Circuit Court Enrollments, June 1836 - July 1875.
Circuit Court Minutes, Oct. 1826 - Jan. 1901.
Guardians' Bonds & Letters, July 1861 - Nov. 1904.
Administrators' Bonds & Letters, Jan. 1854 - June 1859.
Executors' Bonds & Letters, Dec. 1861 - Sept. 1918.
Administrators' Bonds, Jan. 1854 - June 1859.
Administrators' Bonds & Estates, July 1859 - Oct. 1861.
Guardians' Minutes, Sept. 1878 - Apr. 1893.
Insolvent Estates, Oct. 1877 - Apr. 1902.
Inventories of Estates, Apr. 1870 - May 1900.
Marriages, Jan. 1838 - Sept. 1915.
Land Survey, Oct. 1858 - July 1884.
Chancery Minutes, July 1871 - June 1904.
County Court Minutes, Jan. 1824 - Mar. 1900.
Administrators', Executors', & Guardians' Settlements, Sept. 1861 - Feb. 1903.
Wills, Inventories, & Settlements, Oct. 1834 - July 1924.

OBION COUNTY
(continued)

MICROFILMED RECORDS (continued)
  Vital Statistics, 1881.
  Deeds, Feb. 1824 - Oct. 1900.
  Index to Entries, Grants.
  Survey Grants, Feb. 1847 - Apr. 1880.
  Surveyors' Book, Dec. 1820 - Dec. 1863.
  Occupance Entry & Survey Book, Jan. 1836 - Aug. 1904.
  Tax Books, 1825-44; 1849-1900.

MANUSCRIPT MATERIALS (available at the Tennessee State Library
    and Archives):
  Church Records. Hopewell Presbytery of the Cumberland
    Presbyterian Church, 1824-1892, (microfilm #176). Min-
    utes, membership lists, lists of ministers and elders,
    and a statistical report for 1882.
  Church Records. Republican Grove Baptist Church, 1838-1860,
    (microfilm #198). Minutes of business meetings, member-
    ship lists, etc.

ADDITIONAL CHURCH RECORDS (may be purchased from the Historical
    Commission of the Southern Baptist Convention, 127 Ninth
    Ave. N., Nashville, TN 37234):
  Republican Grove Baptist Church, 1838- , (microfilm reel
    #279).
  Union City. First Baptist Church, 1901-02; 1927-72, (micro-
    film reel #290).
  Union City. First Baptist Church, Bulletins, 1946-1953,
    (microfilm reel #348).

OVERTON COUNTY

CREATED: 1806 from Jackson County [1801 from Smith Co.].
COUNTY SEAT: Livingston, TN 38570.

SPECIAL NOTE: (Courthouse fire in 1865 destroyed many records.)

LIBRARY: Overton Co. Public Library, Livingston, TN 38570.

HISTORICAL SOCIETY: Overton Co. Historical Society, 207
    E. University St., Livingston, TN 38570.

PUBLISHED SOURCES:
  Eldridge, R. L. & M. History Of Overton County. [Livingston,
    TN: Enterprise Printing Co., 1976].

OVERTON COUNTY
(continued)

PUBLISHED SOURCES (continued)
Goodpasture, A. V. Overton County. [Livingston, TN: 1870]
Livingston Senior Class, 1952. Echoes From The Foothills.
Whitley, E. R. Tennessee Genealogical Records, Overton
  Co. [Nashville: 1967].

W.P.A. TYPESCRIPT RECORDS (available at the Tennessee State
  Library and Archives):
General Index to Deed Books, A,B,E,I,J,K,N, & O, 1806-1859.
Index to Deed Record Books, C,D,F,G,H,L,M,P, & Q, 1810-1865.
Circuit Court Minute Book, 1815-24.
County Court Minute Book, 1852-56.
Reference Docket, 1818-22; and Receipts for land tax, 1838-40.

MICROFILMED RECORDS (available at the Tennessee Library and
  Archives):
1820-80; 1900-10 Federal Census.
Clerk & Masters' Minutes, Sept. 1846 - Sept. 1854; Nov.
  1885 - Sept. 1906.
Enrollments, May 1866 - Oct. 1889.
Circuit Court Minutes, Sept. 1815 - Mar. 1823; Feb. 1839
  - Feb. 1900.
Enrolling Dockets, June 1850 - June 1852; Oct. 1856 - Aug.
  1874.
Guardians' & Administrators' Settlements, Sept. 1870 -
  July 1907.
Administrators' Bonds & Letters, Mar. 1887 - Aug. 1916.
Guardians' Bonds & Letters, July 1887 - July 1915.
Administrators', Guardians', & Executors' Bonds, Aug. 1871
  - Dec. 1886.
Executors' Bonds & Letters, Oct. 1887 - Feb. 1968.
Insolvent Estates, Aug. 1873 - Apr. 1948.
Inventory of Estates, June 1848 - Apr. 1861.
County Court Minutes, Sept. 1837 - Sept. 1900.
Marriages, Aug. 1867 - Nov. 1927.
Marriage Bonds, Apr. 1894 - Sept. 1918.
Wills, Mar. 1870 - Aug. 1926.
Deeds, Sept. 1801 - Oct. 1901.
Trust Deeds, May 1868 - Aug. 1878; Feb. 1892 - Aug. 1903.
Probate of Deeds, Aug. 1867 - Apr. 1877.
Land Entries, June 1835 - Apr. 1856.
Grants, 1869 - Aug. 1891.
Tax Books, 1872; 1875-79; 1883-1901.
County Court Minutes, Mar. 1852 - Jan. 1856.
Claim Dockets, Nov. 1870 - July 1898.
Road Book, July 1889 - Feb. 1899.

OVERTON COUNTY
(continued)

MANUSCRIPT MATERIALS (available at the Tennessee State Library
and Archives):
Cemeteries for South Carolina and Tennessee, ca. 1850 -
ca. 1956, (microfilm #307). An alphabetical listing,
by county, of tombstone inscriptions from SC and Tennessee counties including some from Overton Co.
Church Records. Hiwassee Baptist Association, Kingston,
TN, 1878-1967, (microfilm #319). Records of marriages,
baptisms, deaths communicants, elders, deacons, etc.

PERRY COUNTY

CREATED: 1821 from Hickman County [1807 from Dickson Co.].
Originally it embraced the territory now in Perry and Decatur
Counties, with Perryville, on the west side of the Tennessee
River established as the county seat until 1846, when the
Tennessee River was made the boundary line and the western
part of the county was erected into Decatur County.
COUNTY SEAT: Linden, TN 37096.

SPECIAL NOTE: (Courthouse fire during the Civil War destroyed
most records.)

LIBRARY: Perry County Public Library, Linden, TN 37096.

PUBLISHED SOURCES:
History Of Tennessee. [Chicago & Nashville: Goodspeed
Publishing Co., 1887]. (Perry Co., pp. 777-88; 889-909.)
Marsh, H. C. Name Index To Goodspeed's History Of Tennessee
...Perry County. [1972].

W.P.A. TYPESCRIPT RECORDS (available at the Tennessee State
Library and Archives):
Minutes of the County Court, 1826-33.
Circuit Court Minutes v.II, 1834-38.
Journal of the Circuit Court v.3, 1838-41.

MICROFILMED RECORDS (available at the Tennessee State Library
and Archives):
1820-80; & 1900-10 Federal Census.
Chancery Court Minutes, Jan. 1854 - Dec. 1868; Mar. 1875
- Nov. 1904.
Enrollment Books, Dec. 1854 - Mar. 1877.
Circuit Court Minutes, Apr. 1834 - Oct. 1855; Apr. 1865
- Aug. 1907.
Enrolling Docket, Oct. 1874 - Feb. 1876.

PERRY COUNTY
(continued)

MICROFILMED RECORDS (continued)
Marriage Records, Apr. 1865 - July 1919.
Minutes, Jan. 1866 - Aug. 1906.
Insolvent Estates Minutes, Jan. 1883 - July 1936.
Vital Statistics, 1881-82; 1908-12.
Wills, Dec. 1863 - Nov. 1959.
Guardians' Settlements, June 1877 - Feb. 1913.
Deeds, Jan. 1844 - Nov. 1900.
Survey Book, Dec. 1820 - June 1974.
Land Entry Book, Nov. 1824 - Oct. 1902.
Trust Deeds, Aug. 1876 - Apr. 1901.
Tax Books, 1873-1902.

PICKETT COUNTY

CREATED: 1879 from Fentress [1823 from Overton & Morgan Cos.]
and Overton County [1806 from Jackson Co.].
COUNTY SEAT: Byrdstown, Tennessee 38549.

SPECIAL NOTE: Courthouse fire in 1934 destroyed essentially
all records.

LIBRARY: Pickett County Public Library, Community Center,
Byrdstown, TN 38549.

PUBLISHED SOURCES:
Huddleston, Tim. Pioneer Families Of Pickett County, Tennes-
see. [Collegedale, TN: College Press, 1968].
_____. History Of Pickett County, Tennessee. [Ooltewah,
TN: 1973].

MICROFILMED RECORDS (essentially all county records were lost
in the 1934 courthouse fire. The standard county records
including deeds, marriages, wills, county court minutes,
etc. dating after 1934 may be found in the county courthouse at Byrdstown, TN.)
1880; & 1900-10 Federal Census (available at the Tennessee
State Library and Archives).

POLK COUNTY

CREATED: 1839 from McMinn [1819 from Cherokee lands ceded
to the U. S. in that year] and Bradley County [1835 from
Cherokee lands ceded to the U. S. in 1819].

COUNTY SEAT: Benton, TN 37307.

LIBRARY: Benton Public Library, Benton, TN 37303.

POLK COUNTY
(continued)

PUBLISHED SOURCES:
History Of Tennessee...(East TN Edition). [Chicago & Nashville: Goodspeed Publishing Co., 1886]. (Polk Co.,
pp. 804-807; 987-994.)
Haynes, E. R. History Of Polk County. [1937].
Studies In Polk County History, No. 1, 1965, Polk Co.
Historical Society, Benton, TN.
1840 Federal Census Of Polk County. (Name of compiler
unavailable during preparation of this work.)

W.P.A. TYPESCRIPT RECORDS (available at the Tennessee State
Library and Archives):
County Court Minutes, 1840-53.
County Court Minutes, v.1, 1844-47.
County Court Minutes, v.2, 1844-48.
Ocoee Baptist Church Minutes, 1836-74.
Ocoee Baptist Association Minutes.

MICROFILMED RECORDS (available at the Tennessee State Library
and Archives):
1840-80; & 1900-10 Federal Census.
Delinquent Tax Dockets, 1939-1945.
Chancery Court Minutes, Feb. 1886 - May 1940.
Enrolling Dockets, Sept. 1866 - May 1871; June 1885 - June
1891; Feb. 1896 - Feb. 1900.
Circuit Court Civil & Criminal Minutes, Jan. 1969 - July
1970.
Circuit Court Criminal Minutes, May 1936 - Dec. 1968.
Circuit Court Civil Minutes, Mar. 1936 - Dec. 1968.
Administrators' Bonds & Letters, Mar. 1890 - Apr. 1965.
Executors' Bonds & Letters, May 1903 - Oct. 1964.
Guardians' Bonds & Letters, Dec. 1894 - Nov. 1963.
Insolvent Estates, Accounts of, Feb. 1895 - Feb. 1932.
Marriages, Sept. 1894 - Sept. 1870.
Quarterly Court Minutes, May 1840 - Mar. 1858; Dec. 1860
- Apr. 1970.
Quorum Minutes, Nov. 1915 - July 1965.
Road Commission Minutes, Nov. 1913 - Oct. 1916.
Physicians' Register, Aug. 1895 - Oct. 1906.
Dentists' Register, Aug. 1919 - June 1929.
Optometrists' Register, Feb. 1907 - Jan. 1929.
Administrators', Executors', and Guardians' Settlements,
May 1894 - July 1970.
Wills, Jan. 1873 - Oct. 1884; Nov. 1893 - July 1970.
Board of Education Minutes, Apr. 1909 - Sept. 1970.
Deeds, Oct. 1894 - Sept. 1970.

138

POLK COUNTY
(continued)

MICROFILMED RECORDS (continued)
Military Discharges, June 1945 - Oct. 1970.
Plats, Jan. 1941 - Oct. 1970.
Trust Deeds, Oct. 1894 - Oct. 1970.
Cash Journals, Dec. 1935 - Oct. 1970.
Tax Books, 1893-94; 1896-97; 1899-1900; 1902-04; 1906-09;
    1911-14; 1923; 1927; 1934; 1938; 1943; 1948; 1953;
    1958; 1960-70.

MANUSCRIPT MATERIALS (available at the Tennessee State Library
    and Archives):
Church Records. Old Friendship Baptist Church, 1879-1943,
    (microfilm #348). Minutes of session; lists of communi-
    cants, elders, deacons, and pastors; lists of baptism
    and deaths; and historical index.
J. D. Clemmens Scrapbook, 1884-1934.

CHURCH RECORDS (may be purchased from the Historical Commission
    of the Southern Baptist Convention, 127 Ninth Ave. N.,
    Nashville, TN 37234):
Benton. First Baptist Church, 1836 - Aug. 1946, (microfilm
    reel #2191).

PUTNAM COUNTY

CREATED: 1842 from White [1806 from Smith], Overton [1806
    from Jackson Co.], Jackson [1801 from Smith Co.], Smith
    [1799 from Sumner Co.], and DeKalb County [1837 from White,
    Warren, Cannon, Wilson, & Jackson Cos.].
COUNTY SEAT: Cookeville, TN 38501.

SPECIAL NOTE: (Courthouse fire in 1899 destroyed most
    records.)
LIBRARIES: Putnam County Library, 50 E. Broad St., Cockeville,
    TN 38501.
Upper Cumberland Regional Library, 208 E. Minnear, Cooke-
    ville, TN 38501.

GENEALOGICAL SOCIETY: Upper Cumberland Genealogical Society,
    48 E. Board St. Cookeville, TN 38501.

PUTNAM COUNTY
(continued)

PUBLISHED SOURCES:
 DeLozier, M. J. Putnam County, 1850-1870. [Cookeville,
   TN: 1979].
 McClain, Walter S. A History Of Putnam County, Tennessee.
   [Cookeville, TN: Q. Dyer & Co., 1925].

W.P.A. TYPESCRIPT RECORDS (available at the Tennessee State
   Library and Archives):
 Richard F. Cooke's Survey or Plat Book, 1825-1839.
 Minutes of the Circuit Court, 1842-1856.
 Tax Book, 1854-1855.
 Family Records.

MICROFILMED RECORDS (available at the Tennessee State Library
   and Archives):
 1850-80; & 1900-10 Federal Census.
 Clerk & Masters' Minutes, Nov. 1895 - June 1900.
 Circuit Court Minutes, May 1842 - Dec. 1856; May 1899 -
   May 1901.
 Marriages, Sept. 1879 - Nov. 1902.
 Marriage Bonds, June 1899 - Oct. 1920.
 Wills, Aug. 1876 - Dec. 1933.
 Administrators' & Executors', & Guardians' Bonds, Jan.
   1875 - Sept. 1894.
 Bonds & Letters, Apr. 1889 - Feb. 1905.
 Guardians' Settlements, Aug. 1899 - Aug. 1918.
 Deeds, July 1854 - July 1902.
 Trust Deeds, July 1876 - Apr. 1880; May 1887 - Dec. 1901.
 Tax Book, 1893-94; 1897-1900.
 Survey Book, 1825-39.

MANUSCRIPT MATERIALS (available at the Tennessee State Library
   and Archives):
 Cemeteries of South Carolina and Tennessee, ca. 1850 -
   ca. 1956, (microfilm #307). Alphabetical listing, by
   county, of tombstone inscriptions including some from
   Putman Co.

CHURCH RECORDS (may be purchased from the Historical Commission
   of the Southern Baptist Convention, 127 Ninth Ave. N.,
   Nashville, TN 37234):
 Cookeville. First Baptist Church, 1873-1956, (microfilm
   reel #724).

RHEA COUNTY

CREATED: 1807 from Roane County [1801 from Knox Co.].
COUNTY SEAT: Dayton, TN 37321.

SPECIAL NOTE: Tornado in 1833 destroyed some of the county records.)

LIBRARY: Dayton Public Library, Dayton, TN 37321.

PUBLISHED SOURCES:
  Allen, V. C. Rhea And Meigs County In The Confederate War. [1908].
  Campbell, T. J. Records Of Rhea: A condensed county history. [Dayton, TN: Rhea Publishing Co., 1940].
  History Of Tennessee...(East TN Edition). [Chicago & Nashville: Goodspeed Publishing Co., 1887] (Rhea Co., pp. 817-21; 1046-1071.)
  McGhee, L. K. Historical Records Of East Tennessee, Rhea County. [Washington, D.C., 1954].
  Wells, Emma M. The History Of Roane County, Tennessee, 1801-1870. [1975].
  Whitley, E. R. Marriages Of Rhea County, Tennessee, 1808-1859. [Baltimore: Genealogical Publishing Co., 1983].

W.P.A. TYPESCRIPT RECORDS (available at the Tennessee State Library and Archives):
  Deed Records, v.A, 1808-09.
  Court of Pleas and Quarter Sessions Minutes, v.B, 1829-34.
  County Court Minute Books C & D, 1834-40; 1840-44.
  County Court Minutes Index, 1844-52.
  Court of Pleas & Quarter Sessions, Minute Docket, 1823-29.
  Marriage Records, 1808-90.
  Wills & Inventories, 1825-40.
  Administrations & Wills, 1841-52.
  Wills & Settlements, 1850-60.
  Minutes of the Quarterly Conference of the Washington Circuit of the Holston Conference of the Methodist Church, South, 1870-79.
  Minutes of the Hiwassee Association of Missionary Baptists, 1891-95.
  Tombstone Inscriptions.

MICROFILMED RECORDS (available in the Tennessee State Library and Archives):
  1830-80; & 1900-10 Federal Census.
  Circuit Court Minutes, Sept. 1815 - Mar. 1969.
  Circuit Court Criminal Minutes, Aug. 1938 - Feb. 1969.

RHEA COUNTY

MICROFILMED RECORDS (continued)
Clerk & Masters' Enrollment Books, Mar. 1823 - July 1843;
   Mar. 1872 - Sept. 1880.
Clerk & Masters' Minutes, Apr. 1865 - Mar. 1969.
Land Sale Records, Apr. 1943 - 1968; Dec. 1958 - Dec. 1959;
   1964.
Birth Records, Feb. 1908 - Oct. 1912.
Administrators' Bonds & Letters, Jan. 1890 - Apr. 1969.
Conservators' Bonds & Letters, Oct. 1956 - Oct. 1968.
Executors' Bonds & Letters, June 1890 - Apr. 1969.
Guardians' Bonds & Letters, Feb. 1890 - Feb. 1969.
Claims against Estates, Jan. 1922 - Apr. 1969.
Common School Record, June 1859 - Oct. 1867.
Insanity Records, Oct. 1919 - May 1966.
Marriage Records, Sept. 1808 - Aug. 1890; Feb. 1896 - Apr.
   1969.
County Court Minutes, May 1823 - Nov. 1828; Aug. 1834 -
   Nov. 1852; Oct. 1866 - Feb. 1969.
Optometry Register, Sept. 1909 - July 1952.
Physicians' Register, June 1908 - Jan. 1951.
Quarterly Court Minutes, Apr. 1949 -Apr. 1959.
Administrators' Settlements, Apr. 1902 - Mar. 1969.
Guardians' Settlements, Apr. 1858 - Feb. 1969.
Wills, Settlements, & Inventories, Aug. 1825 - Dec. 1840;
   July 1852 - Mar. 1902; Feb. 1904 - Nov. 1932; Apr. 1937
   - Sept. 1967.
Deeds, July 1808 - Jan. 1969.
Land Entry Books, Oct. 1819 - Oct. 1905; Aug. 1824 - July
   1889.
Military Discharges, May 1919 - Apr. 1968.
Plat Books, July 1889 - Jan. 1969.
Trust Deeds, Apr. 1899 - Mar. 1969.
Tax Books, 1875; 1895-98; 1907-14; 1917; 1923; 1928; 1933;
   1938; 1943; 1948; 1953; 1958-68 (intermittantly).
Cash Journals (School funds), 1904-12.

MANUSCRIPT MATERIALS (available at the Tennessee State Library
   and Archives):
Church Records. Hiwassee Baptist Association, Kingston,
   1878-1967, (microfilm #319). Session minutes which
   include names and addressed of ordained and licensed
   ministers; list of church clerks; obituaries; and general
   church news.
Church Records. Salem Baptist Church, Dayton, TN, 1807-1937,
   (microfilm #465). Membership list, minutes, etc.

RHEA COUNTY
(continued)

ADDITIONAL CHURCH RECORDS (may be purchased from the Historical
    Commission of the Southern Baptist Convention, 127 Ninth
    Ave. N., Nashville, TN 37234):
Old Friendship Baptist Church, Nov. 1875 - Apr. 1941, His-
    tory, (microfilm reel #5531).
Wolf Creek Baptist Church, 1869 - , formerly, Privett Springs
    Baptist Church, (microfilm reel #4970).
Yellow Creek Baptist Church, 1853-1961, (microfilm reel
    #1607).

ROANE COUNTY

CREATED: 1801 from Knox County [1792 from Greene & Hawkins
    Cos.].
COUNTY SEAT: Kingston, TN 37763.

SPECIAL NOTE: Courthouse fire in 1840 destroyed some records.)

LIBRARY: Kingston City Library, Patton Ferry Road, Kingston,
    TN 37763.

HISTORICAL SOCIETY: Roane Co. Historical Society, Box 165,
    Rockwood, TN 37854.

PUBLISHED SOURCES:
    Harvey, F. M. & W. R. Hutcherson, & M. H. Thornton. 1850
        Roane County, Tennessee Census. [1965].
    History Of Tennessee. [Chicago & Nashville: Goodspeed
        PUblishing Co., 1887]. (Roane Co. pp. 821-25; 1072-1081.)
    Hutcherson, W. & Marilyn McCluen. Marriage Records Of
        Roane County, Tennessee, 1801-1855. [Rockwood, TN:
        1973].
    Hutcherson, W., M. McCluen, & M. Thornton. Tax Lists Of
        Roane County, Tennessee, 1814-1821. [Kingston?, TN:
        1969].
    McCuen, Marilyn. Roane County Abstracts Of Estate Book
        "A", 1801-1824. [1965].
    Pickel, E. A History Of Roane County. Thesis, University
        of Tennessee, Knoxville, TN, 1971.
    Roberts, Snyder E. Roots Of Roane County, Tennessee, 1792-.
        [1981].
    Thornton, M. Pioneers Of Roane County, Tennessee, 1801-1830.
        Rockwood, TN: 1965].

ROANE COUNTY
(continued)

<u>PUBLISHED SOURCES</u> (continued)
Wells, Emma M. <u>The</u> <u>History</u> <u>Of</u> <u>Roane</u> <u>County,</u> <u>Tennessee,</u>
<u>1801-1870</u>. [1927].
Whitley, E. R. <u>Marriages</u> <u>Of</u> <u>Roane</u> <u>County,</u> <u>Tennessee</u>
<u>1801-1838</u>. [Baltimore: Genealogical Publishing Co.,
Inc., 1983].
The Historical Society of Roane County, Tennessee., Sept.
1792 - Nov. 1975.

<u>W.P.A. TYPESCRIPT NOTES</u> (available at the Tennessee State
Library and Archives):
Court of Pleas and Quarter Sessions Minute Book A, 1801-1805.
Book B., 1805-1807.
Book C, 1807-1809.
County Court Minute Book, 1808-1812.
Court of Pleas & Quarter Sessions Minute Book, 1813-15.
County Court Minute Book, 1815-16.
Court of Pleas & Quarter Sessions Minute Book, 1816-18.
County Court Minutes, Book H, 1819-21.
Book I, 1821-23; 1823-26.
General Index to Warranty Deeds, v.1, 1801-60.
Estate Book A, 1802-1828.
Book B, 1829-37.
Book C, 1838-42.
Land Entry Book A, 1807-08.
Marriage Records, 1801-38.
John McClellan's Surveyors Book, 1808-1810.
Revolutionary War Pension Applications, 1793-1855.
Minutes New Hope Cumberland Presbyterian Church,1824-45.
Bible Records, pts. I & II.
Negro Bible Records.
Tennessee Negro Cemetery Records (Roane Co.)

<u>MICROFILMED RECORDS</u> (available at the Tennessee State Library
and Archives):
1830-80; & 1900-10 Federal Census.
Circuit Court Minutes, Mar. 1810 - May 1966.
Criminal & Circuit Minute Books, June 1836 - Dec. 1967.
Clerk & Master Chamber Minutes, Apr. 1951 - Dec. 1967.
Enrollment Books, Aug. 1868 - Aug. 1874.
Clerk & Masters' Minutes, Dec. 1824 - Dec. 1967.
Administrators' Bonds & Letters, Mar. 1875 - Jan. 1968.
Chiropractic Register, May 1923 - Oct. 1943.
Claims against estates, Feb. 1922 - Aug. 1923.
Dentists' Register, Aug. 1919 - Jan. 1957.
Executors' Bonds & Letters, Apr. 1875 - Feb. 1968.

ROANE COUNTY
(continued)

MICROFILMED RECORDS (continued)
 Guardians' Bonds & Letters, Mar. 1875 - Jan. 1967.
 Guardian Books, June 1871 - Jan. 1968.
 Insanity Minutes, June 1919 - Mar. 1926.
 Land Entry Books, Aug. 1807 - June 1808; Feb. 1814 - June
  1815; Aug. 1846 - July 1893.
 Marriage Records, Dec. 1801 - Feb. 1968.
 Militia Companies, Nov. 1806 - Nov. 1838.
 County Court Minutes, Dec. 1801 - Feb. 1968.
 Notary Bond Book, May 1895 - Mar. 1907.
 Nurses' Register, July 1922 - June 1956.
 Optometry Register, Sept. 1909 - Feb. 1952.
 Overseers' Road Books, July 1866 - Jan. 1872; Feb. 1879
  - Apr. 1889.
 Physicians' Register, Apr. 1902 - July 1917.
 Rural Road Plats, June 1948 - Mar. 1956; July 1930 - May
  1937; June 1949 - Apr. 1952; Aug. 1952 - Jan. 1953;
  June 1954 - Oct. 1958.
 Probate Deed Books, Sept. 1913 - Dec. 1967.
 Probate Docket & Claims Records, Feb. 1939 - Nov. 1954;
  Aug. 1948 - Feb. 1968.
 Quarterly Court Minutes, Jan. 1912 - Jan. 1968.
 Veterinarians' Register, Aug. 1945 - June 1958.
 Vital Statistics: Births, Apr. 1881 - Oct. 1881. Deaths,
  Apr. 1881 - Aug. 1881.
 Wills & Estate Settlements, Mar. 1802 - Apr. 1924; Apr.
  1928 - Feb. 1968.
 Wills, Nov. 1940 - Aug. 1967.
 Charter Books, July 1912 - Mar. 1968.
 Deeds, Jan. 1801 - May 1968.
 Discharge Records, Nov. 1944 - Apr. 1968.
 Miscellaneous Records, Jan. 1932 - May 1968.
 Plat Books, Apr. 1890 - Sept. 1945; June 1947 - Apr. 1968.
 Survey Books, Mar. 1807 - Nov. 1813; Mar. 1808 - Sept.
  1810; Jan. 1814 - Apr. 1910.
 Trust Deeds, Aug. 1872 - June 1968.
 Deed Records of School Property, Aug. 1869 - Dec. 1925.
 School Board Minutes, July 1921 - May 1968.
 Tax Books, 1858-59; 1866-67; 1868-70; 1876-1965
  (intermittantly).

MANUSCRIPT MATERIALS (available at the Tennessee State Library
  and Archives):
 Church Records. Cedar Fork Baptist Church, Philadelphia,
  TN, 1844-1968, (microfilm #263). Minutes, membership
  rolls, baptisms, pastors, church clerks, etc. This
  is a Loudon County church which was in an area that
  was once a part of Roane County.

ROANE COUNTY
(continued)

MANUSCRIPT MATERIALS (continued)
    Church Records. Shiloh Primitive Baptist Church, Kingston,
        TN, 1821-1953, (microfilm #220).   Membership lists,
        minutes of session, etc., and some baptismal and death
        records.
    Church Records.   Bethel Presbyterian Church, Kingston,
        1818-1968, (microfilm #264).   Church minutes, membership
        rolls, list of marriages and deaths, etc.
    Church Records.   Hiwassee Baptist Association, Kingston,
        1878-1967, (microfilm #319).   Session minutes, names
        of ordained and licensed ministers, church clerks;
        obituaries, etc.
    Cemetery Records, Anderson Co., TN, 1800-1974, (microfilm
        #506). (Includes some cemetery records from Roane County,
        particularly the Oak Ridge area of Roane and Anderson
        Counties.
ADDITIONAL CHURCH RECORDS (may be purchased from the Historical
        Commission of the Southern Baptist Convention, 127 Ninth
        Ave. N., Nashville, TN 37234.)
    Prospect Baptist Church, July 1826-1862, (microfilm reel
        #526).

ROBERTSON COUNTY

CREATED: 1796 from Tennessee County which was created in
    1788 from Davidson Co. (not completely organized until
    1791), and which was abolished in 1796, and its records
    included in those of Robertson County.
COUNTY SEAT: Springfield, TN 37172.

LIBRARY: Gorham - MacBane Public Library, 405 White St.,
    Springfield, TN 37172.

HISTORICAL SOCIETY: Robertson Co. Historical Society, Gorham
    - MacBane Public Library, 405 White St., Springfield, TN
    37172.

PUBLISHED SOURCES:
    Durrett, Mrs. C. W. & Mrs. R. A. Williams. Cemetery Records
        Of Robertson County, Tennessee. 3 volumes. [Springfield,
        TN: 1973].
    History Of Tennessee.   [Chicago & Nashville: Goodspeed
        Publishing Co., 1886].   (Robertson Co., pp. 827-67;
        1124-1205.)

PUBLISHED SOURCES (continued)
Holman, C. & Jean Durrett. Historic Robertson County, Places & Personalities. [Springfield, TN: 1970].
Marsh, H. C. Index To Goodspeed's History Of Tennessee...Robertson County. [1971].
Morton, J. C. & V. D. Moore, Jr. Robertson County Negro Yearbook, 1938. [Springfield, TN: 1970].
Whitley, E. R. Marriages Of Robertson County, Tennessee 1839-1861. [Baltimore: Genealogical Publishing Co., Inc, 1981].
Winters, Ralph L. Historical Sketches Adams, Robertson County, Tennessee 1779-1968. [1968] Reprinted 1978.

W.P.A. TYPESCRIPT RECORDS (available at the Tennessee State Library and Archives):
Court of Pleas and Quarter Sessions Minute Book 1, 1796-1807. Book 3, 1811-15.
County Court Minute Books, 2, 4, 5, 6, & 7, 1808-11; 1815-24.
General Index to Deeds Book O, 1796-1838.
Wills, Inventories, Bonds, etc., vol.I, 1796-1812.
vol. II, 1812-1818.
vol. III, 1819-1821.
Marriage Records, vol. 1, 1829 (1839) - 1860 (1861).
History of Ilai Metcalfe Account Book.
Records of Red River Church at the mouth of Sulphur Fork of Red River in Tennessee County (now Robertson) Mero District, 1791, and Minutes of Tar River Association in North Carolina beginning in 1769.

MICROFILMED RECORDS (available at the Tennessee State Library and Archives):
1820-80; & 1900-10 Federal Census.
Deeds, 1796 - 1963.
Trust Deeds, 1902-05; 1907-64.
Plat Book, 1941-63; 1955 -.
Military Discharges, 1922-50.
Wills & Inventories, 1796-1959.
Marriage Records, 1839-1965.
County Court Minutes, 1796-1964.
Quarterly Court Minutes, 1931-1960.
Guardians' Settlements, 1858-1961.
Guardians' Bonds & Letters, 1840-1963.
Administrators' & Executors' Bonds, 1869-97; 1906-64.
Inventory & Estate Settlements, 1934-63.
Land Deed Probates, 1833-1856.
Dentists' Register, 1919-48.
Doctors' Register, 1889-1963.

ROBERTSON COUNTY
(continued)

MICROFILMED RECORDS (continued)
    Optometrists' Register, 1907-45.
    Scholastic Population Listing, 1839-51.
    Survey Book, 1824-98.
    Vital Statistics, 1908-1912.
    Circuit Court Minutes, 1832-1962.
    Clerk & Masters' Minutes (Chancery), 1844-1962.
    General Sessions Court Minutes, 1947-64.
    School Board Minutes, 1907-64.
    Tax Books, 1867-72; 1877-80; 1883-84; 1903-1964.
    Tax Books (Misc.) 1873-86; 1893-98.

MANUSCRIPT MATERIALS (available at the Tennessee State Library
    and Archives):
    Cemeteries. Elmwood Cemetery, Springfield, TN, 1890-1968,
    (microfilm #267). Indexed record of individuals interred
    in Elmwood Cemetery. Use with ac. no. 268 (TSLA Collec-
    tion).
    Vital Statistics. Associated Funeral Directors, Springfield,
    TN, 1891-1968, (microfilm #268). Records consisting
    of name, age, race, sex, date and place of death, date
    of and place of burial, and other information.
    Church Records. Oakland Baptist Church, Springfield, 1888-
    1913, (microfilm #371). Minutes; and lists of members,
    baptisms, church services, and some death dates.
    Church Records. Bethlehem Baptist Church, 1853-1955, (micro-
    film #467). Membership lists, minutes, etc., along statis-
    tical table and list of deceased members.
    Church Records. Harmony Baptist Church, Cedar Hill, TN,
    1880-1935, (microfilm #160). Minutes of conference
    meetings, church rolls, correspondence, and a few miscell-
    aneous items.
    Church Records. Spring Creek Primitive Baptist Church,
    1830-1920, (microfilm #504). Membership lists; minutes
    of session, etc.
    Church Records of Fykes Grove Primitive Baptist Church,
    1813-1976, (microfilm #534). Minutes, membership lists,
    etc.

ADDITIONAL CHURCH RECORDS (may be purchased from the Historical
    Commission of the Southern Baptist Convention, 127 Ninth
    Ave. N., Nashville, TN 37234):
    Orlinda. Pleasant Hill Baptist Church, 1849-1979, (microfilm
    reel #5198).
    Red River Baptist Church, 1791-1826, (microfilm reel #289).
    Springfield. Hopewell Baptist Church, 1846-1964, (microfilm
    reel #2131).

RUTHERFORD COUNTY

CREATED: 1803 from Davidson County [1783 from Washington Co., NC].
COUNTY SEAT: Murfreesboro, TN 37130.

LIBRARIES: Linebaugh Public Library, 110 West College St., Murfreesboro, TN 37130. (This library houses a genealogical collection which was inventoried in the Tennessee Genealogical Review quarterly, Vol. 1, no. 2 (March 1980), pp. 9-10.
Todd Library, Middle Tennessee State University, Murfreesboro, TN 37130. (This library houses an extensive genealogical collection of secondary source materials.)
Highland Rim Regional Library Center, 2102 Mercury Blvd., Murfreesboro, TN 37130.

HISTORICAL SOCIETY: Rutherford County Historical Society, Box 906, Murfreesboro, TN 37130. (Publishes historical periodical.)

19TH CENTURY LAND OWNERSHIP MAPS (available from the Library of Congress, Washington, D. C.):
Rutherford Co., 1878. D. G. Beers & Co., Surveyor/Publisher: scales, 1:50,688, map #878.

PUBLISHED SOURCES:
Rutherford County, Tennessee Marriage Records, 1804-1850. [Murfreesboro: Daughters of the American Revolution, Tennessee, Col. Hardy Murfree Chapter. 1966].
Marriage Record, Rutherford County, Tennessee 1851-1872. [Murfreesboro: Col. Hardy Murfree Chapter, NSDAR, & the Rutherford Co. Historical Society].
Garrett, J. K. & I. H. McClain. Some Rutherford County, Tennessee Cemetery Records. [Columbia, TN: 1971].
History Of Tennessee. [Chicago & Nashville: Goodspeed Publishing Co., 1886]. (Rutherford Co. pp 810-940; 1019-1076).
Historical Records Survey...Tennessee. Inventory of the county archives of Tennessee. No. 75, Rutherford County (Murfreesboro). [Nashville: The Survey, 1938].
Houston, Martha Lou. 1810 Census Report.
Jacobs, L. F. Duck River Valley In Tennessee And Its Pioneers. [1908].
Llewellyn, R. M. Others Have Labored (First Presbyterian Church, Murfreesboro). [1962].
Lynch, Louise. Rutherford County, Tennessee Record Book A, No. 1, 1804-1814. [1980].
Marsh, H. C. Name Index To Goodspeed's History Of Tennessee ...Rutherford Co.

RUTHERFORD COUNTY
(continued)

PUBLISHED SOURCES (continued)
    Phillips, Oma Dee. 1860 U.S. Census, Rutherford County,
        Tennessee. [La Mesa, TX: 1970].
    Rutherford County Historical Society Publication, No. 1,
        Summer, 1978.
    Sims, C. C. A History Of Rutherford County, Tennessee.
        [Murfreesboro, TN: 1947].
    Taylor, E. The United Baptist Church Book At Mt. Pleasant,
        Feb. 1846-Apr. 5, 1884. [Amarillo, TX: 1970?].
    Walkup, William. Rutherford County, Tennessee Cemeteries.
        [Smyrna, TN: Stones River Chapter S.A.R. & the Rutherford
        Co. Historical Society, 1975].
    Whitley, E. R. Marriages Of Rutherford County, Tennessee
        1804-1872. [Baltimore: Genealogical Publishing Co.,
        Inc., 1981].
    Wray, H. G. Rutherford County, Tennessee Deed Abstracts,
        1804-1810. [Smyrna, TN: 1968?].

W.P.A. TYPESCRIPT RECORDS (available at the Tennessee State
        Library and Archives):
    Court of Pleas & Quarter Sessions Minutes, Vols. A, B,
        C, D, F, G, H, I, and K, 1807-1817.
    County Court Minutes, Books L, N, O, P, Q, R, S, T, U,
        V, & W, 1817-1830.
    Marriage Records, v.1, 1804-1837.
    Marriage Records, 1838-1845.
    General Index to Deeds, Book 1, 1804-1842.
    Tax Lists, 1809-1813; 1849.
    Wills, Inventories, Settlements, etc., Vols. II through
        VIII, 1804-1832.
    Record Book A, No. 1, 1804-1814.
    History, Minutes and Register of the 1935 Smyrna Presbyterian
        Church, 1887-1912.
    Church Records.
    Bible, Family & Tombstone Records, & Miscellaneous Records.
    Wills, v.6, 1824-1827.

MICROFILMED RECORDS (available at the Tennessee State Library
        and Archives):
    1820-80; & 1900-10 Federal Census.
    Trust Deeds, 1868-1963.
    Deeds, 1804-08; 1811-32; 1834-1963. (Some deeds for the
        years 1813, 1814, 1823, 1824, 1836, 1837, 1852, 1853,
        and 1864 are missing.)
    Chattel Mortgages, 1934-1963.
    Settlement Books, 1885-1963.

RUTHERFORD COUNTY
(continued)

MICROFILMED SOURCES (continued)
Discharge Records, 1919-1958.
Bond Book, 1942-1962.
Judgement Books, 1930-1963.
Lien Book, 1932-1963.
County Court Minutes, 1804-08; 1812-1962.
Marriage Records, 1804-1907.
Marriage Records, 1907-1963.
Marriage License Bonds, 1902-1914.
County Court Record Books, 1804-27; 1830-1914.
Quarterly Minutes Books, 1879-1963.
Guardian Settlements, 1940-1963.
Enrollment Cases, 1867-93.
Will Books, 1879-1963.
Probate Dockets & Record of Claims, 1939-60.
Birth & Death Records, 1881-1912.
Birth Records, 1915-1935.
Inventory Records, 1828-29.
Inventory Books, 1883-1963.
Sales Record, 1883-1954.
Insanity Books, 1919-1964.
Guardian Bond Book, 1877-1948.
Guardian Minute Book, 1874-1910.
Executors' Bond Book, 1806-1945.
Merchants' Bonds, 1842-1848.
Rule Docket Book, 1918-1949.
Register - Physicians' Certificates, 1947-1962.
Trial Sessions, 1807-08.
Trial Docket, 1842-52.
Grant Court, Civil & Criminal Minutes, 1849-51; 1865-1963.
Chancery Court Minutes, 1845-1964.
Rule Docket Books, 1860-1963.
Tax Books, 1809-13; 1867; 1871; 1877-1963.
Misc. Tax Books, 1875.
Marriage Records, 1863-1870.
Executors' Bonds, 1945-60.
Guardians' Bonds, 1948-60.
   Administrators' Bonds, 1873-1900; 1900-1960; 1960-65.
Administrators' Bonds, 1873-1900; 1900-1960; 1960-65.
Land sold for taxes, 1897-1918.
Guardian Receipt Books, 1855-1914.
Claims against estates, 1921-29.
Administrators' Settlements, 1868 -
Administrators' & Executors' Minute Books, 1870-1909.
Physicians' Register, 1907-1946.
Privilege Licenses, 1884-1909.
Records of Bonds, Power of Attorney & bills of sale,1804-14.

RUTHERFORD COUNTY
(continued)

MICROFILMED RECORDS (available at the Tennessee State Library
   and Archives):
Merchants' Bonds, 1832-1903.
Road Books, 1872-99.
Administrators', Executors' & Guardians' Bonds, 1874 -.
Circuit Court Jury List, 1826-41.
Circuit Court Minutes, 1890-1915.
Execution Dockets, 1855-1861.
County Board of Health Minutes, 1954-64.
School Fund Disbursement Book, 1870-96.
School Board Minutes, 1929-60.
School Superintendant's Correspondence, 1945-47.

MANUSCRIPT MATERIALS (available at the Tennessee State Library
   and Archives):
Cemeteries. National Cemetery, Murfreesboro, TN, 1862-1966,
   (microfilm #219). Interments, listed alphabetically,
   gives name, rank, company and number, state, date of
   death, and grave mark. Indexed.
Scrapbooks. Bedford & Rutherford Counties, 1900-1968,
   (microfilm #266). Newspaper clippings of activities
   of school groups; obituaries; club activities; World
   War II veterans; an account of ex-slave Simon Landrum;
   recollections of early days, etc.
Church Records. Rock Spring Church of Christ, 1835-1860,
   (microfilm #170). Membership lists, genealogical data
   on members, meeting records, etc.
Church Records. LaVergne Presbyterian Church, 1887-1972,
   (microfilm #415). Church business records; baptisms,
   deaths, and marriages.
Church Records. Florence Baptist Church, 1915-1970, (microfilm #518). Membership lists; minutes; associational
   letters; church officers and members transferred, etc.
Church Records. First Presbyterian Church, Murfreesboro,
   1812-1967, (microfilm #502). Church histories; registers
   of pastors, elders, deacons, and communicants; abstract
   of deeds; membership list; and church minutes.
Church Records. First Cumberland Presbyterian Church,
   Murfreesboro, 1899-1975, (microfilm #509). Minutes
   of session and official rolls; newsletters; and church
   directories.

ADDITIONAL CHURCH RECORDS (may be purchased from the Historical
   Commission of the Southern Baptist Convention, 127 Ninth
   Ave. N., Nashville, TN 37234):
Murfreesboro. The United Baptist Church, 1835-1897, (micro-
   film reel #2325).

SCOTT COUNTY

CREATED: 1849 from Anderson [1801 from Knox and Grainger Cos.], Campbell [1806 from Anderson & Claiborne Cos.], Fentress [1823 from Morgan & Overton Cos.], and Morgan County [1817 from Roane Co.].
COUNTY SEAT: Huntsville, TN 37756.

LIBRARY: Scott Co. Public Library, Huntsville, TN 37756.

PUBLISHED SOURCES:
  Creekmore, Pollyanna. 1850 Scott County, Tennessee Census. [1980].
  Sanderson, E. S. County Scott And Its Mountain Folk. [Huntsville, TN: 1958].

W.P.A. TYPESCRIPT RECORDS (available at the Tennessee State Library and Archives):
  County Court Minutes, 1850-55.
  Minute Book (Deeds) v.C, 1859-61.
  Marriage Records, Vols. A, B, C, 1854-80.

MICROFILMED RECORDS (available at the Tennessee State Library and Archives):
  1850-80; & 1900-10 Federal Census.
  Chancery Court Minutes, Apr. 1858 - Mar. 1972.
  Chancery Chamber Minutes, Feb. 1961 - Aug. 1972.
  Circuit Court Civil Minutes, Nov. 1928 - Aug. 1972.
  Civil & Criminal Minutes, Nov. 1850 - July 1972.
  Administrators' Bonds & Letters, Mar. 1947 - Sept. 1972.
  Executors' Bonds & Letters, Jan. 1947 - Aug. 1972.
  Guardians' Bonds & Letters, Jan. 1947 - Aug. 1972.
  Claims against estates, Feb. 1923 - Sept. 1950.
  Insanity Records, Feb. 1920 - Sept. 1972, (not available for research).
  Inventories & Settlements of Estates, July 1953 - July 1972.
  Marriages, May 1854 - Sept. 1972.
  County Court Minutes, Oct. 1856 - July 1869; Jan. 1875 - Sept. 1972.
  Professional Licenses Registers, Physicians & Nurses, May 1905 - June 1968.
  Settlements, Executors', Administrators' and Guardians', Aug. 1892 - Apr. 1938; June 1946 - Aug. 1959.
  Wills, Jan. 1929 - Aug. 1972.
  Land Entries, May 1850 - July 1889.
  Military Discharges, June 1919 - Jan. 1938; May 1943 - Oct. 1972.
  Misc. Records: Liens, Leases, Contracts, etc., Apr. 1921 - June 1972.

SCOTT COUNTY
(continued)

MICROFILMED RECORDS (continued)
Oil & Gas Leases, Apr. 1915 - June 1939.
Surveyors' Book, Oct. 1850 - Apr. 1909.
Trust Deeds, Apr. 1892 - Dec. 1972.
Cash Journals, June 1944 - Ocat. 1972.
Tax Books, 1875-78; 1880-1908; 1911-12; 1914-15; 1918-1972
    (intermittantly).

SEQUATCHIE COUNTY

CREATED: 1857 from Hamilton County [1819 from Rhea County].
COUNTY SEAT: Dunlap, TN 37327.

LIBRARY: Sequatchie County Public Library, Rt. 2, Dunlap,
    TN 37327.

PUBLISHED SOURCES:
Brown, Erma Lee S. Sequatchie County, Tennessee Marriages
    1858-1922. [1975].
Layne, O. Sequatchie County: History And Developement.
    [Dunlap, TN: 1969].
Raulston, J. L. & J. W. Livingood. Sequatchie [Knoxville:
    U. T. Press, 1974].

W.P.A. TYPESCRIPT RECORDS (available at the Tennessee State
    Library and Archives):
County Court Minutes, 1858-74.
Wills & Inventories, 1858-74.
Marriage Records, 1858-74.
Church Records.

MICROFILMED RECORDS (available at the Tennessee State Library
    and Archives):
1860-80; & 1900-10 Federal Census.
Circuit Court Minutes, Mar. 1898 - Jan. 1917; Sept. 1923
    - Sept. 1938; Jan. 1939 - May 1948; Sept. 1948 - Jan.
    1969.
Clerk & Master Minutes, Dec. 1869 - Sept. 1877; Mar. 1878
    - Sept 1893; Mar. 1894 - Sept. 1926; Mar. 1927 - May
    1959; Sept. 1959 - Jan. 1969.
Administrators' Bonds, Jan. 1880 - Nov. 1968.
Conservators' Bonds & Letters, Feb. 1955 - Sept. 1968.
Executors' Bonds, Nov. 1880 - May 1967.

SEQUATCHIE COUNTY
(continued)

MICROFILMED RECORDS (continued)
Guardians' Bonds, Jan. 1881 - Oct. 1968.
Marriage Records, Jan. 1858 - Feb. 1969.
County Court Minutes, Jan. 1858 - Feb. 1869.
Quarterly Court Minutes, Jan. 1950 - Jan. 1969.
Physicians' Records, Oct. 1889 - Dec. 1963.
Real Estate Transfers (By Probate), Feb. 1858 - Dec. 1888.
Scholastic District Boundaries; School Commissioners; Scho-
    lastic Population; Estate Insolvencies, 1871-97.
Administrators', Executors', & Guardians' Settlements,
    Apr. 1860 - Aug. 1902 (Guardians' only); July 1925 -
    Jan. 1969.
Birth Records, 1880-1940.
Death Records, 1881-1938.
Wills & Inventories, June 1858 - Apr. 1968.
Deeds, Feb. 1858 - Nov. 1968.
Military Discharges, Jan. 1919 - Apr. 1919; July 1945 -
    Dec. 1968.
Plat Book, May 1964 - Jan. 1968.
Trust Deeds, Mar. 1876 - Jan. 1969.
Board of Education Minutes, May 1908 - June 1910; Apr.
    1923 -Apr. 1937; Mar. 1939 - Jan. 1969.
Tax Books, 1861-71; 1875-1914; 1918; 1923; 1928; 1933;
    1943; 1948; 1953; 1958; 1960-68.

CHURCH RECORDS (may be purchased from the Historical Commission
    of the Southern Baptist Convention, 127 Ninth Ave. N.,
    Nashville, TN 37234):
Dunlap. Ewtonville Baptist Church, 1836-1952, (microfilm
reel #847).

SEVIER COUNTY

CREATED: 1794 from Jefferson County [1792 from Greene &
    Hawkins Cos.].
COUNTY SEAT: Sevierville, TN 37862.

LIBRARY: Sevier Co. Public Library, Court Avenue, Sevierville,
    TN 37862.

HISTORICAL SOCIETY: Smokey Mtn. Historical Society, P. O.
    Box 286, Sevierville, TN 37862.

SEVIER COUNTY
(continued)

PUBLISHED SOURCES:
  Creekmore, Pollyanna & Blanche C. McMahon. Population
    Schedule Of The U.S. Census Of 1830 For Sevier County.
    [Knoxville: 1956].
  _____. U.S. Census Office, 7th Census, 1850. [Knoxville:
    1953].
  History Of Tennessee...(East TN Edition). [Chicago &
    Nashville: Goodspeed Publishing Co., 1887]. (Sevier
    Co., pp. 834-37; 1096-1104.)
  Matthews, F. D. History Of Sevier County, Masters,
    Knoxville, TN, 1950.
  Reagan, D. B. Smoky Mountain Clans. [Knoxville, TN: 1974].
  _____. Cemetery Inscriptions In The Smoky Mountain Area,
    Sevier County, Tennessee. [Knoxville: 1974].
  Smoky Mtn. Historical Society. The 1840 Sevier County
    Census Record.
  _____. In The Shadow Of The Smokies. [1985]. The cemetery
    records of Sevier Co., including inscriptions from 350
    cemeteries.
  Waters, John B. Early Sevier County VIP'S. [Sevierville,
    TN: 1975].

W.P.A. TYPESCRIPT RECORDS (available at the Tennessee State
    Library and Archives):
  Marriage License Record, No. 1, 1857-73.
  Tennessee Negro Cemetery Records.

MICROFILMED RECORDS (available at the Tennessee State Library
    and Archives):
  1830-80; & 1900-10 Federal Census.
  Chancery Court Minutes, Oct. 1854 - Aug. 1900.
  Enrollments, June 1870 - Oct. 1873.
  Circuit Court Minutes, Mar. 1850 - Nov. 1853; Nov. 1857
    - July 1904.
  Enrollment Book, July 1858 - Nov. 1876.
  Guardians' Settlements, July 1871 - Dec. 1905.
  Administrators' & Executors' Settlements, Oct. 1879 - Apr.
    1906.
  Guardians' Bonds and Letters, Sept. 1872 - Dec. 1907.
  County Court Minutes, Apr. 1856 - Sept. 1900.
  Marriages, Apr. 1856 - Dec. 1916.
  Wills, Dec. 1849 - Oct. 1922.
  Inventory of estates, Mar. 1856 - Aug. 1896.
  Vital Statistics, May 1881 - Feb. 1882.
  Deeds, Oct. 1845; Sept. 1909.
  Surveyors' Book, May 1824 - Nov. 1894.
  Trust Deeds, July 1883 - May 1903.
  Tax Books, 1864-67; 1869-72.

SEVIER COUNTY
(continued)

CHURCH RECORDS (may be purchased from the Historical Commission of the Southern Baptist Convention, 127 Ninth Ave., N., Nashville, TN 37234).
Paw Paw Hollow Baptist Church, 1802-1880, (microfilm reel #365).
Providence Baptist Church, 1829 - Oct. 1904, (microfilm reel #1765).

SHELBY COUNTY

CREATED: 1819 from Hardin County [1819 from the Western District (Indian lands).
COUNTY SEAT: Memphis, TN 38102

LIBRARIES:
Memphis-Shelby County Public Library, 1850 Peabody St., Memphis, TN 38104.
Branch Genealogy Library of the Church of Jesus Christ of Latter Day Saints, 4520 Winchester Rd., Memphis, TN 38118.
Memphis State University Library, Memphis, TN 38104.
Memphis Pink Palace Museum, Memphis, TN 38104.

GENEALOGICAL & HISTORICAL SOCIETIES
Tennessee Genealogical Society, P. O. Box 12124, Memphis, TN 38112.
West Tennessee Historical Society, 157 S. Fenwick Rd., Memphis, TN 38111.

PUBLISHED SOURCES:
Elam, Erickson, & Wyckoff-Hunt. Gravestone Inscriptions From Shelby County, Tennessee. Vol. I [Memphis: Milestone Press, 1971]. Vols. II [1974], and Vol III.
Elmwood Cemetery. [Memphis: Boyle & Chapman, printers, 1874].
History Of Tennessee. [Chicago & Nashville: Goodspeed Publishing Co., 1887].
Historical Records Survey. Tennessee. Special Publication Ser. No. 2. [Nashville: The Survey, 1939]. The history and organization of the Shelby County judiciary.
Historical Records Survey. Transcription of the county archives of Tennessee. [Nashville: The Survey, 1941]. V.1, Minutes of the county court of Shelby County, Book no. 1, 1820-24.

SHELBY COUNTY
(continued)

PUBLISHED SOURCES (continued)
"Index to the 1830 Census, Shelby County, Tennessee," by T. J. Hughes, Ansearchin' News, v.16, 1969, no. 3, pp. 109-111.
"Index to the 1840 Census, Shelby County, Tennessee," by T. P.Hughes, Ansearchin' News, v.16, 1969, no. 3, pp. 112-118.
Keating, John M. L. History Of The City Of Memphis And Shelby County, Tennessee. [Syracuse, NY: D. Mason & Co., 1888].
Memphis City Directories, 1844; 1849; 1855-57; 1859-1901.
Shelby County, Tennessee Marriage Records, 1819-1850, compiled by Memphis Genealogical Society, 1957.
Polk's Memphis Surburban Directory.
Whitley, E. R. Marriages Of Shelby County, Tennessee 1820-1858. [Baltimore: Genealogical Publishing Co., Inc., 1982].

W.P.A. TYPESCRIPT RECORDS (available at the Tennessee State Library and Archives):
Minutes of the County Court, Book 1, 1820-24.
   Book 3, 1830-34, pts. I & II.
   Book 4, 1833-43, pts. I, II, & III.
   Book 5, 1843-48, pts. I, II, & III.
   Book 6, 1848-51, pts. I, II, & III.
Old Circuit Court Minutes, #2, 1828-36.
Probate Court Minute Book 2, 1824-29.
Shelby County Court Minute Book 1, 1850-59.
Chancery Court Minute Book #1, 1846-51, pts. I & II.
General Index Record (Deeds), 1821-70.
Will Book #1, Jan. 1830 - May 1847.
   Book 2D, June 1847 - July 1855.
   Book 3E, 1855-62.
Probate Court Will Record C-1, 1830-47.
List of Deaths in the City of Memphis, May 1848 - Dec. 1859.
Marriage Records, Vols. 1, 2, & 3, 1820-65.
Will Book 4A (Probate Court), 1864-67.
Tombstone Inscriptions.

MICROFILMED RECORDS (available at the Tennessee State Library and Archives):
1830-80; & 1900-10 Federal Census.
Journal, July 1853 - Feb. 1870.
Jail Commissioners' Minutes, Jan. 1866 - Apr. 1867.
Shelby County Court Minutes, Jan. 1896 - Jan. 1898.

SHELBY COUNTY
(continued)

MICROFILMED RECORDS (continued)
City of Memphis Census, 1869, for 3rd, 6th, 9th, & 10th
Ward; and City of Memphis Census, 1865.
Deed Book, 1, Shelby County, 1819-20.
*Births, 1881-82; 1908-12.
*Memphis births, 1874-1912.
*Deaths, 1881-82; 1908-12.
*Memphis deaths, 1848-59; 1909-12.
*Chancery Court Minutes, 1846 to present.
*Circuit Court Minutes, 1828 to present.
*County Court Minutes, 1820 to present.
*Deeds, 1821 to present.
*Marriage Records, 1819 to present.
*Probate Records, 1824 to present.
*Wills, 1830 to present.
*Tax rolls, 1838 to present.

*NOTE: These materials available at the courthouse in Memphis,
TN.

MANUSCRIPT MATERIALS (available at the Tennessee State Library
and Archives):
Cemeteries. Elmwood Cemetery, Memphis, 1853-1904, (mf.
#193). Record of names of interred, dates, lot & section
number, and occassional remarks.
Church Records. Cumberland Presbyterian, Calvary Episcopal,
First Presbyterian, Germantown Presbyterian, Lindsay
Ave. Presbyterian, Lauderdale Presbyterian, and Westminster
Presbyterian Churches including session & board meetings,
membership rolls, baptisms, lists of officers, letters,
certificates of dismissal, clippings, sketches, and
photographs.

ADDITIONAL CHURCH RECORDS (may be purchased from the Historical
Commission of the Southern Baptist Convention, 127 Ninth
Ave., N., Nashville, TN 37234):
Coldwater Baptist Church, 1867-1979, (microfilm reel #5073).
Egypt Baptist Church, 1840-1961, (microfilm reel #3323).

SMITH COUNTY

CREATED: 1799 from Sumner County [1796 from Davidson Co.].
COUNTY SEAT: Carthage, TN 37030.

LIBRARY: Smith County Public Library, Carthage, TN 37030.

HISTORICAL SOCIETY: Smith Co. Historical Society, Carthage,
TN 37030.

SMITH COUNTY
(continued)

PUBLISHED SOURCES:
Bowen, J. W. Smith County History.
Smith County, Tennessee Marriage Records 1838-1881, compiled
    by Caney Fork Chapter NSDAR [1980].
Embry,H. Smith County Marriages, 1838, 1845-1854. [Nash-
    ville: 1962].
Gold, W. D. The County Of Smith. [Carthage, TN: The Car-
    thage Post, 1903].
History Of Tennessee. [Chicago & Nashville: Goodspeed
    Publishing Co., 1887] (Smith Co., pp. 821-34; 929-71.
Lynch, Louise. Cemetery Records Of Smith County, Tennnessee.
    [1978].
Marsh, H. C. Name Index To Goodspeed's History Of Tennessee
    ...Smith Co.

W.P.A. TYPESCRIPT RECORDS (available at the Tennessee State
    Library and Archives):
Court of Pleas & Quarter Sessions Minutes, 1799-1800, and
    County Court Minute Book, 1799-1804; 1835.
Court of Pleas & Quarter Sessions Minute Book, 1808-11.
County Court Minute Books, 1811-13; 1813-15; 1815-17; 1817-19.
Minutes of the County Court, No. 8, 1819-1820.
    No. 9, 1820-22.
    No. 10, 1822-24.
Will Book, 5, Smith County, 1805-09.
Wills & Inventories, 1812-14.
Wills & Inventories, 1814-16.
Will Book, 4, Smith County, 1820-23.
Will Book, No. 4, 1816-20.
Bible & Tombstone Records.
Church Minutes, 1807-11.
United Baptist Section Minutes, 1838-50.
Dixon's Creek Baptist Church Minutes, 1799-1853.
Dixon's Creek Baptist Church Minutes, 1812-18.

MICROFILMED RECORDS (available at the Tennessee State Library
    & Archives):
1820-80; 1900-10 Federal Census.
General Sessions Minutes, Sept. 1960 - June 1966.
Circuit Court Minutes, Civil & Criminal, Nov. 1811 - Oct.
    1820; Apr. 1823 - June 1966.
Clerk & Masters' Chambers Minutes, Sept. 1847 - May 1966.
Clerk & Masters' Minutes, May 1825 - Mar. 1966.
Administrators' Bonds & Letters, Feb. 1860 - June 1866.
Administrators' & Executors Settlements, Sept. 1846 - Mar.
    1966.

160

SMITH COUNTY
(continued)

MICROFILMED RECORDS (continued)
Administrators' Receipts, Nov. 1854 - Dec. 1904.
County Court Minutes, Dec. 1799 - June 1966.
Dentist Register, Aug. 1891 - Mar. 1915.
Executors' Bonds, Feb. 1860 - Apr. 1966.
Guardians' Bonds & Letters, Feb. 1860 - Apr. 1966.
Guardians' Minutes, Apr. 1867 - Feb. 1914.
Guardians' Receipts, Nov. 1854 - Apr. 1916.
Guardians' Settlements, Apr. 1834 - Jan. 1966.
Inventory & Will Book, Feb. 1823 - May 1966.
Judgements, Aug. 1834 - Oct. 1852.
Juvenile Court Minutes, Apr. 1912 - Sept. 1932.
License Register, Oct. 1848 - Oct. 1867.
Marriage Licenses & Bonds, Feb. 1838 - July 1966.
Medical Examiner, May 1907 - Aug. 1950.
Merchants' & Tipplers' Bonds, Jan. 1872 - Mar. 1882.
Physicians' Records, Dec. 1898 - June 1906.
Osteopathy Records, May 1900 - July 1902.
Optometry Register, Apr. 1916 - Mar. 1941.
Quarterly Court Minutes, Oct. 1930 - Apr. 1966.
Report of Common School Commissions, Oct. 1850 - Apr. 1868;
    Aug. 1870 - June 1876.
Road Books, Aug. 1841 - July 1893.
Vital Statistics: Births and Deaths, 1881-82; 1908-12.
Workhouse Minutes, Jan. 1908 - Apr. 1928.
Will Books, Nov. 1805 - Mar. 1809; Sept. 1812 - Nov. 1895;
    Jan. 1897 - Apr. 1966.
Inventories, Feb. 1823 - Oct. 1827.
Charter Books, Jan. 1911 - June 1966.
Deeds, Apr. 1801 - July 1966.
Military Discharges, June 1919 - May 1966.
Oil & Gas Leases, June 1896 - May 1960.
Plat Book, Aug. 1952 - June 1966.
Ranger & Entry Book, Dec. 1842 - Nov. 1885.
Entry Book, July 1865 - Nov. 1885.
Survey Books, July 1824 - Aug. 1917.
Trust Deeds, July 1877 - July 1966.
School Board Minutes, Apr. 1914 - June 1966.
Minutes of Board of Aldermen, Gordonsville, 1909-60.
Scholastic Reports, 1856-68.
Tax Books, 1875 - 1965.
Supplement
    Board of Carthage; Hartsville Turnpike Co. Minutes,
    Nov. 1857 - Dec. 1873.
    Note Books, Register's Office, May 1876 - May 1915.
    Tax Books, 1860; 1866-85.

SMITH COUNTY
(continued)

MANUSCRIPT MATERIALS (available at the Tennessee State Library
and Archives):
Associations, Institutions, etc. Smith Co. Debating Club,
1849-50; 1855-78, (microfilm #130). Contains minutes,
bylaws, proceedings of debating club; miscellaneous
birth, death, & marriage notations; records of Knob
Spring and Plunkett Creek churches; family accounts;
and home remedies.
Associations, Institutions, etc. Masonic Records, 1867-1962,
(microfilm #221). (Restricted). Records of Carthage
Benevolent Lodge No. 14; Carthage Lodge No. 128; Martin
Lodge, No. 141; and Snow Creek Lodge.
Church Records. Brush Creek Primitive Baptist Church,
1802-1971, (microfilm #389). Church business records;
birth, death, some marriage records, and cemetery records.
Church Records. Plunkett Creek Missionary Baptist Church,
1913-1977, (microfilm #551). Contains information on
births, baptisms, marriages, and deaths.
Church Records. Peyton's Creek Baptist Church, 1834-1953,
(microfilm #216). Membership rolls and minutes.

ADDITIONAL CHURCH RECORDS (may be purchased from the Historical
Commission of the Southern Baptist Convention, 127 Ninth
Ave. N., Nashville, TN 37234):
Brush Creek Baptist Church Records, 1828-1951, (microfilm
reel #4296].
Hickman Baptist Church, Sept. 1828 - Dec. 1980 (lacking
Nov. 1851 - Aug. 1870), (microfilm reel #5219).

STEWART COUNTY

CREATED: 1803 from Montgomery County [1796 from Tennessee
Co.].
COUNTY SEAT: Dover, TN 37058.

SPECIAL NOTE: Courthouse fire during Civil War destroyed
some records.)

LIBRARY: Stewart Co. Public Library, Courthouse, Dover,
TN 37058.

STEWART COUNTY
(continued)

PUBLISHED SOURCES:
"The 'Lost' Minute Book of Stewart County, Tennessee, 1804-1807," by Duncan. Ansearchin News, v.7 (1960), no. 3, pp. 61-62; no. 4, pp.88-99; v.8 (1961) no. 1, pp. 16-19; no. 2, pp. 43-48; no. 3, pp. 87-94; no. 4, pp. 118-21; v.9 (1962) no. 1, pp. 28-33; no. 2, pp. 63-64; no. 3, pp. 104-115; no. 4, pp. 135-47.

History Of Tennessee. [Chicago & Nashville: Goodspeed Publishing Co., 1886]. (Stewart Co., pp. 894-920; 1289-1329.)

McClain, I. H. History Of Stewart County. [Columbia, TN: Garrett-McClain, 1965].

Marsh, H. C. Name Index To Goodspeed's History Of Tennessee ...Stewart Co.

Simmons, Don. Marriage Records Of Stewart County, Tennessee, 1838-1848. [Murray, KY: 1974?].

_____. Marriage Records, Stewart County, Tennessee, 1849-1866. [Murray, KY: 1973].

_____. Marriage Records Of Stewart County, Tennessee, 1865-1881. [Murray, KY: 1973].

Whitley, E. R. Marriages Of Stewart County, Tennessee, 1838-1866. [Baltimore: Genealogical Publishing Co., Inc., 1982].

W.P.A. TYPESCRIPT RECORDS (available at the Tennessee State Library and Archives):
General Index to Deeds, v.1, 1804-43.
Deed Record Book v.3, 1789-1818.
Deed Record Book v.4, 1810-1813 Abstract.
Deed Record Book v.1, 1804-06.
Marriage Record Book v.4, 1838-1848.
Marriage Record Book v.5, 1849-1866.
County Court Minute Docket, 1804-07.
Tax Book v.2, 1808-1812.
Minutes of the County Court v.3, 1811-12.
County Court Minutes, 1813-15; 1815-19.

MICROFILMED RECORDS (available at the Tennessee State Library And Archives):
1820-80; & 1900-10 Federal Census.
Circuit Court Minute Books, Sept. 1821 - Oct. 1967 (incomplete).
Clerk & Master Chamber Minutes, Feb. 1954 - Sept. 1967.
Clerk & Master Enrollment Book, Feb. 1866 - Feb. 1877.
Clerk & Master Minute Books, June 1865 - Oct. 1967.
Administrators' Bonds & Letters, Dec. 1883 - Nov. 1899; June 1925 - Sept. 1947; Dec. 1947 - Oct. 1967.

STEWART COUNTY
(continued)

MICROFILMED RECORDS (continued)
  Administrators' Settlements (on microfilm roll #139 (Insanity
    Records).
  Automobile Registrations 1916-1917.
  Claims against estates, Dec. 1921 - June 1934.
  Conservators' Bonds & Letters, Oct. 1958 - Aug. 1967.
  Constable & Magistrate Bonds, Aug. 1924 - Sept. 1956.
  County Officials Bonds, Sept. 1942 - Aug. 1966.
  Executors' Bonds & Letters, Apr. 1901 - Jan. 1941.
  Guardian Bonds & Letters, Oct. 1883 - Feb. 1967.
  Guardian Minute Book, July 1895 - Jan. 1915.
  Guardian Settlements, July 1842 - Nov. 1967.
  Insanity Minutes & Records, 1919-1921 (not available for
    research).
  Insolvent Estates, Aug. 1870 - Jan. 1914.
  Inventories of estates, Apr. 1903 - Oct. 1966.
  Land Sale Minutes, Oct. 1911 - June 1967.
  Land Sales Records, Sept. 1896 - 1936.
  Marriage Records, Jan. 1849 - Dec. 1967.
  Merchants' Bonds & Oaths, Nov. 1894 - Aug. 1897; June 1907
    - Apr. 1921.
  County Court Minutes Books, 1804; 1808; 1812 - Jan. 1968
    (incomplete).
  Minutes of Workhouse Commission, Aug. 1895 - Dec. 1903.
  Physicians' Records, 1889-1905; June 1907 - Aug. 1919.
  Probate Deed Books, Oct. 1894 - July 1947.
  Quarterly Court Minutes, July 1900 - Dec. 1905; Jan. 1916
    - Oct. 1928; July 1929 - Apr. 1944; July 1944 - Nov.
    1967.
  Road Books, June 1870 - Apr. 1913.
  Settlements & Bonds, May 1812 - May 1814; Nov. 1814 - Feb.
    1929; Apr. 1829 - Jan. 1968.
  Tipplers' Bonds & Oaths, Oct. 1897 - Apr. 1901.
  Vital Statistics, 1881-82 (Birth); 1908-11 (Birth & Death);
    1912 (Birth & Death).
  Wills, Mar. 1899 - Nov. 1966.
  Board of Health Minutes, Jan. 1963 - Feb. 1966.
  Contracts, Charters, Releases, etc., Nov. 1921 - Aug. 1928;
    Oct. 1928 - Jan. 1968.
  Deed Books, Dec. 1796 - Feb. 1968.
  Entry Takers' Book, Nov. 1829 - June 1905.
  File Books, Apr. 1904 - Feb. 1968.
  Military Discharge Records, 1917; Nov. 1918 - Jan. 1968.
  Oil & Gas Leases, June 1920 - June 1967.
  Trust Deed Books, Aug. 1868 - Jan. 1968.
  Board of Education Minutes, July 1907 - Jan. 1939; Mar.
    1939 - Sept. 1967.

STEWART COUNTY
(continued)

MICROFILMED RECORDS (continued)
Tax Books, 1808; 1827-33; 1836-38; 1841-65; 1877-1959.
(see also, County Court Minutes, 1808, microfilm roll
#38).
Tax Book & Administrators' Settlements, Apr. 1837 - Dec.
1839.

MANUSCRIPT MATERIALS (available at the Tennessee State Library
and Archives):
Church Records. Indian Mound Methodist Church includes
list of pastors 1881-1905; Membership list, 1842-1946;
Revised membership list, 1945-1962; and a partial listing
of baptisms, marriages, and deaths, 1882-1927, (microfilm
roll #128).

ADDITIONAL CHURCH RECORDS (may be purchased from the Historical
Commission of the Southern Baptist Convention, 127 Ninth
Ave. N., Nashville, TN 37234):
Cumberland Association. Cross Creek Baptist Church, 1851-
1953, Sept. 1956 - Jan. 1969, (microfilm reel #2193).

SULLIVAN COUNTY

CREATED: 1779 from Washington County [1777 from Washington
District, NC, which had been detached from Wilkes & Burke
Cos., NC].
COUNTY SEAT: Blountville, TN 37617.

SPECIAL NOTE: (Courthouse fire in 1863 destroyed some
records.)

LIBRARIES: Sullivan Co. Public Library, 205 Main St.,
Blountville, TN 37617.
Bristol Public Library, 701 Goode St., Bristol, VA 24201.
J.F. Johnson Memorial Library, Broad & New St., Kingsport,
TN 37660.
Branch Genealogical Library, Church of Jesus Christ of Latter
Day Saints, Netherland Inn Dr., Kingsport, TN 37662.

PUBLISHED SOURCES:
Allen, Penelope Johnson. Tennessee Soldiers In The
Revolution, A Roster Of Soldiers Living During The
Revolutionary War In The Counties Of Washington And
Sullivan. [1935].

SULLIVAN COUNTY
(continued)

PUBLISHED SOURCES (continued)

"Early East Tennessee Taxpayers, VII, Sullivan County, 1796," by Pollyanna Creekmore; East TN Historical Society Publications, no. 31 (1959) pp. 112-121.

Historical Records Survey. Tennessee. Inventory of the county archives in Tennessee. No. 82, Sullivan Co. [Nashville: The Survey, 1942].

History Of Tennessee...(East TN Edition). [Chicago & Nashville: Goodspeed Publishing Co., 1887]. (Sullivan Co., pp. 912-21; 1300-1312.)

The New Bethel Sesquicentennial, 1782-1932. [Bristol, TN: 1932].

Veterans Of Foreign Wars Of U.S. [Bristol: Patton-Crosswhite Post 706975].

Taylor, Oliver. Historic Sullivan. [Bristol, TN: The King Printing Co., 1909].

Vineyard, Mrs. John. First Land Owners Of Sullivan County, Tennessee. [Drake, MO: 1974].

W.P.A. TYPESCRIPT RECORDS (available at the Tennessee State Library and Archives):

Deed Books, v.1, 1775-90; v.2, 1784-96; v.3, 1795-1802; v.4, 1802-1807; v.5, 1807-08 & 1834-1838; v.6, 1809-1815.

Will Book #1, 1830-70.

Marriage Records (unbound), 1861-70.

Rhea Papers from the Collection of Mrs. Charles R. Hyde of Chattanooga, TN.

New Bethel Church Minutes.

Tombstone Records.

New Bethel Presbyterian Church Records.

MICROFILMED RECORDS (available at the Tennessee State Library and Archives):

1830-80; & 1900-10 Federal Census.

Enrollment Books, July 1858 - Nov. 1867.

Chancery Court Minutes, May 1852 - Jan. 1902.

Circuit Court Enrollment Books, Nov. 1871 - July 1874.

Circuit Court Minutes, Mar. 1879 - Jan. 1909.

County Court Enrollment Book, Sept. 1874 - Nov. 1874.

Estate, Insolvent, Feb. 1881 - Oct. 1942.

Guardian Bonds & Letters, Oct. 1882 - Sept. 1907.

Executors' Bonds & Letters, June 1875 - May 1929.

Administrators' Bonds & Letters, Mar. 1875 - July 1904.

Marriages, 1863-1915.

County Court Minutes, May 1861 - Sept. 1900.

SULLIVAN COUNTY
(continued)

MICROFILMED RECORDS (continued)
    Physicians' Register, Apr. 1889 - Oct. 1971.
    Road Book, July 1883 - Mr. 1891.
    Inventories, Apr. 1864 - Nov. 1907.
    Settlements with estates, Jan. 1878 - Mar. 1901.
    Death Records, May 1881 - Sept. 1894.
    Birth Records, Apr. 1881 - June 1882; 1908-12.
    Wills, Aug. 1838 - Mar. 1915.
    Deeds, May 1775 - Nov. 1901.
    Land Entries, Nov. 1832 - Apr. 1903.
    Land Surveys, Apr. 1824 - Aug. 1841.
    Tax Books, 1877 - 1900.

MANUSCRIPT MATERIALS (available at the Tennessee State Library
    and Archives):
    Confederate Veterans Association of Upper East Tennessee,
        1861 - ca. 1895, (microfilm #167). Roster containing
        the name, county, state, date of enlistment, company
        and regiment, rank, wounds received, date and cause
        of discharge, and general remarks about members of the
        association living in several counties including Sullivan
        Co., TN.
    Cemeteries. Greene, Sullivan, Unicoi, and Washington
        Counties, TN, ca. 1780-1960, (microfilm #320). The
        Sullivan County records include Newland, Fain, Mauk,
        Latture or Wilson, Droke Denton, Dishner, Harr, Abraham,
        Deck, Seneker-Steele, Leonard, Hold, Mottern, Lilley,
        Massengill, Bachman, Waterman, Claud, Groseclose, Yoakley,
        and Gaines family cemeteries; also, church cemetery
        records for the following denominations: Baptist,
        Methodist, Lutheran, Missionary Baptist, and Freewill
        Baptist.
    Church Records. Baptist Churches, Washington & Sullivan
        Counties, TN, (microfilm #327). Yearbook and Directory,
        1927, of the Calvary Baptist Church of Bristol, which
        contains an historical sketch of the church for the
        period 1900-27.
    Church Records. Lutheran Conference, 1821, (microfilm
        #465).

SUMNER COUNTY

CREATED: 1786 from Davidson County [1783 from Washington County].
COUNTY SEAT: Gallatin, TN 37066.

LIBRARY: Edward Ward Carmack Public Library, Hartsville, Pike, Gallatin, TN 37066.

HISTORICAL SOCIETY: Sumner Co. Historical Society, Belvedere Drive, Gallatin, TN 37066.

19TH CENTURY LAND OWNERSHIP MAP (available from the Library of Congress, Washington, D.C.)
Sumner Co., 1878; D. G. Beers Co., Surveyor/Publisher; scale 1:50,688, map #880.

PUBLISHED SOURCES:
Absher, L. A. Some Early Settlers Of Upper Sumner County, Tennessee. [Knoxville, TN, 1966].
"Petitioners of Sumner County, Tennessee," (those petitioning to form Wilson Co.), Ansearchin News, v.7 (1960), no. 2, pp. 38-39; v.7, no. 3, pp. 63-64; v.9, (1962), no. 1, pp. 10-11.
Bamman, Mrs. Gale W., C. G. Sumner County, Tennessee Abstracts Of Inventories, Settlements, And Guardian Accounts, Vol.A 1808-1821.
Cisco, J. G. Historic Sumner County, Tennessee. [Folk-Keeling Printing Co., 1909].
Dry Fork Cumberland Presbyterian Church, Sumner Co., Aug. 30, 1831-Oct. 25, 1852.
Durham, Walter. Old Sumner, A History of Sumner Co. 1805-1861. [Gallatin, TN: Sumner Co. Public Library Board, 1972].
_____. The Great Leap Westward: A History of Sumner Co. [Gallatin, TN: Sumner Co. Public Library Board, 1969].
Fulcher, Richard C. 1770-1790 Census Of The Cumberland Settlements. [Brentwood: 1986]. (Includes a seperate section on Sumner County.)
History Of Tennessee. [Chicago & Nashville: 1887]. (Sumner Co., pp. 797-821; 848-929.)
Marsh, H. C. Name Index To Goodspeed's History Of Tennessee ...Sumner Co.
The Montgomery County Genealogical Journal (quarterly); beginning with Vol. 9, no. 1, "Old Sumner County Records."
Roddy, Vernon. The Lost Town Of Bledsoesborough, Tennessee. [1984]. (Established in 1797, the site of the town today is in the western edge of Smith Co., TN, 2 miles south of Dixon Springs.)

SUMNER COUNTY
(continued)

PUBLISHED SOURCES (continued)
Station Camp, Tennessee United Baptist Church of Christ
Minutes, 1867-1919.
Whitley, E. R. Marriages Of Sumner County, Tennessee,
1787-1838. [Baltimore: Genealogical Publishing Co.,
Inc., 1981].
_____. Sumner County, Tennessee Will Books 1 And 2 Ab-
stracts, 1788-1823. [Nashville: 1956].
Yorgason, Joan H. & Margaret C. Snider. Sumner County,
Tennessee Cemetery Records. [1981].

W.P.A. TYPESCRIPT RECORDS (available at the Tennessee State
Library and Archives):
County Court Minutes, v.I, 1787-91; v.II, 1791-96; v.III,
1796-1802; v.IV, 1801-04; and v.V, 1804-05.
Index of County Court Minute Books, v.1-5, 1788-1805.
Record of Tax, 1787-94.
Marriage Records, 1787-94.
Will Book v.I, 1789-1822.
Shiloh Presbyterian Church, 1793-1847.
Minutes of Beech Cumberland Presbyterian Church, v.1, 1838-39;
v.2, 1869-99.
Bible, Family & Tombstone Records (miscellaneous).
Miscellaneous Church Records.

MICROFILMED RECORDS (available at the Tennessee State Library
and Archives):
1820-80; & 1900-10 Federal Census.
Circuit Court Minute Books, Oct. 1810 - Oct. 1964.
Enrolling Dockets, Nov. 1826 - June 1874.
Clerk & Masters' Minute Book, Oct. 1840 - Dec. 1966.
Records of Letters Testamentary (labled & filmed in a Mar-
riage Volume, 1865-1860). Sept. 1840 - Feb. 1852.
Administrators' Bonds & Letters, May 1876 - July 1967.
Adminstrators' & Executors' Settlements, 1870 - July 1967.
Conservators' Bonds, Aug. 1856 - May 1967.
County Court Minutes, Apr. 1785 - June 1787; 1805 - Mar.
1967.
Executors' Bonds & Letters, July 1796 - 1816; Nov. 1876
- July 1967.
Guardian Settlement Book, Mar. 1901 - Sept. 1909; Oct.
1919 - July 1967.
Inventories & Settlements, Mar. 1808 - Feb. 1821; May 1826
- May 1879.
Marriage Records, 1787-1838; Jan. 1845 - June 1854; June
1865 - Jan. 1967.

SUMNER COUNTY
(continued)

MICROFILMED RECORDS (continued)
Minutes County Board of Commissioners, Dec. 1867 - Jan. 1892.
Minutes & Insanity Records, Dec. 1933 - May 1966 (not available for research).
Physicians' Register, 1907.
Quarterly Court Minutes, Jan. 1926 - Oct. 1967.
Revenue Dockets, Feb. 1828 - Nov. 1859.
Settlements, Oct. 1927 - July 1963.
Birth Records, 1908-12.
Death Records, 1881.
Will Books, July 1789 - Jan. 1967.
Deed Books, Aug. 1793 - Sept. 1966.
Military Discharge Records, July 1920 - May 1967.
Land Grant Book, Apr. 1786 - Sept. 1806; Sept. 1813 - Feb. 1833.
Oil & Gas Leases, Apr. 1917 - June 1959.
Plat Books, July 1945 - Jan. 1967.
Trust Deeds, Jan. 1887 - July 1966.
School Board Minutes, Sept. 1938 - Oct. 1967.
Tax Books, 1891; 1909-65.
Marriage Records, 1787-1915.
County Court Clerk Minutes, Apr. 1787 - June 1805.
Enrollments, June 1808 - Mar. 1810.

MANUSCRIPT MATERIALS: (available at the Tennessee State Library and Archives):
Church Records. First Presbyterian Church and Shiloh Presbyterian Church, Gallatin, TN, 1793-1968, (microfilm #257). The records, 1793-1968, of the First Presbyterian Church include minutes of sessions and congregational meetings; registers of pastors, elders, deacons, communicants, baptisms, marriages, deaths, dismissals, retired rolls, etc.
Records of Shiloh Presbyterian Church, 1793-1934, include historical sketches and registers of pastors, elders, and communicants.
Church Records. Spring Creek Baptist Church in which are included records, 1823-79, of the West Station Primitive Baptist Church, Sumner Co., TN, consisting of membership lists for both white and black members, (microfilm #504).
Church Records. Beech Cumberland Presbyterian Church Records, 1798-1961, (ac. no. 24). Minutes of the Session, 1899-1961; Registers of Elders, 1855-1960; Registers of the Deacons, 1865-1960; Registers of the Pastors 1798-1950; and Registers of the Communicants, 1865-1961.

TENNESSEE COUNTY

CREATED: 1788 from Davidson County [1783 from Washington Co.].

SPECIAL NOTE: Abolished in 1796; its' territory divided into Robertson and Montgomery County; and its' records included in those of Robertson County.

PUBLISHED SOURCE:
Fulcher, Richard C. 1770-1790 Census Of The Cumberland Settlements. [Brentwood: 1986]. (Contains a seperate section for Tennessee County.)

TIPTON COUNTY

CREATED: 1823 from the Western District (Indian lands).
COUNTY SEAT: Covington, TN 38019.

LIBRARY: Tipton Co. Public Library, 300 W. Church St., Covington, TN 38019.
HISTORICAL SOCIETY: Tipton County Historical Society, 535 S. Tipton, Covington, TN 38019.

PUBLISHED SOURCES:
Carpenter, V. K. Tipton County, Tennessee 1850 Federal Census. [1971].
Historical Records Survey. Tennessee. Inventory of the county archives of Tennessee. No. 84, Tipton County. [Nashville: The Survey, 1941].
History Of Tennessee. [Chicago & Nashville: Goodspeed Publishing Co., 1887]. (Tipton Co., pp. 808-18; 885-921.)

W.P.A. TYPESCRIPT RECORDS (available at the Tennessee State Library and Archives):
Direct & Reverse Index to Deeds, 1824-78, pt. I, A-L; pt. II, M-Y.
County Court Minute Book A, 1823-31.
County Court Minute Book B, 1831-33.
County Court Minute Book C, 1834-45.
Minutes of the County Court Book D, 1846-53, pts. I & II.
Marriage Records Book B, 1840-60.

MICROFILMED RECORDS (available at the Tennessee State Library and Archives):
1830-80; & 1900-10 Federal Census.
Chancery Court Minutes, July 1854 - Sept. 1901.

TIPTON COUNTY
(continued)

MICROFILMED RECORDS (continued)
Circuit Court Minutes, June 1832 - Oct. 1900.
Marriages, Apr. 1840 - Nov. 1900.
Administrators' Bonds & Letters, Jan. 1835 - Dec. 1842;
Dec. 1876 - Dec. 1901.
Wills, Aug. 1824 - Aug. 1973.
Entry Book, Oct. 1820 - Oct. 1870.
Surveyor Books, Feb. 1821 - Mar. 1822; May 1831 - June 1831;
1832-1903.
Deeds, 1824 - June 1900.

TROUSDALE COUNTY

CREATED: 1870 from Sumner [1786 from Davidson Co.], Macon
[1842 from Smith & Sumner Cos.], Smith (1799 from Sumner
Co.], and Wilson County (1799 from Sumner Co.].

COUNTY SEAT: Hartsville, TN 37074.

SPECIAL NOTE: (1904 Courthouse fire destroyed most records.).

LIBRARY: Trousdale County Public Library, 217 Whiteoak St.,
Hartsville, TN 37074.

PUBLISHED SOURCES:
McMurtry, J. C. History Of Trousdale County. [Hartsville,
TN: Vidette, 1970].
History Of Tennessee. [Chicago & Nashville: Goodspeed
Publishing Co., 1887]. History & biography of Sumner,
Smith, Macon, and Trousdale Counties, Tennessee.

MICROFILMED RECORDS (except for census, available at the
courthouse in Hartsville, TN):
1830-80; & 1900-10 Federal Census.
Vital Statistics: Births, 1909-1912; Deaths, 1809-1912.
Deeds, 1905 to present.
Circuit Court Minutes, 1906 to present.
Chancery Court Minutes, 1903 to present.
Marriages, 1905 to present.
Wills, 1905 to present.

UNICOI COUNTY

CREATED: 1875 from Washington [1777 from Washington District, NC, which had been detached from Wilkes & Burke Cos., NC], and Carter County [1796 from Washington Co.].
COUNTY SEAT: Erwin, Tennessee 37650.

LIBRARY: Unicoi Co. Public Library, S. Main Ave., Erwin, TN 37650.

PUBLISHED SOURCES:
   History Of Tennessee...(East TN Edition). [Chicago & Nashville: Goodspeed Publishing Co., 1887].
   Masters, R. A. The Valley Of The Longhunters. [Parsons, WV: McClain Printing Co., 1969].

MICROFILMED RECORDS (available at the Tennessee State Library and Archives):
1880; & 1900-10 Federal Census.
Chancery Court Minutes, July 1876 - Nov. 1908.
Circuit Court Minutes, Apr. 1876 - Sept. 1919.
Administrators' Settlements, Apr. 1884 - Aug. 1944.
Guardian Bonds, Apr. 1870 - Feb. 1940.
Guardian Settlements, Aug. 1878 - Feb. 1928.
Inventory of estates, Sept. 1876 - Mar. 1950.
Marriages, Jan. 1876 - Mar. 1904.
County Court Minutes, Oct. 1875 - Oct. 1905.
Wills, Apr. 1878 - Apr. 1947.
Deeds, Feb. 1876 - Feb. 1903.
Land Entries, Oct. 1900 - July 1903.
Trust Deeds, Dec. 1876 - Oct. 1905.
Tax Book, 1876 - 1899.

MANUSCRIPT MATERIALS (available at the Tennessee State Library and Archives):
   Cemeteries: Greene, Sullivan, Unicoi, and Washington Counties, (microfilm #320). Unicoi County records include the Sames, Day, Tinker, Edwards, Beals, Tilson, Ray, Peoples, and McInturff family cemeteries; also, the Clear Branch Baptist Church and Divide Church cemetery.

CHURCH RECORDS (may be purchased from the Historical Commission of the Southern Baptist Convention, 127 Ninth Ave. N., Nashville, TN 37234.)
   Erwin. First Baptist Church, 1822-1970. Formerly Indian Creek. (Microfilm reel #3571.)

UNION COUNTY

CREATED: 1850 from Grainger [1796 from Hawkins & Knox Cos.],
Claiborne [1801 from Grainger & Hawkins Cos.], Campbell
[1806 from Anderson & Claiborne Cos.], Anderson [1801 from
Knox & Grainger Cos.], and Knox County [1792 from Greene
& Hawkins Cos.].
COUNTY SEAT: Maynardville, TN 37807.

LIBRARY: Union Co. Public Library, Maynardville, TN 37807.

PUBLISHED SOURCES:
History Of Tennessee...(East TN Edition). [Chicago &
Nashville: Goodspeed Publishing Co., 1887].
Graves, K. G. & W. P. McDonald. Our Union County.
[Maynardville, TN: Heritage, 1978].
Early Marriage Records, Union County, Tennessee, 1864-1900.
(Name of compiler, publisher, and intended publishing
date unavailable to this compiler for this work.)

MICROFILMED RECORDS (available at the Tennessee State Library
and Archives):
1850-80; & 1900-10 Federal Census.
Administrators' Settlements, Aug. 1859 - Aug. 1899.
Wills & Inventories, June 1875 - Aug. 1911.
Guardians' Settlements, Apr. 1856 - Dec. 1862; Aug. 1869
- Jan. 1902.
Estates Claims, Nov. 1872 - 1915.
Marriages, July 1864 - Oct. 1916.
County Court Minutes, Feb. 1854 - Apr. 1909.
Vital Statistics, 1881-1882.
Deeds, Feb. 1856 - Oct. 1900.
Trust Deeds, Feb. 1869 - Aug. 1906.
Tax Duplicates, 1854 - 1860; 1869-74; 1893; 1898.

MANUSCRIPT MATERIALS (available at the Tennessee State Library
and Archives):
Church Records. Warwick Chapel Missionary Baptist Church,
Union Co., TN, (microfilm #531). Records include
membership rolls.

VAN BUREN COUNTY

CREATED: 1840 from White [1806 from Smith Co.], Warren [1807
from White Co.], and Bledsoe County [1807 from Roane Co.].

COUNTY SEAT: Spencer, TN 38585.

VAN BUREN COUNTY
(continued)

PUBLISHED SOURCES:
  Carpenter, V. K. Van Buren County, Tennessee 1850 Federal
    Census. [1971].
  Rhienhart Margaret. Our People. The Tombstone Inscriptions
    Of Van Buren County, Tennessee, With Genealogical Notes.
    [1983]. Includes Big Fork, Beech Cove, Blankenship,
    Boyd, Phronie Boyd, Crain Hill, Cummingsville, Simon
    Dodson, Drake, Old Drake, Gillentine, Gravel Hill,
    Graveyard Ridge, Heaton, Head, Arch Hills, Blackstone
    Hills, John Hillis, Hodges, Hollingsworth, Laurel Creek,
    Old Laurel Creek, Lanewood, Long, McElroy, Miller, Molloy,
    Moneyham, Myers, Neal, Pleasant Hill, Ray, New Rocky,
    Old Rocky, Savage, Seitz, Shockley, Old Sodom, Sparkman,
    Bryant Sparkman (or Charlie Holland), John R. Sparkman,
    Town of Spencer, Walling, White Hill, and Yates
    cemeteries.

W.P.A. TYPESCRIPT RECORDS (available at the Tennessee State
    Library and Archives):
  County Court Records of 1840.
  Marriage Records, Vol. A, 1840-61.
  Tombstone Inscriptions.

MICROFILM RECORDS (available at the Tennessee State Library
    and Archives):
  1840-80; & 1900-10 Federal Census.
  Circuit Court Minutes, Aug. 1840; Jan. 1850; May 1850 -
    Dec. 1859; Apr. 1860 - June 1863; Aug. 1865 - Aug. 1872;
    Dec. 1872 - Apr. 1890; Aug. 1890 - Apr. 1943; Oct. 1943
    - Apr. 1963; Oct. 1963 - Oct. 1968.
  Enrollment Book, Oct. 1868 - Nov. 1875.
  Land Sale Records, 1896 - 1923 (Individuals): 1899 - 1914;
    1916-22 (State).
  Minutes, Clerk & Masters', Dec. 1868 - Oct. 1882; Apr.
    1883 - Feb. 1895; Apr. 1895 - Oct. 1916; Mar. 1917 -
    Apr. 1929; Apr. 1930 - Jan. 1969.
  Administrators', Executors', & Guardians' Bonds, July 1888
    - Dec. 1968.
  Land Sale Records, 1898-1962.
  Marriage Records, May 1840 - May 1861.
  Marriage Records, Aug. 1866 - Sept. 1878; Sept. 1881 -
    Jan. 1969.
  County Court Minutes, Apr. 1840 - Aug. 1840.
  County Court & Quarterly Minutes, Apr. 1840 - Jan. 1969.
  Administrators', Executors', and Guardians' Settlements,
    July 1851; Oct. 1852 - Nov. 1868.
  Tax Aggregate Books, 1840-62; 1865-74.

VAN BUREN COUNTY
(continued)

MICROFILMED RECORDS (continued)
  Vital Statistics: Births & Deaths, 1908-11.
  Wills & Inventories, Apr. 1840 - Nov. 1860; Aug. 1865 -
    July 1899; (wills after July 1899, are filed in Court
    Court Minute Books.)
  Deeds, May 1840 - Mar. 1866; Jan. 1870 - Jan. 1969.
  Land Entry Takers' Book, July 1836 - Aug. 1849.
  Military Discharges, Jan. 1919 - May 1968.
  Plat Book, May 1906 - June 1965.
  Surveyors' Book, Nov. 1840 - Mar. 1904.
  Trust Deeds, Sept. 1907 - Feb. 1969.
  Board of Education Minutes, June 1913 - June 1921; Dec.
    11, 1952 & Oct. 22, 1952; July 1921 - Sept. 12, 1968.
  Tax Books, 1866-89; 1892-1914; 1918; 1923; 1928; 1933;
    1938; 1943; 1948; 1953; 1958-1968.

WARREN COUNTY

CREATED: 1807 from White County [1806 from Smith Co].
COUNTY SEAT: McMinnville, TN 37110.

SPECIAL NOTE: (Some county records destroyed during the
  Civil War.)

LIBRARY: Magness Community House & Library, Main St.,
  McMinnville, TN 37110.

PUBLISHED SOURCES:
  History Of Tennessee. [Chicago & Nashville: Goodspeed
    Publishing Co., 1887]. (Warren Co., pp. 812-27; 884-921.)
  Greathouse. Warren County, Tennessee 1860 Census. [1981].
  Killebrew, J. B. Warren County. [Nashville: 1871].
  Marsh, H. C. Name Index To Goodspeed's History Of Tennessee
    ...Warren Co.
  Census Of 1850 For Warren County, Tennessee. [McMinnville,
    TN: Womack Printing Co., 1958]
  Marriage Records, Warren County, Tennessee, 1852-1900.
    Vol. 1, [McMinnville, TN: Womack Printing Co., 1965].
  Womack, W. McMinnville At A Milestone: History Of
    McMinnville And Warren County. [McMinnville, TN: Lomond
    Press, 1960].

WARREN COUNTY
(continued)

W.P.A. TYPESCRIPT RECORDS (available at the Tennessee State
Library and Archives):
Deeds, v.1, Book A, 1808-18.
Deeds, v.B, 1812-19, pts. I & II.
Deed Book, v.C, 1818-20.
Deed Book, v.E, 1823-26.
Inventories, Sale Bills, Statements, etc., Book 1, 1827-44,
pts. I & II.
Marriage License Records, v.A, 1852-64.

MICROFILMED RECORDS (available at the Tennessee State Library
and Archives):
1820-80; & 1900-10 Federal Census.
Circuit Court General Sessions Minutes, Feb. 1949 - Jan.
1959; May 1959 - July 1968.
Circuit Court Minutes, May 1842 - Sept. 1846; Oct. 1856
- Sept. 1868.
Clerk & Masters' Chamber Minutes, Mar. 1931 - July 1968.
Enrolling Books, June 1870 - Mar. 1903.
Minute Books, Mar. 1847 - July 1968.
Administrators' Letters of Testamentary, June 1870 - June
1989 - Apr. 1905 - July 1913.
Claims against estates, May 1921 - Apr. 1966.
Administrators' & Guardians' Bonds, Apr. 1870 - June 1891;
Nov. 1900 - Dec. 1934; Jan. 1936 - Jan. 1968.
Guardians' Minute Book, Apr. 1870 - June 1893.
Guardians' Settlements, Feb. 1866 - Dec. 1926; Aug. 1927
- June 1968.
Insanity Minutes, June 1920 - July 1920.
Insolvent Estates, Mar. 1860 - Sept. 1942.
Marriage Records, June 1852 - Aug. 1968.
County Court Minutes, May 1948 - Aug. 1968.
Physicians' Record Books, July 1889 - Oct. 1962.
Nurses, Record of trained, Oct. 1930.
Optometry Register, Nov. 1909 - June 1931.
Dentist Register, July 1919 - Sept. 1941.
Veterinary Register, May 1921.
Quarterly Court Minutes, July 1899 - Oct. 1967.
Road Books, June 1870 - Feb. 1891.
Vital Statistics: Births, June 1881 - Aug. 1898. Deaths,
July 1908 - Aug. 1912.
Wills, Aug. 1888 - Aug. 1968.
Wills, Inventories, Sales, and Settlements, Apr. 1827 -
Dec. 1858; Feb. 1863 - Aug. 1968.
Deeds, Mar. 1814 - Nov. 1967.
Military Discharges, June 1919 - June 1968.

WARREN COUNTY
(continued)

MICROFILMED RECORDS (continued)
Grant Books, Apr. 1824 - Feb. 1838; July 1895 - May 1901.
Mortage Records, Federal Farm Loan, Oct. 1917 - Sept. 1930.
Oil & Gas Leases, Sept. 1896 - Feb. 1897; Oct. 1919 - Aug.
1921; Sept. 1921 - Oct. 1922; July 1927 - May 1934;
Feb. 1947 - Oct. 1966.
Plat Books, June 1824 - June 1968.
Trust Deeds, Sept. 1870 - Mar. 1968.
School Board Minutes, July 1911 - May 1924; June 1934 -
June 1963.
Tax Books, 1876-83; 1885; 1887; 1889-1966.
Mayor & Board of Aldermen of McMinnville Minutes, Aug.
1859 - Oct. 1934.

MANUSCRIPT MATERIALS (available at the Tennessee State Library
and Archives):
Church Records. Caney Fork Primitive Baptist Church,
1816-1935, (microfilm #178). Membership lists and
business records, which contain the names of many early
settlers in Warren County.
Church Records. Liberty Cumberland Presbyterian Church
in McMinnville, and Friendship Baptist Church, 1831-1912,
(microfilm #259). Minutes, and a membership roll
containing death dates and other notations of the Liberty
Cumberland Presbyterian Church. Original minutes located
in the Tennessee State Library and Archives. Also,
the membership roll, 1849-1912, of the Friendship Baptist
Church.
Church Records of Main Street Presbyterian Church in
McMinnville, 1871-1949, (microfilm #262). Minutes;
lists of elders, deacons, communicants, baptisms,
marriages, and deaths; and statistical reports of the
presbytery.
Church Records for Methodist Churches in Warren and Coffee
Counties, 1898-1967, (microfilm #375). Church history,
1898-1910, and membership lists of the Viola Methodist
Church of Warren County; and membership list of Mt.
Zion Methodist Church of Warren County.
Thomas J. Barnes Papers containing historical and
genealogical data on Warren County and its inhabitants;
including some cemetery and church records in addition
to some public records.

ADDITTIONAL CHURCH RECORDS (may be purchased from the
Historical Commission of the Southern Baptist Convention,
127 Ninth Ave. N., Nashville, TN 37234):
McMinnville. Magness Memorial Baptist Church, 1838-1915,
(microfilm reel #1068).

WASHINGTON COUNTY

CREATED: 1777 from the Washington District, NC, which was detached from Wilkes and Burke Counties.
COUNTY SEAT: Jonesboro, TN 37659.

LIBRARIES:
Jonesboro-Washington County Library, Jonesboro, TN 37659.
Sherrod Library, East Tennessee State Library, Johnson City, TN 37601.
Watauga Regional Library Center, Johnson City, TN 37601.
Library, East TN State University, Johnson City, TN 37601.

GENEALOGICAL SOCIETY: Wautauga Association of Genealogists, 301 Sherrod, Johnson City, TN 37601.

HISTORICAL SOCIETY: Tipton-Haynes Historical Association, Erwin Highway and Buffalo Road, Johnson City,TN 37601.

PUBLISHED SOURCES:
Allen, Penelope Johnson. _Tennessee Soldiers In The Revolution. A Roster Of Soldiers Living During The Revolutionary War In The Counties Of Washington And Sullivan._ [1935].
"County Court Records of Washington County," American Historical Magazine, v.5 (1900), pp. 326-81; v.6 (1901), pp. 51-93; 191-92; 283-88.
Bennett, C. M. _Washington County, Tennessee Tombstone Inscriptions_, plus Genealogical Notes. [Nashville: 1977].
Burgner, Goldene F. _Washington County, Tennessee, Wills, 1777-1872._ [1983].
Burns, W. A. _Death & Obituary Notices Appearing In The Herald & Tribune_, published in Jonesboro, TN. [Pheonix, Ariz.: 1967].
"Early East Tennessee Taxpayers, X, Washington County, 1778," by Creekmore. East Tennessee Historical Society Publications, no. 34 (1962), pp. 118-131.
"Early East Tennessee Taxpayers, XI, Washington County, 1787," by Creekmore. East Tennessee Historical Society Publications, no. 35 (1963), pp. 106-117.
Finchum, G. A. _Washington County Court, 1796-1836._ [Johnson City, TN: 1959].
History Of Tennessee...(East TN Edition). [Chicago & Nashville: Goodspeed Publishing Co., 1887]. (Washington Co., pp. 891-904; 1262-1286.)
Grammer, N. R. & M. D. Mullins. _Marriage Records Of Washington County, Tennessee, 1787-1840._ [Fort Worth, TX: 1940].

WASHINGTON COUNTY
(continued)

PUBLISHED SOURCES (continued)
McCowan, M. H. Washington County, Tennessee Records.
[Johnson City, TN: 1964].
"Marriage Records of Washington County, Tennessee,
1805-1820," Tennessee Historical Magazine, v.9 (1925),
pp. 66-70.
"Marriage Records of Washington County, Tennessee,
1821-1830," Tennessee Historical Magazine, v.1, ser.
2 (1930), pp. 71-80.

W.P.A. TYPESCRIPT RECORDS (available at the Tennessee State
Library and Archives):
General Index to Deeds & Mortgages, vol. 1, 1779-1866.
Inventories of estates, v. OO, 1779-1821.
Vol. O, 1822-31.
Vol. 1, 1826-43.
Settlements of estates, v. OO, 1790-1841.
Vol. O, 1841-60.
Will Book, v.1, 1779-1858.
Tax List, 1814-19.
Marriage Records, vol. 1, 1838-46.
Superior Court Minutes Book, 1793-95; Book A, 1791-1804;
Book B, 1791-1804; vol. 3, 1804-1815; 1800-1803;
1804-1808.
Superior Court Docket, 1803-1806 (1809).
Minutes of the Superior Court of Law & Equity, 1791-99.
County Court of Pleas & Quarter Sessions, vol. 1, Sections
1 & 2, 1778-85; 1787-98; 1802-06 (1809); 1822-24; 1824-26;
1826-27; 1828-29; 1829-31; 1832-33; 1833-37.
County Court Minutes, 1837-42; Sept. 1842 - Mar. 1847.
Court of Pleas & Quarter Sessions Minutes, 1798-99; 1809-17.
Tombstone Records.
Marriage Records, 1787-1859.
County Court of Pleas & Quarter Sessions, 1819-22.

MICROFILMED RECORDS (available at the Tennessee State Library
and Archives):
1830-80; & 1900-10 Federal Census.
Enrolling Dockets, Jan. 1819 - Nov. 1837; Mar. 1838 - June
1846; Jan. 1849 - Mar. 1853; Aug. 1867 - May 1875.
Circuit Court Civil & Criminal Minutes, Nov. 1809 - Oct.
1968.
Circuit Court Civil Minutes, Apr. 1891 - Feb. 1968.
Enrollment Books, Dec. 1870 - Mar. 1877.
Guardians' Settlements, Dec. 1930 - Nov. 1935.
Land Sales Records, 1911-14.

WASHINGTON COUNTY
(continued)

MICROFILMED RECORDS (continued)
Clerk & Masters' Minutes, Sept. 1836 - May 1968.
Clerk & Masters' Minutes (Johnson City), June 1891 - Nov. 1968.
Administrators' Bonds & Letters, Apr. 1875 - Dec. 1968.
Birth & Death Records, July 1908 - Sept. 1913.
Board of Equalization Minutes, June 1900 - July 1910.
Executors' Bonds & Letters, May 1875 - Dec. 1968.
Guardians' Bonds & Letters, Apr. 1875 - Dec. 1968.
Guardians' Settlements, Sept. 1841 - Aug. 1968.
Insanity Proceeding Records, July 1929 - Jan. 1969.
Insolvent Estates Accounts, Sept. 1852 - Sept. 1867.
Inventories of Estates, Feb. 1779 - Dec. 1968.
Jonesboro Education Society, Aug. 1885 - Jan. 1923.
Marriage Bonds & License Books, Oct. 1886 - June 1929.
Marriage Records, Sept. 1787 - Jan. 1969.
W.P.A. Miscellaneous Records Book, 1778-1900.
County Court & Quarterly Court Minutes, Jan. 1778 - Jan. 1817; Apr. 1819 - Nov. 1968.
Optometry Register, Oct. 1909 - Aug. 1936.
Physicians' Registers, Aug. 1889 - Nov. 1949.
Administrators' & Executors' Settlements, May 1796 - July 1862; July 1865 - Jan. 1969.
Superior Court Minutes, Aug. 1791 - Mar. 1817.
Tax Release Records, 1887-1902; 1905-13.
Will Books, Aug. 1779 - Nov. 1968.
Deed Books, Oct. 1782 - July 1969.
Military Discharges, June 1943 - June 1969.
Plat Books, Nov. 1924 - June 1969.
Surveyors' Books, 1824-96.
Trust Deed Books, Oct. 1872 - Sept. 1968.
Board of Education Minutes, June 1919 - June 1923; July 1929 - Nov. 1969.
Cash Journal, Sept. 1927 - Mar. 1934.
Tax Books, 1778-1853; 1856-71; 1875-1914; 1918; 1923; 1928; 1933; 1939-44; 1951-68.

MANUSCRIPT MATERIALS (available at the Tennessee State Library and Archives):
Associations, Institutions, etc. Confederate Veterans Association of Upper East Tennessee, 1861 - ca. 1895, (microfilm #167). Roster containing name, county, state, date of enlistment, company and regiment, rank, wounds received, date and cause of discharge, and general remarks about members of the association living in Washington and other East Tennessee counties and Fulton Co., GA.

WASHINGTON COUNTY
(continued)

MANUSCRIPT MATERIALS (continued)
County Records. Cumberland District, Davidson & Washington
Counties, Tenessee, 1779-1806, (microfilm #224). Records
for Tennessee Courts of Pleas and Quarter Sessions in
the Cumberland District, Davidson County, and Washington
County when those areas were still a part of North Caro-
lina. Records list includes land grants, tax accessments,
wills probated, members of the county court, and commis-
sioners appointed.
Cemeteries of Greene, Sullivan, Unicoi, and Washington
Counties, ca. 1780-1960, (microfilm #320). Washington
County records include May and Peoples, Galloway, Gyer,
Carr, Bowman, Sherfey, Speedwell, Thomas, Garber, Keplin-
ger, Barnes, Berry, Walters, Clark-Dodson, Deakins,
McCrary, Gibson, Fulkerson, White, Howard, Keebler,
Grisham, Houston, Krous, Harvey, Young, France, Slagle-
Huffine, Leach, Archer, Dunkard, Pritchett, Ledford,
Beard, Bacon, Hartman, and Ford family cemeteries; Bap-
tist, Cumberland Presbyterian, Freewill Baptist, Metho-
dist, Church of the Brethern, and Church of Christ ceme-
teries.
Church Records of Cherokee Baptist Church, Jonesboro, TN,
1787-1923, (microfilm #523). Minutes; lists of members,
clerks, ministers, deacons, and deaths.
Church Records of Boone's Creek Church of Christ, 1834-1892,
(microfilm #48). Subscriptions lists, deeds, miscellaneous correspondence, etc.
Church Records for Baptist Churches, Washington & Sullivan
Counties, 1845-1927. Primarily membership lists and
minutes.

ADDITIONAL CHURCH RECORDS (may be purchased from the Historical
Commission of the Southern Baptist Convention, 127 Ninth
Ave. N., Nashville, TN 37234):
Nolichucky Baptist Association. Liberty Baptist Church
Records, Oct. 1842 - Dec. 1876. New County Line Baptist
Church Records, 1876-1941.
Buffalo Ridge Baptist Church, 1827-1874, (microfilm reel
#398).

WAYNE COUNTY

CREATED: 1817 from Hickman [1807 from Hickman Co.] and Humphreys County [1809 from Stewart Co.].
COUNTY SEAT: Waynesboro, TN 38485.

LIBRARY: Wayne Co. Public Library, Waynesboro, TN 38485.

HISTORICAL SOCIETY: Wayne Co. Historical Society, Box 451, Waynesboro, TN 38485.

PUBLISHED SOURCES:
  Dean, Vera L. Family Name Index To Goodspeed's History Of Wayne County, Tennessee, 1886.
  History Of Tennessee. [Chicago & Nashville: Goodspeed Publishing Co., 1886]. (Wayne Co., pp.763-77; 849-89.)
  Marsh, H. C. Name Index To Goodspeed's History Of Tennessee. [Chicago & Nashville: Goodspeed Publishing Co., 1886]. (Wayne Co., pp. 763-77; 849-89.)

W.P.A. TYPESCRIPT RECORDS (available at the Tennessee State Library and Archives):
  Circuit Court Execution Docket, 1837-40.
  Wills & Inventories, Settlement, V.O, 1848-57.
  Marriages, 1857-98.

MICROFILMED RECORDS (available at the Tennessee State Library and Archives):
  1820-80; & 1900-10 Federal Census.
  Circuit Court Minutes, May 1851 - Mar. 1968.
  Clerk & Master's Enrolling Dockets, Mar. 1871 - Apr. 1877.
  Clerk & Master's Minutes, Aug. 1861 - Mar. 1868.
  Administrators' Bonds, Jan. 1874 - Mar. 1968.
  Guardians' Bonds, Jan. 1856 - June 1966.
  Guardians' Minutes, Dec. 1968 - Sept. 1893.
  Guardians' Settlements, Aug. 1870 - Mar. 1968.
  Insolvent Estates, July 1872 - June 1952.
  Inventories, Wills & Settlements, Sept. 1848 - Feb. 1968.
  Inventories, Nov. 1894 - Nov. 1967.
  Marriage Records, Jan. 1851 - Apr. 1968.
  County Court Minutes, Sept. 1848 - Apr. 1968.
    Optometry Register, Nov. 1913 - Mar. 1937.
  Physicians' Register, June 1907 - Mar. 1937.
  Quarterly Court Minutes, Apr. 1907 - Jan. 1968.
  Road Order Minutes, Aug. 1854 - Apr. 1885.
  Vital Statistics: Deaths, 1881-82; Birth & Deaths, 1908-12.
  Deeds, Mar. 1821 - May 1968.
  Entry Takers' Books, Oct. 1820 - Apr. 1901.
  Military Discharge Books, Mar. 1919 - May 1968.

WAYNE COUNTY
(continued)

MICROFILMED RECORDS (continued)
Miscellaneous Records, Feb. 1960 - Apr. 1968.
Oil & Gas Leases, Feb. 1917 - Nov. 1917.
Plat Book, June 1965.
Survey Books, Dec. 1820 - Sept. 1907.
Trust Deeds, Dec. 1873 - June 1868.
Cash Journals, 1941-68 (incomplete).
Tax Books, 1873-1967.
School Board Minutes, Jan. 1913 - Dec. 1967.

MANUSCRIPT MATERIALS (available at the Tennessee State Library
and Archives):
Church Records of Cumberland Presbyterian Church, 1838-1920,
(microfilm #21). Indexed church register; minutes of
session 1866-1920; and lists of elders, deacons,
communicants, baptisms, marriages, and deaths.
Church Records of Salem Primitive Baptist Church, 1821-1929,
(microfilm #419). Minutes of session, membership lists,
church organization, etc.

WEAKLEY COUNTY

CREATED: 1823 from the Western District (Indian lands).
COUNTY SEAT: Dresden, TN 38225.

LIBRARIES:
Weakley Co. Public Library, Church St., Dresden, TN 38225.
Reelfoot Regional Library Center, Highway 45 South, Martin,
TN 38237.

PUBLISHED SOURCES:
Weakley County, Tennessee Cemetery Listings, Vols. 1 &
2, compiled by James Buckley Chapter NSDAR. 1980.
History Of Tennessee. [Chicago & Nashville: Goodspeed
Publishing Co., 1887]. (Weakley Co., pp. 831-42;
985-1024.)
Prins, D. E. The Life And Times Of Greenfield, With Sketches
Of Weakley County. [Greenfield, TN: Greenfield
Historical Society, 1965].

W.P.A. TYPESCRIPT RECORDS (available at the Tennessee State
Library and Archives):
Grant Book, 1794-1844.
Will & Record Book, 1828-42.

WEAKLEY COUNTY
(continued)

P.A. TYPESCRIPT RECORDS (continued)
Reccord & Will Book B, 1840-61.
Reccord of Occupant Entry, 1827-33.
Minutes of the County Court, v.1, 1827-35, pts. I, II,
    & III; 1835-46, pts. I & II; 1853-57, pts. I & II.
Marriage License Record No. 1, 1843-53; and No. 2, 1846-54.

CROFILMED RECORDS (available at the Tennessee State Library
    and Archives):
1830-80; & 1900-10 Federal Census.
Chancery Court Enrollments, Oct. 1827 - Mar. 1828; May
    1834 - Feb. 1843; Jan. 1859 - Aug. 1892.
Chancery Minutes, Nov. 1827 - Oct. 1838; July 1901.
County Court Minutes Project Settlements, Jan. 1855 - Nov.
    1902.
Circuit Court Minutes, Feb. 1844 - Oct. 1848; Feb. 1850
    - July 1902.
Enrollments, Oct. 1868 - June 1884.
Administrators' Bonds, Sept. 1867 - Jan. 1900.
Administrators' Letters, Apr. 1881 - Feb. 1923.
Administrators' & Executors' & Administrators' Settlements,
    Jan. 1851 - Feb. 1867.
Guardians' Bonds, Apr. 1868 - Jan. 1910.
Guardians' Letters, Sept. 1874 - Jan. 1901.
Guardians' Settlements, Apr. 1843 - Nov. 1851; Apr. 1854
    - Mar. 1886; Dec. 1897 - Mar. 1909.
Inventory of estates, Jan. 1852 - Aug. 1904.
Claims of Insolvent Estates, May 1867 - Aug. 1903.
Marriages, June 1843 - June 1945.
Marriage Bonds, Nov. 1878 - June 1910.
County Court Minutes, Oct. 1828 - July 1901.
Probate of Deeds, 1866-70.
Vital Statistics: Births, 1908-12.
Wills, 1828 - June 1861; Sept. 1866 - Aug. 1900.
Order Book, Guardians' & Administrators', Jan. 1867 - Sept.
    1891.
Land Sales, Sept. 1899 - Aug. 1904.
Road Order Book, May 1866 - Apr. 1880.
Auto Registration, June 1911 - Jan. 1916.
Dog Registration, May 1901 - June 1902.
Horse Pedigree, 1884-88.
Deeds, July 1822 - Aug. 1900.
Trust Deeds, July 1868 - Sept. 1900.
Survey Book, 1784 - Apr. 1867.
Entry Book, Dec. 1820 - May 1835.
Entry Takers' Book, Jan. 1827 - Mar. 1847.
Tax Books, 1842 - 1874.
Tax Duplicates, 1875 - 1900.

WEAKLEY COUNTY
(continued)

MANUSCRIPT MATERIALS (available at the Tennessee State Library
and Archives):
Church records for Hopewell Presbytery of the Cumberland
Presbyterian Church, 1824-92, (microfilm #176). Minutes,
membership lists, lists of ministers and elders, and
a statistical report of 1882.
Church Records of Macedonia Primitive Baptist Church, Martin,
1824-1969, (microfilm #288). Membership lists, minutes
of meetings, church covenant, etc. Records for Mud
Creek and Ralston Primitive Baptist Churches are also
included.

WHITE COUNTY

CREATED: 1806 from Jackson County [1801 from Smith Co.].
COUNTY SEAT: Sparta, TN 38583.

LIBRARIES:
White Co. Public Library, 144 S. Main, Sparta, TN 38583.
Caney Fork Regional Library, 25 Rhea St., Sparta, TN 38583.

PUBLISHED SOURCES:
Fancher, F. T. The Sparta Bar. [Milford, NH: 1950].
History Of Tennessee. [Chicago & Nashville: Goodspeed
Publishing Co., 1887]. (White Co., pp. 797-812; 860-84.)
Marsh, H. C. Name Index To Goodspeed's History Of Tennessee
...White Co.
Mitchell, M. F. White County, Tennessee Oldest Marriage
Book, 1809-1859. [1977].
Rogers, E. G. Memorable Historical Accounts Of White County.
[Collegedale, TN: College Press, 1972].
Seals, Monroe. History Of White County, Tennessee. [Sparta,
TN: Sparta Civitan Club, 1935].

W.P.A. TYPESCRIPT RECORDS (available at the Tennessee State
Library and Archives):
Tax Book, 1811-15.
Inventories & Will Books, A, 1810-28; 1831-40 (incomplete).
County Court Minutes, 1806-11; 1811-12; 1812-14; 1814-17,
pts. I & II; 1819-20.
Minutes of the Court of Pleas & Quarter Sessions, 1817-19;
1820; vol. 6, 1820-23, pts. I & II; 1824-27, pts. I,
II, & III; 1835-41, pts. I & II.

WHITE COUNTY
(continued)

MICROFILMED RECORDS (available at the Tennessee State Library
     and Archives):
1820-80; & 1900-10 Federal Census.
Circuit Court Minute Books, Jan. 1859 - Dec. 1966.
General Sessions, Mar. 1953 - Dec. 1966.
Clerk & Master Chamber Minutes, July 1950 - Dec. 1966.
Chancery Court Minutes, Apr. 1842 - Nov. 1966.
Administrators' Bonds & Letters, Oct. 1866 - Jan. 1967.
Administrators' Letters, Aug. 1886 - June 1915.
Claims against estates, Feb. 1930 - May 1961.
Constables' Bonds, Aug. 1912 - Sept. 1960.
County Court Minutes, Oct. 1806 - Nov. 1966.
County Officials' Reports, Sept. 1838 - Dec. 1884.
Guardians' Bonds, Sept. 1886 - Jan. 1967.
Guardians' Receipt Book, Sept. 1854 - Mar. 1875.
Inventory Books, Mar. 1841 - Nov. 1966.
Magistrates' Bonds, Sept. 1888 - Oct. 1954.
Marriage Records, Jan. 1838 - Jan. 1967.
Merchants' Bonds, Aug. 1884 - Dec. 1916.
Minutes & Insanity Records, 1930-55.
Nurses Register, Sept. 1936 - Oct. 1949.
Optometry Register, Oct. 1909 - May 1942.
Physicians' Register, 1889-1952.
Probate Deed Books, Mar. 1833 - Nov. 1947.
Road Commissioners' Books, Apr. 1891 - Dec. 1899.
Settlements & Wills, May 1831 - Jan. 1967.
County Court Will Books, Feb. 1810 - Apr. 1828.
Vital Statistics, May 1881 - Apr. 1882; 1908-09.
Will Books, Oct. 1944 - May 1965.
County Officials Bond Record, Sept. 1942 - Oct. 1966.
Deeds & Trust Deeds, Feb. 1801 - Feb. 1967.
Lease Book, June 1896 - June 1966.
Liens Records, Feb. 1955 - Dec. 1966.
Military Discharges, Oct. 1943 - Oct. 1966.
Register of Miscellaneous Records, Sept. 1930 - Feb. 1967.
Register's Office, Note Bonds, Jan. 1842 - Aug. 1962.
Plat Book, May 1956 - Mar. 1967.
Trust Deeds, Nov. 1882 - Dec. 1966.
School Board Minutes, July 1920 - Jan. 1967.
Tax Books, 1811-1965.

MANUSCRIPT MATERIALS (available at the Tennessee State Library
     and Archives):
Church Records. First Methodist Church, Sparta, TN, 1825-
     1962, (microfilm #271). Registers of pastors; membership
     lists; marriages, 1906-17 & 1930-31; baptisms, 1906-15
     & 1921-56; deaths, ca. 1953-62; U. S. Military service
     roll, 1945; and historical sketch of the church.

WHITE COUNTY
(continued)

MANUSCRIPT MATERIALS (continued)
Church Records. Sparta Methodist Episcopal Church, 1825-1964,
(microfilm #532). Registers of pastors, infant baptisms,
marriages, and members; and other church records.
Church Records. Bon Aire Methodist Episcopal Church, South,
1906-1972, (microfilm #456). Registers of pastors,
baptisms, and members.
Church Records. Mount Gilead Methodist Episcopal Church,
1830-1933, (microfilm #507). Registers of pastors,
members, and baptisms.
Church Records. Methodist Episcopal Church, Sparta, 1882-1937,
(microfilm #508). Minutes and roll of Quarterly Conference of the Methodist Episcopal Church, South, attended
by members of this church.

WILLIAMSON COUNTY

CREATED: 1799 from Davidson County [1783 from Washington
Co., NC].
COUNTY SEAT: Franklin, TN 37064.

LIBRARIES:
Williamson County Public Library, Five Points, Franklin,
TN 37064. (This library houses a substantial collection
of secondary sources and several family histories, which
were inventoried in the Tennessee Genealogical Review
(quarterly), v.1, no. 10 (Dec. 1980), pp. 61-64. The
library also houses a collection from the files of Edythe
R. Whitley.)
Brentwood Public Library, Brentwood, TN 37027.

GENEALOGICAL SOCIETIES:
Brentwood Historical & Genealogical Society, P.O. Box 21,
Brentwood, TN 37027.
Middle Tennessee Society of Professional Genealogists,
P. O. Box 21, Brentwood, TN 37027.

HISTORICAL SOCIETY: Williamson Co. Historical Society, Franklin, TN 37064.

PUBLISHED SOURCES:
Bejack, W. R. & L. J. Gardiner. Williamson County, Tennessee
Marriage Records, 1800-1850. [Memphis, TN: 1957].
Bowman, Virginia. Historic Williamson County. [Nashville:
Blue-Gray Press, 1971].

WILLIAMSON COUNTY
(continued)

PUBLISHED SOURCES (continued)
"Revolutionary Soldiers buried in Williamson County,"
Bicentennial Tabloid, 1976. Brentwood Historical Society,
Brentwood, TN.
History Of Tennessee. [Chicago & Nashville: Goodspeed
   Publishing Co., 1887]. (Williamson Co., pp. 787-810;
   865-1019.)
Hamilton, Edmond K. Williamson County, Tennessee Marriage
   Records 1804-1850. [1981].
Hays. Williamson County, Tennessee Will Book. v.1-5.
   [Franklin, TN: 1949].
Little, T. Vance. Williamson 101. [1970].
_____. Cemeteries In 16th District Of Williamson County.
   [Brentwood, TN: 1967].
Lynch, Louise. Bible Records, Williamson County, Tennessee.
   [Franklin, TN: 1970].
_____. Tax Book I, Williamson County, Tennessee 1800-1813.
   [Franklin, TN: 1971].
_____. Wills & Inventories Of Williamson County, Tennessee,
   Book I, July 1800 - April 1813. [Franklin, TN: 1969].
_____. U.S. Census Office, 7th Census 1850. [Franklin,
   TN: Williamson Co. Historical Society, 1970].
_____. Our Valiant Men. [1976]. Sketches of Revolutionary
   Soldiers with Williamson Co. connections.
_____. County Court Of Williamson County, Tennessee Law-
   suits, 1821-1872, Books 2-8. [Franklin, TN: 1974].
_____. Miscellaneous Records Of Williamson County, Tennes-
   see. Vols. 1-4.
_____. Record Book, Letters Of Administrators (1838-1855).
   [Franklin, TN: 1971].
_____. Wills & Inventories, Book 2, Oct. 1812 - Oct.
   1818.
McRaven. Life And Times Of Edward Swanson. [Nashville:
   1937]. List of Revolutionary Soldiers buried in William-
   son County on front lining paper.
Marshall, Park. Williamson County. [Franklin, TN: 1970].
Family Records. [Franklin, TN: Old Glory Chapter NSDAR,
   1925].
Marriage Bonds, 1804-1820. [Franklin, TN: Old Glory Chapter
   NSDAR].
Whitley, E. R. Marriages Of Williamson County, Tennessee
   1804-1850. [Baltimore: Genealogical Publishing Co.,
   1982].
Directory Of Burials In Williamson County, Tennessee, pt.
   I & II. [Franklin, TN: Williamson County Historical
   Society.]
Williamson County Historical Society periodical publication.

WILLIAMSON COUNTY
(continued)

W.P.A. TYPESCRIPT RECORDS (available at the Tennessee State
  Library and Archives):
  County Court Minute Book v.1, pt. I, 1800-12; v.2, 1812-15.
  Minutes of the Court of Pleas & Quarter Sessions, v.3,
  1816-17.
  Will Book, v.1, 1800-12; v.3, 1819-25, pts. I, II, & III.
  Record of Wills, 1825-30, pts. I & II.
  Bible, Family and Tombstone Records.
  Tax Book, no. 1, 1800-13.
  Wills and Inventories, v.B, 1811-18.

MICROFILMED RECORDS (available at the Tennessee State Library
  and Archives):
  1820-80; & 1900-10 Federal Census.
  Clerk & Masters' Minutes (Chancery), May 1825 - Dec. 1963.
  Circuit Court Civil & State Minutes, Jan. 1810 - Nov. 1876.
    Civil Minutes, Mar. 1877 - May 1964.
    State Minutes, Feb. 1872 - Dec. 1963.
  County Court Minutes, Feb. 1800 - Feb. 1966.
  County Court of Pleas & Quarter Sessions Minutes, Dec.
    1817 - Mar. 1872.
    Quarterly Court Minutes, Oct. 1900 - Oct. 1965.
  Juvenile Court Minutes, Nov. 1911- Apr. 1920.
  Marriage Records, Feb. 1800 - Jan. 1836; Jan. 1838 - Aug.
    1964.
  Will Books, July 1800 - Mar. 1963.
  Guardians' Bonds, Jan. 1859 - Aug. 1961.
  Guardians' Settlements, Jan. 1822 - Sept. 1837; May 1845
    - Aug. 1857; Oct. 1865 - May 1880; Feb. 1882 - Jan.
    1963.
  Miscellaneous Guardians' Records, 1838-45; Dec. 1856 -
    Aug. 1918; Oct. 1860 - Sept. 1916.
  Administrators' Letters, Feb. 1838 - Feb. 1878.
  Administrators' Bonds, Jan. 1858 - Nov. 1888; Jan. 1876
    - Feb. 1888.
  Administrators' Bonds & Letters, Feb. 1888 - Mar. 1966.
  Executors' Bonds & Letters, May 1904 - Mar. 1960.
  Administrators' & Executors' Receipts, Apr. 1857 - Feb.
    1881.
  Claims against estates, June 1939 - Jan. 1965.
  Land Sales Register, Aug. 1877 - Aug. 1900.
  Vital Statistics, May 1881 - Oct. 1882; 1908-1912.
  Physicians' Register, Apr. 1890 - June 1958.
  Dentist Licenses Records, June 1910 - May 1920.
  Notary Public Bonds, July 1900 - Apr. 1961.
  Contract Book, Oct. 1865 - May 1866.

WILLIAMSON COUNTY
(continued)

MICROFILMED RECORDS (continued)
Road Books, Jan. 1834 - Oct. 1872.
Ranger Books, 1829 - 1869.
Freight Book, Mar. 1832 - Mar. 1837.
Board of Health Minutes, Jan. 1954 - Mar. 1966.
Deeds, Nov. 1799 - Mar. 1966.
Trust Deeds, June 1868 - Mar. 1966.
Land Entry Books, Apr. 1824 - July 1902.
Survey Book, Mar. 1827 - Dec. 1832.
Plat Books, Feb. 1938 - Mar. 1966.
Military Discharges, Aug. 1918 - Oct. 1955; Feb. 1936 -
    Mar. 1966.
Common School Commissioners' Report, Apr. 1871 - July 1884.
School Board Minutes, 1936-40; July 1940 - June 1941; July
    1944 - Oct. 1965.
Tax Books, 1800-36; 1838-41; 1844-61; 1866; 1871; 1873-1963.

MANUSCRIPT MATERIALS (available at the Tennessee State Library
    and Archives):
Church Records. St. Paul's Episcopal Church, Franklin,
    1827-1954, (microfilm #22). Minutes; registers of commun-
    icants, baptisms, marriages, confirmations, and burials.
Church Records. Belleview Cumberland Presbyterian Church,
    1852-1908, (microfilm #429). Church history; registers
    of baptisms, marriages, deaths, elders, deacons, etc.
Church Records. Church of Christ, Boston, 1855-88, (microfilm
    #43). Lists of members, elders, deacons, and ministers;
    records of marriages, baptisms, deaths, and other church
    records.
Church Records. Wilson Creek Primitive Baptist Church,
    1804-1945, (microfilm #90). Minutes of services and
    business meetings; membership list by race and sex;
    lists of deaths; and records of early legal cases settled
    by the church.
Church Records. Harpeth Presbyterian Church, 1837-1889.
    Marriage records, baptismal records, lists of members,
    etc.
Church Records. Cool Springs Primitive Baptist Church,
    1829-1934. Church minutes; lists of members from 1835-
    1934; etc.
Thomas Fearn Perkins Henderson's Diaries, Memoirs, etc.,
    (microfilm #10). Along with records of his activities
    in Europe in World War I, he gives a list of Williamson
    County soldiers in World War I, the Spanish-American,
    and Civil Wars.

WILLIAMSON COUNTY
(continued)

MANUSCRIPT MATERIALS (continued)
Scrapbooks. Susie Gentry Scrapbook, 1911, (microfilm #418).
Contains "A list of Revolutionary Soldiers of Tennessee
and data relating to them." including numerous letters
tracing lineages, reciting battles, and other related
information. Indexed.
Scrapbook of Susie Gentry (1860-1944) for 1901-1937; (microfilm #58). Contains sketches of historical events,
prominent men and women, historic houses; list of Revolutionary War veterans and cemeteries; accounts of activities of the D.A.R. and U.D.C.
Cemeteries. Confederate Cemetery in Franklin, 1864, (microfilm #209). Records listing Confederate soldiers killed
in the Battle of Franklin, 1864.
Cemeteries. South Carolina and Tennessee, ca. 1850 - ca.
1856, (microfilm #307). Alphabetical listing, by county,
of tombstone inscriptions from 25 South Carolina and
48 Tennessee cemeteries including information from Williamson County.

WILSON COUNTY

CREATED: 1799 from Sumner County [1786 from Davidson Co.].
COUNTY SEAT: Lebanon, TN 37087.

LIBRARY: Lebanon-Wilson County Library, 108 S. Hatton Ave.,
Lebanon, TN 37087.

HISTORICAL SOCIETY: Historical Associates of Wilson County,
Cumberland College, Lebanon, TN 37087.

PUBLISHED SOURCES:
Carpenter, V. K. Wilson County, Tennessee 1850 Federal
Census. [1971].
Carver, R. P. Cemetery Records Of Davidson & Wilson Coun-
ties. [Donelson, TN: 1957].
Drake, J. V. A Historical Sketch Of Wilson County. [Nash-
ville: Tavel, Eastman & Howell, 1874].
History Of Tennessee. [Chicago & Nashville: Goodspeed
Publishing Co., 1887]. (Wilson Co., pp. 840-61; 1077-
1125.)
The Historian. History Associates of Wilson Co., Vol.
1, Mar. 1965.
Historical Records Survey. Inventory of the county archives
of Tennessee. No. 95. [Nashville: The Survey, 1938].

WILSON COUNTY
(continued)

PUBLISHED SOURCES (continued)
Marsh, H. C. Name Index To Goodspeed's History Of Tennessee
...Wilson Co.
Merritt, D. The History Of Wilson County. [Nashville:
Benson Printing Co., 1961].
Partlow, Thomas E. Wilson County, Tennessee Wills, Books
1-13 (1802-1850). [1981].
_____. Wilson County, Tennessee Miscellaneous Records
1800-1875. [1982].
_____. The People Of Wilson County, Tennessee 1800-1899.
[1983].
_____. Early Families Of Wilson County, Tennessee. [Leba-
non, TN: 1973].
_____. Selected Cemeteries In Wilson County, Tennessee.
[Lebanon, TN: 1974].
_____. Minutes U.C.V. Camp #941, 1897-1928. [1975].
Whitley, E. R. Marriages Of Wilson County, Tennessee 1802-
1850. [Baltimore: Genealogical Publishing Co., Inc.,
1981].

W.P.A. TYPESCRIPT RECORDS (available at the Tennessee State
Library and Archives):
Minutes of County Court, v.1, 1803-07; 1809-19; 1816-19;
1822-24.
Grant Book v.C, 1807-09.
Wills & Inventories, v.1, 1803-14.
Cumberland Presbyterian Church Minutes, Lebanon, TN, 1845-67,
and Minutes of the Cumberland Church, v.2, 1880-95.
Bible, Family, & Tombstone Records.
Wills & Inventories, 1814-19.

MICROFILMED RECORDS (available at the Tennessee State Library
and Archives):
1820-80; & 1900-10 Federal Census.
Deeds, 1789-1965.
Trust Deeds, 1829-1965.
Military Discharges, 1945-65.
Plat Books, 1919-63.
Quarterly Court Minutes & Actions, 1803-07; 1812-1965.
Marriage Records, 1802-1965.
Wills & Inventories, 1802-1965.
Birth Records, 1881-82; 1908-12.
Death Records, 1908-12.
United Confederate Veterans Minutes, 1897-1926.
Administrators' Bonds & Letters, 1838-45; 1862-1965.
Guardians' Bonds & Letters, 1858 - 1965.
Administrators' & Executors' Settlements, 1839-44; 1850-1965.

WILSON COUNTY
(continued)

MICROFILMED RECORDS (continued)
  Guardians' Settlements, 1836-1965.
  Tax Books, 1803; 1807; 1821-1964.
  Chancery Court Minutes, 1837-1965.
  Circuit Court Minutes, 1810-1965.
  Common School Commissioners Reports, 1838-51.
  School Board Minutes, 1923-64.
  Land Entry Book, 1824-1945.
  Surveyors' Plat Book, 1824-30; 1836-74.
  Clerk & Masters' Enrollment Books, Sept. 1836 - Sept. 1839;
    July 1842 - May 1877.

MANUSCRIPT MATERIALS (available at the Tennessee State Library
    and Archives):
  Church Records. Fall Creek Baptist Church, Lebanon, TN,
    1822-1973, (microfilm #443). Membership lists which
    include both white and black members; church constitution
    and organization; minutes; and obituaries.
  Church Records. Cedar Lick Baptist Church, 1815-1881,
    (microfilm #329). Minutes of session, historical sketch,
    membership, and baptismal rolls.
  Church Records. Cedar Lick Creek Baptist Church, 1881-1861,
    (microfilm #339). Minutes of session and membership
    lists.
  Church Records. Mount Olivet Baptist Church, Mount Juliet,
    TN, 1801-1975, (microfilm #511). Membership lists,
    minutes, etc.

STATEWIDE GENEALOGICAL REFERENCES

PERIODICALS:
ANSEARCHIN' News (Quarterly), Tennessee Genealogical Society, Vol. 1, 1954.
ECHOES, East Tennessee Historical Society, Knoxville, TN, Vol. 1, Apr. 1955.
FAMILY FINDINGS, Tennessee Genealogical Society, Jackson, TN, Vol. 1, Apr. 1969.
HISTORICAL MAURY, Maury County Historical Society, Vol. 1, No. 1, May 1965.
TENNESSEE GENEALOGICAL REVIEW (Quarterly), Richard C. Fulcher, publisher. Brentwood, TN, Vol. 1, 1980.
THE TENNESSEE RESEARCHER, Vol. 1-4, Mar. 1962 - Dec. 1965.

BIOGRAPHY, HISTORY & GENERAL REFERENCES:
Allen, Penelope J. Leaves From The Family Tree. [1980]. 151 family articles from the Chattanooga, TN Sunday newspaper between 1933-1936.
Allison, John. Notable Men Of Tennessee. [Atlanta: 1905].
Arnow, Harriett L. Seedtime On The Cumberland. [New York: Macmillan, 1960].
_____. Flowering Of The Cumberland. [New York: Macmillan, 1963].
"Surnames abstracted from Cherokee Indian Agency Records, Tennessee, 1801-1804," William A. Burns, compiler; ANSEARCHIN' News, v.6, no. 3 (1959), pp. 3-4.
Edwards, Olga J. & I. W. Frizzell. The "Connection" In East Tennessee. [Washington College, TN: Pioneer Printers, 1969].
Fain, J. T. Fain's Critical And Analytical Index And Genealogical Guide To Ramsey's Annals Of Tennessee. [Nashville: 1920].
Haywood, John. Civil And Political History Of The State Of Tennessee From Its Earliest Settlement up to the year 1796 including the Boundaries of the State. [Knoxville: Heiskell & Brown, 1923].
Huguenot Society Of The Founders Of Manakin In The Colony Of Virginia, Tennessee branch. [Nashville: 1949?].
Jones, Billy M. Heroes Of Tennessee. [1979].
Moore, John Trotwood. Tennessee The Volunteer State 1769-1923.
Ogle, G. A. Memoirs And Biographical Records, Part II, An Illustrated Compendium of Biography and Biographical Sketches of the Cumberland Region of Tennessee. [1898]. Contains 343 biographical sketches of persons in the Cumberland region of East Tennessee.

BIOGRAPHY, HISTORY & GENERAL REFERENCES:(continued):
Putnam, A. W. History Of Middle Tennessee: or, Life and
    Times of Gen. James Robertson. [1859]. Reprinted 1971.
Ramsey, J. G. Annals Of Tennessee To The End Of The 18th
    Century. [1853].
Ray, Worth S. Tennessee Cousins: A History of Tennessee
    People. [Austin, TX: 1950].
Robertson, Clara H. Kansas Territorial Settlers Of 1860
    Who Were Born In Tennessee, Virginia, North Carolina,
    And South Carolina. [1976].
Satz, Ronald N. Tennessee's Indian Peoples: From White
    contact to Removal, 1540-1840. [1979].
Shepperson, Wilbur S. A Welsh Colonizer In Civil War
    Tennessee. [1961].
Speer, William S. Sketches Of Prominent Tennesseans.
    [1888].
Steely, Skipper. Six Months From Tennessee. [Paris, TX:
    The Wright Press].
Blount Journal, 1790-1796. Tennessee Historical Commission,
    1955.
Tennessee House Journal, 1861-1862. Tennessee Historical
    Commission, 1957.
Commission Book Of Governor John Sevier, 1796-1801.
    Tennessee Historical Commission, 1957.
Williams, Samuel C. Beginnings Of West Tennessee.
_____. Early Travels In The Tennessee Country.
_____. History Of The Lost State Of Franklin.
Whitley, E. R. Red River Settlers. [1933].

SOURCE RECORDS:
Acklen, Jeanette T. Tennessee Records, Vol. 1, Tennessee
    Tombstone Inscriptions. Vol. 2, Tennessee Bible Records.
    [Nashville: 1931].
Baker, Russell P. Marriages And Obituaries From The
    Tennessee Baptist, 1844-1862. [1979].
Bamman, Gale W. & Debbie W. Spero. Tennessee Divorces
    1797-1858. [1985].
Fulcher, Richard C. 1770-1790 Census Of The Cumberland
    Settlements. [Brentwood, TN: 1986]. The only "census"
    available on the early Tennessee country - but - more
    than just list of names, this census cites various records
    in which each settler are found.
Garrett, Jill K. Obituaries From Tennessee Newspapers,
    1851-1899. [1980].
Sistler, Byron & Barbara. U.S. Census, 5th Census (1830),
    East, Middle, & West Tennessee. [Evanston, IL: 1971].
_____. 1850 Census Of Tennessee.
_____. 1860 Census Of Tennessee.
_____. 1890 Civil War Veterans Census, Tennessee.
    [Evanston, IL: 1978].
_____. Tennessee Church Records.

SOURCE RECORDS (continued)
  Tennessee. American Centennial Newspapers, 1876. Collection
    of newspapers from across Tennessee commemorating the
    centennial celebration of the Revolution.
  Tennessee. State Census Enumerations taken in 1805, 1812,
    1819, 1826, 1833.
  Tennessee State Library and Archives. Marriages From Early
    Tennessee Newspapers, 1794-1851. [1980].
  _____. Obituaries From Early Tennessee Newspapers,
    1794-1851. [1978].
  _____. Tennessee Newspapers; a cumulative list of
    microfilmed Tennessee newspapers in the State Library
    and Archives. [1978].
  _____. Index To The Interments In Nashville City Cemetery,
    1845-1962.
  Whitley, E. R. Tennessee Genealogical Records: Records
    of Early Settlers. [1980].

MILITARY RECORDS:
  Allen, Penelope J. Tennessee Soldiers In The Revolution.
    [Baltimore: Genealogical Publishing Co., reprint 1975].
  Armstrong, Zella. Some Tennessee Heroes In The Revolution.
    [1933]. Reprinted 1975.
  _____. Twenty-Four Hundred Tennessee Pensioners,
    Revolutionary War, War Of 1812. [1937]. Reprinted
    1977.
  Bates, Lucy Womack. Roster Of Soldiers And Patriots Of
    The American Revolution Buried In Tennessee. [NSDAR,
    1974].
  Campbell, Mrs. George E. Colonial Dames Of The XVII Century,
    Tennessee. [Chattanooga, TN: 1958].
  National Society Of The Colonial Dames Of America, Tennessee.
  Index: Roster And Soldiers, The Tennessee Society Of The
    D.A.R., compiled by members. [Nashville: 1976].
  Draper, Lyman C. Battle Of King's Mountain And Its Heroes.
    [1895].
  McCown, M. H. & Inez E. Burns. Soldiers Of The War Of
    1812 Buried In Tennessee. [Johnson City, TN: Tennessee
    Chapter U.S.D. of 1812, 1959.
  McGhee, Lucy K. Tennessee Military Records, Pension
    abstracts of Revolutionary War, of 1812 and other wars.
    [Washington, D.C.: 1968].
  _____. Tennessee Revolutionary War Pensioners And Other
    Patriots' Records. [Washington, D.C.].
  Moore, Mrs. John T. Record Of Commissions Of Officers
    In The Tennessee Militia, 1796-1815. [1942].
  Sistler, Byron & Barbara. 1890 Civil War Veterans Census,
    Tennessee. [Evanston, IL: 1978].
  The Tennessee Civil War Questionaires. 5 vols. [Easley,
    SC: Southern Historical Press, 1985].

MILITARY RECORDS (continued):
   Tennesseans In The Civil War. 2 vols. [Tennessee Historical
      Commission, 1964]. Vol. 1 contains the regimental history
      of Tennessee regiments in both Confederate and Federal
      service. Vol. 2 contains an alphabetical list of all
      Tennessee soldiers in both Confederate and Federal Service.
   Index To Tennessee Confederate Pension Applications. Tennes-
      see State Library and Archives.
   Records Of Commissions Of Officers In The Tennessee Militia
      1796-1815, from the Tennessee Historical Quarterly, Vols.
      I-IX, & XV (1942-1950). [1956].
   Whitley, E. R. Membership Roster & Soldiers, D.A.R. Tennes-
      see. 2 vols. [Nashville: 1961-1970].

RESEARCH AIDS:
   Tennessee Genealogical Research. [Salt Lake City: Ancestry,
      Inc.].
   Fulcher, Richard C. Guide To County Records And Genealogical
      Resources In Tennessee. [Baltimore: Genealogical Publish-
      ing Co., Inc., 1987]. (This is the book you are now
      using.)
   Hailey, Naomi. Guide To Genealogical Research In Tennessee.
      [1979].
   Hathaway, Beverly W. Genealogy Research Sources In Tennessee.
      [1972].
   Historical Records Survey. Check List of Tennessee Imprints,
      1793-1840, In Tennessee Libraries. Vol. 16. [Nashville:
      The Survey, 1942].
   _____. Check List of Tennessee Imprints, 1841-1850, in
      Tennessee Libraries. Vol. 20. [Nashville: The Survey,
      1941].
   _____. Instructions for using the county records as source
      materials. [Nashville: The Survey, 1939].
   Kellogg, Louise P. et al. Calender Of The Tennessee And
      King's Mountain Papers Of The Draper Collection. [1929].
   McCay, Betty. Sources For Genealogical Searching In Tennes-
      see.
   McKay, Eleanor. The West Tennessee Historical Society:
      Guide to Archives and Collections. [1979].
   Morris, Eastin. The Gazeteer Of Topographical Dictionary.
      [1834].
   Owsley, H. C. Guide To Processed Manuscripts Of The Tennessee
      Historical Society. [Nashville: Tennessee Historical
      Commission, 1969].
   Smith, Sam B. Tennessee History: A Bibliography. [1974].
   Schweitzer, George K. Tennessee Genealogical Research.
      [1981].

MANUSCRIPT SOURCES (Tennessee State Library and Archives):
Church Records. Assemblies of God Churches, 1914-1965, (microfilm #241). Minutes, lists of ministers, missionaries, churches; etc.
Church Records. Disciples of Christ Churches, 1848-1964, (microfilm #242). Yearbooks, some containing names of preachers; church histories; etc. (See also, Disciples of Christ Historical Society in Davidson County section of this work.)
Church Records. Churches of Christ, 1906-1965, (microfilm #243). Directories of preachers, members; lists of missionaries; congregational histories; congregations in U. S. and other countries, etc.
Church Records. Congregational Churches, 1852-1961, (microfilm #244). Yearbooks; council minutes; biographical sketches; obituaries; historical sketches of churches and schools; information on slavery, education of freedmen, Indian affairs; names and members of church organizations, etc.
Church Records. Eastanallee Baptist Association; 1891, 1903-13, 1916-23, (microfilm #276). Records of annual meetings giving names of representatives from member churches in Bradley, McMinn, Meigs, and Polk counties, TN.
Church Records. Lutheran Synods of Tennessee and North Carolina, 1813-1828, (microfilm #23). Minutes, primarily in German, of the meetings of the North Carolina and Tennessee Synods of the Lutheran Church for the years, 1813, 1818, 1820, 1827, and 1828.
Church Records. Methodist Episcopal Churches in Tennessee, 1879-1892, (microfilm #44). Minutes of the 66th through the 79th annual Tennessee conferences including conference attendance rolls, 1812-1892.
Church Records of the Methodist Churches in Tennessee, 1866-1870, (microfilm #46). Minutes, statistical records, names, and biographical sketches of some of the district ministers.
Church Records. Churches of God, 1906-1974, (microfilm #473). Minutes of annual assemblies, and a church directory for 1972-74.
Church Records for Tennessee Presbyteries and Synods, 1840-1951, (microfilm #472). Records consisting of the Minutes of the Cumberland Presbytery; Memphis Presbytery; Nashville Presbytery; Shiloh Presbytery; West Tennessee Presbytery; Synod of Memphis; Synod of Nashville; and Synod of Tennessee.
Collier Collection, 1833-1896. Along with correspondence, legal documents, clippings, and store records, there are approximately 200 inquiries from prospective emigrants

(continued next page)

MANUSCRIPT SOURCES (continued)
    who are residents of Ohio, Indiana, and Missouri, requesting information about the political, social, and religious conditions existing in Tennessee.

Lyman Copeland Draper Papers, 1542-1916, (microfilm #29). These papers, which cover a broad geographical area of the U.S. from the East Coast to the Mississippi River, are classified primarily under names of important figures. Much information on the early history of Tennessee can be found in these papers.

Andrew Jackson Papers, 1775-1860, (microfilm #30). Primarily public, private, and military papers of Andrew Jackson, including general correspondence; orders, muster rolls, and other military records; and various record books.

Militia Records, 1838-1849. This volume contains the Court-Martial Records of the 146th and 150th Regiments of Tennessee Militia giving names of those appearing before the court, judgements, appeals, officers, executions, costs and returns.

National Archives Records. Freedman's Bureau, 1865-1872, (microfilm #32-34). Selected records of the Tennessee Field Office of the Bureau of Refugees, Freedmen, and Abandoned Lands - containing correspondence, reports, orders, complaints, leases for abandoned lands, and labor contracts.

William Polk Papers, 1785-1890, (microfilm #17). The collection includes Tennessee land surveys, 1785-1814; a parish register for St. John's Episcopal Church in Ashwood, Maury County, TN; some letters of William Polk; and inventories relating to the sale of Hamilton Place in Ashwood.

Photographs, Drawings, etc., Tennesseans, 1813-1902, (microfilm #255). Contains 756 pictures of Tennesseans prominent in business, education, religion, medicine, politics, etc. Published in 1902 by Speed Publishing Co.

School Records, University of Nashville, 1785-1963, (microfilm #153). Collection includes historical memoranda; degrees conferred; graduates; trustees and faculty; minutes of Board of Trustees; class rolls and record books, etc.

182749